THE
EVERYTHING®
THAI COOKBOOK
2ND EDITION

Dear Reader,

My most vivid memories of my childhood are of cooking. I remember sitting on the floor, handing my grandmother ingredients while she made dinner and pounded curry pastes. I spent so much time watching my mother and grandmother cook, I knew I would be able to do it on my own if I was just given a chance.

I lived at home until I moved to Austin, Texas, in 2001, where I started to cook for my college roommates and new friends. I had dinner parties all the time, and after graduating with my master's degree, I began teaching Thai cooking classes. I had found my passion: sharing my knowledge with others.

Thai cooking is driven by what ingredients are available and in season. From the beginning of my cooking days, I have used a variety of ingredients like summer and winter squashes, turnips, rutabaga, and others available at farmers' market stands. I learned very quickly that the best tasting meal is the meal that uses the freshest ingredients. I am overjoyed to share my passion for cooking with you. *Kin Kao*, or let's eat, as we Thais always say.

Jam Sanitchat

Welcome to the EVERYTHING® Series!

These handy, accessible books give you all you need to tackle a difficult project, gain a new hobby, comprehend a fascinating topic, prepare for an exam, or even brush up on something you learned back in school but have since forgotten.

You can choose to read an Everything® book from cover to cover or just pick out the information you want from our four useful boxes: e-questions, e-facts, e-alerts, and e-ssentials.

We give you everything you need to know on the subject, but throw in a lot of fun stuff along the way, too.

We now have more than 400 Everything® books in print, spanning such wide-ranging categories as weddings, pregnancy, cooking, music instruction, foreign language, crafts, pets, New Age, and so much more. When you're done reading them all, you can finally say you know Everything®!

QUESTION

Answers to
common questions

FACT

Important snippets
of information

ALERT

Urgent
warnings

ESSENTIAL

Quick
handy tips

PUBLISHER Karen Cooper

MANAGING EDITOR, EVERYTHING® SERIES Lisa Laing

COPY CHIEF Casey Ebert

ASSOCIATE PRODUCTION EDITOR Mary Beth Dolan

ACQUISITIONS EDITOR Lisa Laing

ASSOCIATE DEVELOPMENT EDITOR Eileen Mullan

EVERYTHING® SERIES COVER DESIGNER Erin Alexander

Visit the entire Everything® series at *www.everything.com*

THE
EVERYTHING®
THAI
COOKBOOK

2ND EDITION

Jam Sanitchat

Avon, Massachusetts

This book is dedicated to my late grandmother, Ubon
Wasuwat, and my parents, Orawan and Banjong
Sanitchat. Thank you for sharing your love and lives
with me, and for always believing in me.

An Everything® Series Book.
Everything® and everything.com® are registered trademarks of F+W Media, Inc.

Published by Adams Media, a division of F+W Media, Inc.
57 Littlefield Street, Avon, MA 02322. U.S.A.
www.adamsmedia.com

ISBN 10: 1-4405-6154-0
ISBN 13: 978-1-4405-6154-2
eISBN 10: 1-4405-6155-9
eISBN 13: 978-1-4405-6155-9

Printed in the United States of America.

10 9 8 7 6 5 4 3 2 1

Always follow safety and common-sense cooking protocol while using kitchen utensils, operating ovens and stoves, and handling uncooked food. If children are assisting in the preparation of any recipe, they should always be supervised by an adult.

Photos by Jam Sanitchat.

This book is available at quantity discounts for bulk purchases.
For information, please call 1-800-289-0963.

Contents

Acknowledgments

I thank my beloved husband and life partner, Bruce Barnes, for allowing me to follow my passion. Without you, Bruce, our son would have missed more baths and bed times.

I would like to thank our son Leo for being patient while I was working on this book. Thank you both for being the easiest family to take care of and for all your support as I was finishing this book. I love you both so much.

I would like to thank my late grandmother, Ubon Wasuwat, for showing me her secrets while she was whipping out dinner after dinner using only a wood-burning stove. Thanks to my parents, Banjong and Orawan Sanit-chat, for having such great passion for great cooking. Thank you Mom for always believing in me, and thank you Dad for always making me believe in myself. I have learned greatly from you and I am so grateful I am your daughter.

Thank you to my team at Thai Fresh. Thank you Nicole Butler and Marc Fidelman for managing while I was gone. Thank you to Aly, Casey, Kaylee, Monica, Tomas, Kyle, Saul, David, Daniel, Maggie, Colin, Robert, and Jess, for doing such a great job creating all the amazing dishes and great customer service.

Thank you to my dear friend Kathy McCarty for the final and last-minute editing. You are amazing.

Lastly, I would like to thank my late professor Leslie Jarmon, who polished my writing skills and enriched my love for writing while I was in graduate school. You have touched my life in many different ways.

I am truly privileged to have all of you as my family and friends. I thank you for fulfilling this dream for publishing.

Introduction

THAI COOKING IS ALL about taste and balance. The five flavors—sweet, sour, salty, spicy, and bitter—are always present, either in a single dish or throughout a meal. Each ingredient has a unique role to play, adding specific flavors and textures. You will use your senses to create each dish, as if you are creating a piece of artwork. You'll find yourself adding a little bit of fish sauce, balancing it slightly with sugar, or adding extra lime to balance the sweetness. After time, when you have gained experience, your instincts will begin to guide you through this process. Eventually you won't even need to think about it.

Just as you create balance within a particular dish, when planning a meal try to create balance between the different dishes you are serving. For example, if you are cooking a spicy curry, a plain vegetable stir-fry will complement the curry perfectly. Condiments are always present at the Thai dinner table as well; and each one can be used to fine-tune the balance of the five flavors. For example, lime juice, tamarind water, and white vinegar all add sourness to food. Some cooks prefer to use lime juice, because of its strong sharp taste, while some prefer to use tamarind water for a more rounded and sweeter taste. Balance is always the goal.

Thailand is blessed with an abundance of food. There is plenty of seafood, fresh meat, fruit, and vegetables; most grow all year round. Thai dinners tend to revolve around which ingredients are currently available. A Thai cook starts with what she's got in the kitchen, then considers which ingredients are in season when deciding what to cook for dinner. Recipe books were not a part of Thai kitchens until the 1980s—in fact, some Thai cooks have never picked up a recipe book in their lives.

When using this book, have fun with it. Remember, there are no terribly strict rules. The measurements in the recipes are there to give you a rough idea. That is why a recipe will often call for 1–2 tablespoons of an ingredient. The amount you will use ultimately depends on your taste and those whom you are cooking for. If your guests aren't very adventurous as far as spices go, tone it down, and add fewer chilies. Learn by using your senses and always taste as you go along. One good way to master Thai flavors is to taste a dish every time you add an ingredient, just to see the difference each one makes. Once you are familiar with what each ingredient adds to the dish, you will be more confident about substitutions when you need to make them. Remember: start small. Once an ingredient is added, you cannot take it out, but you can always add more if you don't use too much to begin with.

The serving sizes given are just rough estimates. Thais usually eat many dishes in the same meal, and the actual serving size depends on how many dishes you are making for that meal. Most dishes, apart from fried rice and noodles, are served with rice. When tasting the food during preparation, remember that rice will be served; so make the seasoning in your dishes a little bit stronger. This way, when eaten with rice, it will be balanced and not bland.

Cooking is not a contest; it is a joy. It is a journey and oftentimes therapeutic. Give yourself time. The most important thing is to have fun while cooking. Enjoy the process and remember to trust your instincts!

CHAPTER 1

An Introduction to Thailand and Thai Cooking

Thailand's roots can be traced back to the T'ai tribesmen, who lived in the shadow of the Chinese in what are now the Chinese provinces of Yunnan and Sichuan, which lie along important east-west trading routes. The first true Thai kingdom, Sukhothai, was established in the thirteenth century after the Thais were freed from the power of Angkor. The era was referred to as the "Dawn of Happiness." During this era, the Thai adopted their first alphabet and the tenets of Buddhism.

The most common name outsiders use for Thailand is Siam. The origin of the name is uncertain, but the name Siam was used to refer to modern-day Thailand until the twentieth century, when it was changed to Thailand in 1949.

Cultural Influences

The thriving seaport city of Ayutthaya became the capital of Siam in 1350, and a monarchy was established. Portugal set up the first embassy there in 1511. By 1662, Holland, Denmark, England, and France all had embassies in the city. The French began amassing troops in Siam beginning in 1675, intent on colonizing the area, but in 1688, the Siamese forcibly removed the *farang* (slang for "French" at the time, the word now means "foreigner") from the country and sealed its borders for 150 years. Thailand is the only Asian country never to have been colonized by a European power, although it has been occupied by the Khmer, the Burmese, and the Japanese.

FACT

Thai food is simply a mixture of Chinese and Indian cuisine. Food travels from India (south of Thailand) and from China (north of Thailand) with the people who migrate. Therefore, the food is milder and uses less dried spices in the north, and is spicier and uses more dried spices in the south.

During his reign from 1824 to 1851, King P'ra Nang Klao began developing trade with China and reopened the borders of the Thai kingdom. The country saw a wave of democracy surge in the 1930s, and in 1932 a constitutional monarchy was formed. Soon after, the country was officially renamed Thailand, meaning "Land of the Free." Today, 75 percent of the population are ethnic Thais, roughly 11 percent are Chinese, and 3.5 percent are Malays. The rest is a combination of Vietnamese, Khmer, and various others. There are only a very small number of non-Asian permanent immigrants.

Weather

Thailand has a monsoon climate. The peninsula has two seasons: wet from November through July, and dry from August through October. The mainland experiences three seasons: wet from May through November, dry and cool from November through February, and dry and hot from March through April. Yet, these definitions are deceiving. From a Western perspective, Thailand is hot and humid all year round; it just varies in degrees. The only real escape from the heat is heading to the mountains in the northern part of the country.

Agriculture

Thailand's fertile delta region, in combination with its hot and humid climate, makes for very good growing conditions, especially for rice. Archeologists believe that what is now central Thailand was the first true agricultural site on the planet, and that rice has been cultivated there since between 4000 and 3500 B.C. Agricultural products account for 66 percent of Thailand's exports, and Thailand produces 36 percent of the world's rice. Other important products include coconut, tapioca, rubber, sugar, pineapple, jute, soybeans, and palm oil. Sixty-five percent of the Thai labor force is involved in agriculture.

Food Culture

Achieving harmony is the most important goal when it comes to Thai cooking. The balance of sweet, salty, sour, spicy (or hot), and bitter is essential, not only within most individual dishes, but also within the context of the overall Thai meal. The key flavoring agents found in a Thai kitchen include lime, chili, garlic, ginger, lemongrass, cilantro, and fish sauce (derived from fermenting fish and salt for a long period of time). These ingredients are as basic as salt and pepper are to a Western kitchen.

All of these ingredients are indigenous to the Asian continent with one notable exception: chilies, which the Portuguese introduced to Asia in the sixteenth century after discovering them in the New World. This is perhaps one of the most profound influences on Thai cuisine, as modern Thai cooking is almost impossible to imagine without the heat of chilies. However, the Portuguese are not the only people to have significantly influenced Thai cuisine as we know it today. The Chinese introduced the concept of stir-frying, and the Indians brought curries and dried spices to the mix.

Thai cuisine reflects the country's ample waterborne resources. Both saltwater and freshwater fish are eaten in abundance. Fish sauce is as common as ketchup and is used as a condiment, a salt substitute, and a general flavoring agent. Shrimp paste is used as we use anchovy paste in the United States. The cuisine also reflects Thailand's tropical climate with an almost endless supply of exotic fruits that are eaten in salads, savory dishes, desserts, and by themselves.

FACT

Thais use spoons and forks when eating their meals. Because the spoon is used in place of a knife, everything is cut into bite-size pieces to reduce the need for cutting. The spoon is the main tool used. Chopsticks are only used in noodle soups.

By far, the most important food in Thailand is rice. It is farmed everywhere from mountaintops to floodplains. It is Thailand's number one export. Rice is so important in Thai culture that the word for rice is the same as the word for food. When Thais say "*kin kao*," or "eat," they are literally saying "eat rice." It is eaten with every meal and made into different forms, from stir-fries to beverages to puffed cakes and desserts. The goddess of rice is Mae Po Sop. Rice is considered the core of existence and is celebrated in several Thai festivals and ceremonies, including births, weddings, and funerals.

Rice is a type of grass, the grain of which can only be extracted by milling or pounding. Thai people take great pride in the quality of their rice, and the whiter and more perfumed the rice is, the better. For this reason, jasmine rice is the long-grained variety preferred above all others. Meat, although readily consumed, is not the centerpiece of a Thai meal, but instead is looked upon as a special treat. Theravada Buddhism, which forbids the killing of animals but not the eating of meat, is practiced by 95 percent of the population of Thailand. To make meat more palatable to the Buddhist psyche, meat is almost always shredded or cut into very small pieces. Rarely will you find a steak or chop served.

Dinner in Thailand is not served in courses, but rather soups, starters, rice, noodles, side dishes, and main courses are all served together to allow the cook to enjoy his or her guests. The meal is always served family style where everyone shares the dishes at the main table. Only dessert is served separately. Condiments such as dried chilies, chili paste, chopped peanuts, fish sauce, and soy sauce are usual additions to the Thai table, just as salt and pepper are in Western countries. Fresh fruits are the typical end to a Thai meal. Desserts such as sticky rice and mango are usually served only at the end of a fancy banquet. Heavy in fish, vegetables, fruits, and rice, and low in meats, Thai cuisine is great for your health. These foods are rich in carotenoids, flavonoids, and antioxidants, all of which are known to reduce cancer. In fact, the Thai have the lowest incidence of digestive tract cancer of all cultures.

Some Cooking Basics

The following are some guidelines that should make your cooking experience more satisfying, no matter what your level of expertise.

- Read the recipe in its entirety before you begin—twice is even better.
- Thai cooking is based on taste. When adding any flavoring ingredient like fish sauce, soy sauce, or sugar, add a small amount and taste first. Add some more if needed.
- Make sure you have all of the ingredients, pans, and utensils, have enough time, and understand the methodology.

- Use seasonal ingredients whenever possible. Thai food is designed around what is in season. Because of the climate, most Thai ingredients are available all year in Thailand. Utilize fresh ingredients from your farmers' market or your garden in the recipes.
- Be prepared. Have your ingredients prepped before you begin cooking—vegetables diced or sliced, dry and wet ingredients properly measured, etc.
- Take meat out of the refrigerator about fifteen minutes before you are going to cook it, allowing it to come to room temperature. It will cook faster and more evenly and be less likely to stick to the pan. Marinate meat in light soy sauce or oyster sauce before using for stir-fries.
- Use freshly ground pepper, if you can. Pepper begins to lose its flavor and pungency as soon as it is ground.

ESSENTIAL

Many Thai ingredients can be frozen up to six months. Consider buying extra ingredients like galangal, lemongrass, lime leaves, and Thai chilies. Those ingredients freeze very well. Once thawed, they have to be used immediately and should not be refrozen.

Basic Cooking Methods

The following are some of the more common cooking methods used, not only in Thai cooking, but all over the world. A basic understanding of these methods will help you with all of your cooking.

Stir-Frying or *Pad*

Stir-frying involves cooking in an open pan over high temperatures, turning and tossing constantly. Stir-frying is a Chinese method of cooking that was adopted by Thais and is usually done in a carbon steel wok for smoky flavor.

In an effort to alleviate the difficulty of cleaning a wok, aluminum woks were made around the mid-nineteenth century. Make sure to season your carbon steel wok before using. Heat up the wok over high heat until hot.

Thinly spread vegetable oil over the entire surface and wipe excess oil. Continue heating until the surface turns somewhat black.

Cooking fats should be relatively free of flavor and have a high smoking point. The best are vegetable oil and peanut oil. The pan must be hot before adding the oil. This will give the pan a somewhat nonstick surface and help prevent the oil from smoking while heating the pan. If the pan is hot, oil will heat up very quickly. Make sure the oil is hot, but not smoking, before adding the spices. Turn down the heat at the beginning to brown the spices properly. Be careful—spices burn easily. Continuous tossing of the spices will prevent burning.

Grilling

Grilling is a cooking method where food is cooked by exposing it to direct (usually intense) heat over hot coals or some other heat source. This method is typically fast; the direct heat chars the surface of the food, giving it great flavor. Thai recipes that call for the grilling method usually have oil as an ingredient in the marinade. Oil will prevent the food from sticking to the grill.

Simmering

Simmering is a technique that involves cooking food in liquid. The cooking liquid is first brought to a boil and then the heat is reduced in order to obtain less active bubbling. This slow and low cooking method is used to ensure that the meat or vegetables are not overcooked or toughened, but cooked through. Cooking whole chicken or ground pork for *larb* are good examples of this method. Only a few foods are actually boiled—vegetables are the most common ingredient to be boiled. Protein tends to get tough if cooked at a rapid boil.

Blanching

You can use boiling water to blanch fruits and vegetables before they are exposed to another cooking method or if you want to keep them tender-crisp. Blanching involves placing the ingredients in boiling water briefly and then plunging them into cold water to help retain color and flavor. This method is used for ingredients that require very little cooking time to remove bitter or raw flavors. It is also used for noodles in noodle soup.

Steaming

Another cooking process that involves water is steaming. For this method, the food is placed in a steamer over boiling water. The pot is always covered to ensure that the steam remains in the pot to cook the food thoroughly. Thais commonly use this method to cook sticky rice. Another great steamed dish is whole fish; a whole fish is scored, put on a plate with seasonings, and steamed in a large metal steamer.

Deep-Frying

Woks and high-sided pans are great for deep-frying. You will need enough oil to cover the food completely. The oil should be hot, at about 350°F. You can use a thermometer to take the temperature, or stick a wooden spoon in hot oil—if the oil sizzles around the spoon, it's ready to go. Remember that as you add food to the hot oil, you're reducing the temperature. Drop items into the hot oil in small batches and fry until they float to the top, then drain on paper towels. When done properly, deep-fried food will not be excessively oily.

What You'll Need

Thai cooking really doesn't require a kitchen full of fancy gadgets. Most often you will use standard mixing bowls and measuring cups, pots and pans, ladles, spatulas, spoons, and knives. Here are a few items that will make your Thai cooking easier and more enjoyable.

KNIVES
- **Paring knife:** a short-bladed knife (usually 2–4 inches) used to trim fruits and vegetables
- **Chef's knife:** a medium-bladed knife used for chopping and slicing
- **Cleaver:** a large knife used to chop bone-in meats or for slicing and mincing meat

SPECIALTY UTENSILS

- **Mortar and pestle:** probably the most important tool in a Thai kitchen for making curry pastes and relishes. Nothing makes curry pastes as smooth as a mortar and pestle. A food processor or blender will cut spices into small pieces, but a mortar and pestle will grind the spices to a fine paste, allowing the fragrant oil to be released. There are two kinds of mortar and pestles that Thais use. A clay mortar with wooden pestle is used to make salad, particularly *Som Tum* (Green Papaya Salad in Chapter 4). A granite mortar and pestle set is used to make curry pastes and relishes or to grind rice or dried shrimp to a fine powder.
- **Wok:** a high-sided, sloping, small-bottomed pan designed to cook food quickly and evenly. American stovetops are not designed to hold a wok, and it can be difficult to get a wok hot enough to cook the food quickly. A good substitution for a wok is a large, high-sided pan like a sauté pan or a Dutch oven. The bigger bottom surface will ensure the high heat while the higher sides will help the food to stay inside the pot while cooking.
- **Rice cooker:** an electric appliance that makes cooking rice a stress-free experience.
- **Food processor:** the workhorse of the kitchen when it comes to mixing, chopping, puréeing, and shredding.

QUESTION

How do I serve a Thai meal?
Thai meals are all about the balance of different flavors and texture. Thai meals are almost always eaten family style. When cooking a Thai meal, make sure to take into consideration the balance of salty, sweet, sour, spicy, and bitter. And don't forget the rice!

Thai Ingredients and Tips on Substitutions

Some ingredients cannot be substituted. In many cases, omitting those ingredients is a better alternative than substituting them. The items that cannot be substituted include galangal (cannot be substituted with ginger) and kaffir limes or kaffir lime leaves (cannot be substituted with regular limes or lime leaves.) A lot of fresh Thai ingredients are easy to grow in a warmer climate. Many online Thai grocery stores also sell fresh ingredients that you can purchase and freeze for later use. If you have to substitute, here are some tips on some of the ingredients.

▼ **THAI SUBSTITUTIONS**

Fish sauce	Thai soy sauce (not the saltier and less sweet Japanese soy sauce)
Thai soy sauce	Chinese soy sauce
Long beans or snake beans	Green beans
Shallots	Red onions
Homemade curry paste	Store-bought curry paste
Thai chilies	Serrano peppers

Thai Pantry

These are things you should always have in your pantry or freezer. These essential ingredients will transform fresh ingredients into many delicious Thai dishes.

Bamboo Shoots (*Nor Mai*)

Bamboo shoots are excellent in curries and stir-fried dishes. Raw bamboo shoots are a little bitter, but the bitterness is reduced after cooking. If you buy canned bamboo shoots, rinse them before using.

Chilies (*Prik*)

Thai chilies are available in Asian supermarkets. The flavor of the Thai chili is unique, and it should not be substituted with other kinds of chilies. Small bird's-eye chilies are hard to come by in the United States, but the slightly less hot chilies you'll find are good enough for Thai cooking. Thai chilies can be frozen for up to six months.

Coconut Milk (*Kati*)

Coconut milk is used in curry dishes and in desserts. Coconut milk can be made fresh by shredding coconut meat in a food processor and adding water to extract cream from the meat. The first round of extraction will yield creamy white coconut cream, and the second round is called coconut milk.

Curry Paste (*Nam Prik Kaeng*)

Canned curry pastes are available in Asian supermarkets, but you can easily make your own. Making your own paste with a mortar and pestle, or even with a blender or food processor, will definitely yield better-tasting curries than canned paste. However, there are a few good quality premade pastes you can use. If you use a canned paste, add a little freshly ground white peppercorn to the paste to revive it.

Fish Sauce (*Nam Pla*)

Almost all Thai dishes use fish sauce. Add this amazing seasoning to anything, and it will do wonders. On its own, fish sauce smells and tastes very pungent. But when cooked in a dish, fish sauce completes the unique taste of Thai cooking as it blends and supports other flavors.

Galangal (*Kha*)

Galangal is a rhizome that is used widely in Thai cooking. Galangal can be purchased fresh or frozen at Asian supermarkets. Dried galangal has a more pungent flavor, so use 30 percent less.

Garlic (*Gratium*)

Garlic is used in almost all curry pastes. Minced garlic is used in almost all stir-fried dishes. Minced garlic is usually fried in vegetable oil until golden brown before adding other ingredients into stir-fried dishes. Always mince fresh garlic right before using. Bottled minced garlic has lost much of its flavor.

Kaffir Lime Leaves (*Bai Magrood*)

Kaffir lime leaves add great flavor to curries and soups like *Tom Yum* or *Tom Kha*. They may be difficult to find in the market, but if you do find them, remember that they'll keep in the freezer for up to six months. Kaffir lime plants can also be found in some nurseries.

Lemongrass (*Ta Krai*)

Lemongrass is used in curries and soups like *Tom Yum* and *Tom Kha* and in curry pastes. You can easily grow your own lemongrass. Place a stalk in water for two weeks and then plant it in a large pot (or in the soil if you live in a warmer climate). Keep the soil moist. Fresh stalks can be frozen for up to six months.

Oil (*Nam Maan Puet*)

Vegetable oil is used for most Thai dishes. Pork or chicken fat is also used in many recipes.

Oyster Sauce (*Nam Man Hoi*)

Although of Chinese origin, oyster sauce adds flavor to many Thai stir-fried dishes. Keep a bottle at home to use interchangeably with soy sauce and sugar. It is salty and sweet.

Peppercorn (*Prik Thai*)

White peppercorns are commonly used in Thai cooking. Freshly ground peppercorns have a much more robust flavor than preground pepper.

Rice (*Kao*)

The favorite Thai rice is the long-grain jasmine rice, *kao hom mali*.

Shrimp Paste (*Kapi*)

Shrimp paste is the heart of Thai cooking. It is used to season almost all curry pastes and many stir-fried dishes. The smell of shrimp paste is extremely pungent. You can buy shrimp paste at Asian supermarkets or make your own. Thai shrimp paste is different from other countries' shrimp paste, so make sure you buy shrimp paste from Thailand. Shrimp paste will keep for up to one year in the refrigerator.

Soybean Paste (*Tao Jeuw*)

Soybean paste is often used to make many Chinese-influenced dishes. The soybeans are salted and then fermented with rice mold. It is used in sauces, soups, steamed dishes, and some stir-fried dishes.

Soy Sauce (*Sii Euy*)

Thin soy sauce has a rich salty flavor and is used for many stir-fries and soup dishes. Thick soy sauce is used to add golden brown color to stir-fried dishes or soupy dishes. Sweet soy sauce is simply thick soy sauce with more sugar. You can make sweet soy sauce by adding one part sugar to two parts thick soy sauce.

Sticky Rice (*Kao Neuw*)

Sticky rice is eaten with many salads or is used to make desserts. Although it's also called glutinous rice, sticky rice does not contain any gluten.

Sugar (*Nam Tarn*)

Palm sugar (*nam tarn peep* or *nam tarn maproa*) is rich in flavor and is preferred when cooking Thai food. Palm sugar is available in bottles. White sugar (*nam tarn sai*) can usually be used as a substitute for palm sugar; however, there are only a few dishes that will be distinctively different when using palm sugar. The recipes will indicate if palm sugar is necessary.

Tamarind (*Ma Kaam Piak*)

Tamarind is used to add a sour taste to dishes. Tamarind pulp can be bought at Asian grocery stores. To make 1 cup of tamarind water, add warm water to ⅓ cup of tamarind pulp. Leave it for a few minutes until softened, then squeeze and work the pulp to get the juice out of it. Strain the remaining pulp. Thick tamarind water can be added to curries, soups, or other Thai dishes.

The Basics

Coconut Milk (*Kati*)

Coconut milk can be purchased in a can or made with shredded coconut meat. You can find shredded coconut meat in the frozen section at Asian grocery stores.

INGREDIENTS | YIELDS 2 CUPS

2 cups frozen shredded coconut meat

3–4 cups water

Storing Coconut Milk

Coconut milk can be frozen for later use. If you use coconut milk from a can, it will keep for four days after opening, but once opened, be sure to transfer it to a different container and store it in the refrigerator.

1. In a large bowl, add enough water to coconut meat to cover. Squeeze the meat with your hands until the liquid becomes white and thick. Strain through a fine mesh strainer. This first round of the liquid is called coconut cream or the "head" of coconut milk.

2. Repeat the process by adding more water to cover the coconut meat. Strain the second round of liquid. This second round of liquid is called coconut milk or the "tail" of coconut milk. When making dessert, most often, only the head is used. When making curries, both the head and tail are used. Store-bought coconut milk is a mixture of head and tail.

Jasmine Rice (*Kao*)

Rice is a crucial part of Thai cuisine. It is so important that the term "eat rice" means to eat a meal.

INGREDIENTS | YIELDS 2 CUPS

1 cup white jasmine rice

1½ cups water

Cooking Perfect Rice

The common recipe of 1 part rice to 2 parts water often yields overcooked rice. Jasmine rice contains more moisture than other long-grain white rice, so 1 part rice to 1½ parts water is ideal. Another easy method of measuring the right amount of water is to cover the rice with water, stir it, then level the top of the rice. Touch the top of the rice with your index finger. The water should be one knuckle above the rice.

Add rice and water to a medium saucepan and stir. Bring the water to a boil, turn the heat down to very low, cover the pan, and let the rice simmer for about 10–12 minutes. Check after 10 minutes. When the water is all absorbed, the rice is done. Keep the cover on for another 5 minutes so the rice will fluff up. Serve.

Sticky Rice (*Kao Neaw*)

Sticky rice, or sweet rice, has a higher starch level than regular white rice. It is sometimes called glutinous rice, not because it contains gluten, but because of its glue-like texture once cooked.

INGREDIENTS | YIELDS 3 CUPS

1 cup sticky or sweet rice

1. Soak rice in room-temperature water for at least 4 hours and up to 12 hours. Steam in a bamboo or any type of steamer for 15 minutes.

2. Alternatively, wrap soaked sticky rice in a dampened towel and place on a plate. Microwave the rice for 3 minutes and check to see if it is done (rice is done when it is completely translucent). Cook in 1-minute increments until the rice is done.

Green Curry Paste (*Kaeng Kiew Wan*)

Green curry is considered one of the spiciest coconut milk–based curries. It is a great curry for all kinds of meat and seafood. Garnish with Thai basil to complete the dish.

INGREDIENTS | YIELDS ½ CUP

15 green Thai chilies

1 teaspoon roasted coriander seeds

1 teaspoon roasted cumin

1 teaspoon white peppercorn

1 tablespoon finely chopped galangal

1 tablespoon chopped lemongrass (about 1 stalk)

1 teaspoon chopped cilantro roots or stems

3 shallots, coarsely chopped

9 cloves garlic

½ teaspoon kaffir lime zest (optional)

1 teaspoon shrimp paste

1 teaspoon salt

Make a paste using a mortar and pestle by adding ingredients one at a time in the order given. Pound one ingredient until it's broken up in small pieces before adding the next one. When all ingredients are added, continue pounding until it forms a fine paste. Alternatively, place coarsely chopped ingredients in a blender and blend until smooth, adding water as needed.

Red Curry Paste (*Kaeng Daeng*)

Red curry paste uses large dried red chilies instead of fresh chilies. It's a little smoky compared to green curry. Almost any type of meat can be used with this curry paste.

INGREDIENTS | YIELDS ½ CUP

- 7 dried large red Thai chilies, soaked and seeded
- 1 teaspoon salt
- 1 teaspoon coriander seeds, toasted
- 1 teaspoon cumin seeds, toasted
- 1 tablespoon chopped lemongrass (about 1 stalk)
- 1 tablespoon finely chopped galangal
- 1 teaspoon kaffir lime zest (optional)
- 2 teaspoons chopped cilantro roots or stems
- 5 shallots, chopped
- 10 garlic cloves, chopped
- 1 teaspoon shrimp paste

Make a paste using a mortar and pestle by adding ingredients one at a time in the order given. Pound one ingredient until it's broken up in small pieces before adding the next one. When all ingredients are added, continue pounding until it forms a fine paste. Alternatively, place coarsely chopped ingredients in a blender and blend until smooth, adding water as needed.

Panang Curry Paste

Panang curry is a thicker and creamier curry that uses more coconut cream than other curries. This classic version uses roasted peanuts, but peanuts are often not added to the curry found in restaurants and markets. Beef is the most common meat used in this curry.

INGREDIENTS | YIELDS ½ CUP

- 10 dried large red Thai chilies, soaked and seeded
- 1 teaspoon salt
- 1 teaspoon ground white pepper
- ½ nutmeg, broken, roasted, and ground
- 4 tablespoons chopped roasted peanuts
- 1 tablespoon chopped lemongrass
- 1½ tablespoons finely chopped galangal
- ½ teaspoon kaffir lime zest (optional)
- 5 shallots, chopped
- 10 garlic cloves, chopped
- 1 teaspoon chopped cilantro roots or stems
- 1 teaspoon shrimp paste

Make a paste using a mortar and pestle by adding ingredients one at a time in the order given. Pound one ingredient until it's broken up in small pieces before adding the next one. When all ingredients are added, continue pounding until it forms a fine paste. Alternatively, place coarsely chopped ingredients in a blender and blend until smooth, adding water as needed.

Southern (or Massaman) Curry Paste

Massaman is the most complex of Thai curries. It was influenced by Malaysian curry, with the addition of more dried spices.

INGREDIENTS | YIELDS ½ CUP

5 dried large red Thai chilies, soaked and seeded

1 teaspoon salt

1 teaspoon coriander seeds, toasted and ground

1 teaspoon cumin seeds, toasted and ground

2 cloves, toasted and ground

1 teaspoon ground white pepper

1 tablespoon chopped lemongrass

1 tablespoon finely chopped galangal

1 teaspoon kaffir lime zest (optional)

2 teaspoons chopped cilantro

3 shallots, roasted

2 garlic cloves, roasted

1 teaspoon shrimp paste

Make a paste using a mortar and pestle by adding ingredients one at a time in the order given. Pound one ingredient until it's broken up in small pieces before adding the next one. When all ingredients are added, continue pounding until it forms a fine paste. Alternatively, place coarsely chopped ingredients in a blender and blend until smooth, adding water as needed.

Northern (or Jungle) Curry Paste (*Kaeng Pa*)

Jungle curry is a spicy stock-based curry from the north of Thailand. It is simple and uses only fish sauce to season the curry. Sometimes a little sugar is added. It is never made with coconut milk and it often combines different kinds of vegetables in the curry.

INGREDIENTS | YIELDS 2 CUPS

15–20 fresh red or green Thai chilies, or dried small red Thai chilies

¼ teaspoon salt

1 tablespoon chopped galangal

2 tablespoons lemongrass, chopped (about 1 stalk)

2 teaspoons minced cilantro roots or cilantro stems

2 tablespoons chopped wild ginger or lesser galangal (*grachai*)

1 or 2 shallots, chopped

1 tablespoon chopped garlic

1 teaspoon shrimp paste

Make a paste using a mortar and pestle by adding ingredients one at a time in the order given. Pound one ingredient until it's broken up in small pieces before adding the next one. When all ingredients are added, continue pounding until it forms a fine paste. Alternatively, place coarsely chopped ingredients in a blender and blend until smooth, adding water as needed.

Yellow Curry Paste (*Kaeng Karee*)

Yellow curry is influenced by the Indian spices curry powder and turmeric.
This curry is less spicy but more pungent with dried spices.

INGREDIENTS | YIELDS ½ CUP

4 dried long red Thai chilies, soaked and seeded

3 shallots, toasted

7 cloves garlic, toasted

1 teaspoon minced ginger, toasted

1 teaspoon minced galangal, toasted

1 tablespoon chopped lemongrass

1 tablespoon coriander seeds, toasted

1 teaspoon cumin seeds, toasted

2 teaspoons curry powder

1 teaspoon salt

1 teaspoon shrimp paste (optional)

Make a paste using a mortar and pestle by adding ingredients one at a time in the order given. Pound one ingredient until it's broken up in small pieces before adding the next one. When all ingredients are added, continue pounding until it forms a fine paste. Alternatively, place coarsely chopped ingredients in a blender and blend until smooth, adding water as needed.

Homemade Curry Powder

Making your own curry powder ensures that no additives like tapioca flour or wheat flour are added.

INGREDIENTS | YIELDS ½ CUP

1 tablespoon black peppercorns

3 tablespoons coriander seeds

2 tablespoons cumin seeds

1 tablespoon cloves, whole

15 white Thai cardamom pods

2 tablespoons ginger powder

¼ cup turmeric powder

3 dried long Thai chilies or dried long New Mexico chilies

1. Toast whole dried spices separately in a dry frying pan over low heat until fragrant. Cumin seeds will take about 1 minute, while the rest of the spices take about 2 minutes.

2. Combine all ingredients in a coffee grinder, working in batches if necessary. Store in a jar with a tight lid for three months.

Sriracha Sauce

Sriracha is the name of a town on the eastern seaboard of Thailand.
This sauce is used in various dishes or as a dipping sauce.

INGREDIENTS | YIELDS 1 CUP

10 dried long red Thai chilies (dried Serrano is a good substitution)

1 cup whole garlic cloves

1 teaspoon salt

¼ cup sugar

1½ cups water

3 tablespoons white vinegar

1. Combine chilies, garlic, salt, sugar, and water in a saucepan. Bring to a boil and simmer until chilies and garlic are tender, about 5–7 minutes. Let cool.

2. Add vinegar to the mixture and purée until smooth.

Chilies in Vinegar

This is a classic condiment for Pad See Ew and many other stir-fried noodle dishes.
It's easy to make and keeps well when refrigerated.

INGREDIENTS | YIELDS 3 CUPS

3 cups sliced jalapeño or Serrano peppers

Distilled white vinegar

In a medium bowl or glass jar, cover sliced peppers with vinegar. Let sit for at least 30 minutes. Store in the refrigerator for up to three months.

Condiments

Thais are big on condiments. There are always little bowls of sauces at the table for you to adjust each dish to your preferred taste. Condiments add balance to the dish.

Pickled Chilies and Garlic

*This is a simple, yet complex-tasting sauce to add to any noodle soup.
It's a great sauce for stewed meats as well.*

INGREDIENTS | YIELDS 1 CUP

1 cup Serrano peppers
3 Thai chilies
4 cloves garlic, peeled
2 teaspoons salt
1 teaspoon sugar
1 cup white vinegar

Purée all ingredients in a blender until smooth. Transfer to a jar, seal, and refrigerate for up to three months.

Tamarind Water

Tamarind water or concentrate is a key ingredient in many Thai recipes. It is tart and a little sweet, and once it is made, the water or paste can be frozen indefinitely.

INGREDIENTS | YIELDS 1 CUP

½ cup tamarind pulp
1½ cups water

Soak tamarind pulp in 1 cup of water for a few minutes to soften. Work the pulp to dissolve the meat. Strain and reserve the thick brown water. Repeat by adding the other ½ cup of water and strain.

Tamarind
Tamarinds can be sweet or sour. Sweet tamarind is eaten like a snack in Thailand, while the sour kind is used in cooking.

Thai Chili and Fish Sauce (*Nam Pla Prik*)

This is the main condiment at every Thai dining table, at home or in restaurants. Chilies pickled in fish sauce become less spicy.

INGREDIENTS | YIELDS ½ CUP

¼ cup red or green fresh Thai chilies, sliced

⅓ cup fish sauce to cover

Combine all ingredients in a bowl and let sit for 30 minutes.

Thai Chili and Fish Sauce with Lime, Shallots, and Garlic

This is a more complex version of chili and fish sauce. It is a perfect condiment for rice dishes, and adds a lively sour element to any dish.

INGREDIENTS | YIELDS 1 CUP

¼ cup fresh red or green Thai chilies, sliced

½ cup fish sauce

1 clove garlic, thinly sliced

1 small shallot, thinly sliced

3 tablespoons lime juice

Combine all ingredients in a bowl and let sit for 30 minutes.

Thai Chilies

Small, thin-skinned, long Thai chilies are known for their heat. Serrano peppers or other hot peppers can be used in place of Thai chilies. However, they are not as spicy and will require quite a few more chilies to achieve the same level of heat.

Roasted Thai Chili Flakes (*Prik Pon*)

Roasted Thai chilies are a simple and fast way to add heat to your dishes.
Once made, ground roasted chilies will keep for six months in an airtight container.
Toasting chilies first before grinding helps release the heat and aroma of the chilies.

INGREDIENTS | YIELDS 1 CUP

4 cups dried small Thai chilies

Roasting Chilies

Make sure that the kitchen is properly ventilated when dry-roasting chilies. The smoke can irritate your eyes and throat.

1. Heat a dry pan over low heat. Add chilies to the pan and toss until slightly brown and fragrant. Alternatively, heat the oven to 350°F. Place dried chilies on a baking sheet and roast for 3 minutes or until fragrant. Remove from heat and let cool.

2. Grind roasted chilies in a food processor and store in an airtight container in the pantry.

Fried Chilies with Shallots and Garlic

Enjoy this flavorful chili paste with many different dishes like
Curried Egg Noodle Soup with Beef (see Chapter 6).

INGREDIENTS | YIELDS ½ CUP

1 cup vegetable oil
3 shallots, chopped
2 garlic cloves, chopped
15 dried small Thai chilies
¼ teaspoon salt
½ teaspoon palm sugar

1. Heat oil in a pot to about 325°F. Deep-fry shallots and garlic until golden, about 1 minute. Drain and set aside.

2. Deep-fry dried chilies until fragrant, about 1 minute, and drain on paper towels.

3. Combine all ingredients, including salt and palm sugar, in a small food processor with 2 tablespoons of the oil from deep-frying and blend until smooth.

Chicken Stock

Homemade chicken stock is hard to beat. Chicken stock is a great addition to soups, curries, or stir-fries. Cooked chicken left over from making chicken stock can be used in many dishes like Chicken and Rice (see Chapter 9) or Rice Congee (see Chapter 9).

INGREDIENTS | YIELDS 12 CUPS

1 whole chicken (about 3 pounds)
3 cloves garlic, crushed
5 slices ginger, ¼"-thick
10 stalks cilantro stems
2 teaspoons salt

1. Combine all ingredients in a large stockpot. Add enough water to cover the chicken. Bring to a boil over high heat, then reduce heat to medium-low. Cover and let simmer for 25 minutes.

2. Remove chicken from the stock and let sit. Strain stock and let it cool. Stock can be frozen for up to six months.

Vegetable Stock

This stock can be made with all or some of the vegetable ingredients. It is mainly designed to use whatever is left in your fridge. The outer leaves of a cabbage are also a great ingredient for the stock.

INGREDIENTS | YIELDS 8 CUPS

2 celery stalks
1 daikon or Japanese white radish, sliced
3 cloves garlic, smashed
1 yellow onion, chopped
2 teaspoons salt
1 teaspoon sugar
3 cilantro stalks

Combine all the ingredients in a stockpot. Cover with water about 6" above the vegetables, bring to a boil over high heat, then reduce heat to medium-low. Cover and let simmer for 1 hour. Strain.

Marinade for Meat

This is a classic Thai marinade. It is the most used marinade recipe for deep-frying, grilling, or sautéing meats. This mixture will marinate ½ pound of meat.

INGREDIENTS | YIELDS ½ CUP

1 teaspoon chopped cilantro roots or stems
¼ teaspoon salt
2 teaspoons chopped garlic
½ teaspoon freshly ground white pepper
2 teaspoons palm sugar
2 tablespoons light soy sauce
Dash of dark soy sauce (optional)

1. Combine the cilantro, salt, garlic, and white pepper, and make into a paste with a mortar and pestle.

2. Mix in sugar and soy sauce.

Dark Soy Sauce

The dark soy sauce will enrich the color of the marinade to a darker brown and add smoky flavor. It is used mainly for grilled items because the sugar in dark soy sauce will caramelize and enhance the flavor and the look of the dish.

Boiled Eggs (*Kai Tom*)

Though boiled eggs are often eaten with relishes, they are also used as an ingredient in many different recipes. Perfectly boiled eggs will have bright yellow yolks.

INGREDIENTS | SERVES 5

5 eggs
Water to cover
2 teaspoons vinegar
1 teaspoon salt

1. Place eggs in a pot in one layer and cover with cold water that reaches 2" above the eggs.

2. Add vinegar and salt to the water. Bring water to a boil and remove the pan from heat.

3. Cover the pot and let sit for 10–12 minutes.

4. Place eggs in ice water or cool them off under cold running water.

5. Cooked eggs can be stored for up to five days.

Easy-Peeling Eggs

For easy-peeling eggs, use older eggs. After a week in the refrigerator, the egg's membrane does not stick to the shell as much as it did when the egg was fresh. Salt added to boiling water will make peeling your eggs an easier task.

Fried Eggs (*Kai Tod*)

Fried eggs are great with some Thai chilies in fish sauce. A fried egg is also a perfect complement to any Thai fried rice (see recipes in Chapter 9) and Basil Fried Rice with Shrimp (see Chapter 9).

INGREDIENTS | YIELDS 1 EGG

½ cup vegetable oil
1 egg

1. Heat a pan or wok until hot.

2. Add oil to the pan and wait 30 seconds.

3. Crack egg into hot oil and let fry for 30 seconds.

4. Flip the egg and let fry on the other side for another 30 seconds.

5. For a more well-done and crispier egg, fry for a few seconds longer on each side.

Deep-Fried Minced Garlic

Garlic becomes sweet and fragrant when deep-fried.
Deep-fried garlic is often added to noodle soups and stews.

INGREDIENTS | YIELDS ½ CUP

½ cup oil
⅓ cup minced garlic

Browning Garlic

When using garlic in Thai stir-fries, it is fried until slightly brown before adding other ingredients. In Thai cuisine, garlic is added to hot oil so it will brown quickly. This is different from Western cuisine where garlic is added to cold oil and brought to heat together to prevent it from browning.

1. Heat a pan or wok until hot.

2. Add oil to the pan and wait 30 seconds.

3. Add garlic to hot oil and turn the heat to medium-low.

4. Stir constantly to brown the garlic and make sure garlic is covered with oil. Add more oil if needed. Do not let the garlic sit in hot oil without stirring, as it will burn.

5. When garlic pieces are slightly golden brown, about 30 seconds–1 minute. Turn off the heat and transfer to a jar. Fried garlic will keep in an airtight jar for three days.

Salted Duck Eggs (*Kai Kem*)

Duck eggs are immersed in salted water for twenty-one days. The result is very firm egg yolk and denser egg white. Salted duck eggs can be eaten with boiled rice, with other dishes, or made into a spicy salad.

INGREDIENTS | SERVES 5

8 cups water
2 tablespoons salt
5 duck eggs

Duck Eggs

Duck eggs are used for salting instead of chicken eggs because they have thicker shells and won't break as easily.

1. Bring water and salt to a boil and let it cool completely.

2. Put duck eggs in a large mason jar and pour the salt water over the eggs to the top of the jar.

3. Break a bamboo skewer to fit inside the jar opening and place it above the eggs to prevent them from floating above the water.

4. Close the lid and label the jar with the date.

5. Let sit for twenty-one days.

Salted Shrimp (*Kung Haeng*)

Salted shrimp is added to a lot of dishes, including Green Papaya Salad (see Chapter 4). You can buy dried shrimp at most Asian grocery stores, but making your own will ensure that there are no additives in the shrimp. Once made, it can be refrigerated for a few weeks or it can be frozen for up to one year.

INGREDIENTS | YIELDS 2 CUPS

4 cups small shrimp
2 teaspoons salt
1 tablespoon fish or soy sauce
1 teaspoon sugar

Traditional Salted Shrimp

Shrimp are traditionally salted and dried in direct sun for days until completely dried. Cheesecloth is used to cover the shrimp while drying to protect it from debris. Often, packaged dried shrimp contains preservatives and/or artificial coloring.

1. Halve the shrimp lengthwise. Cut shrimp into smaller pieces, about ½" long.

2. Mix together salt, fish or soy sauce, and sugar. Add shrimp and marinate for at least 2 hours.

3. Spread shrimp on a baking sheet and dry in an oven at 200°F with the door ajar for about 1 hour.

Rendered Pork Fat

Pork fat or lard is a flavorful cooking ingredient. It adds great flavor and texture to the dish. Even dishes that do not contain pork can be made with lard. The crispy pork fat or skin makes a great addition to spicy, dry relishes.

INGREDIENTS | YIELDS 1 CUP

1 pound pork skin and fat, chopped into 1" pieces
Water to cover

1. Place pork fat in a pan and cover with water.

2. Simmer at medium heat until boiling. Turn the heat down to low and stir occasionally. When the fat is rendered, the skin pieces are crispy and golden, and all the water is evaporated, about 15 minutes, strain the fat and store in the refrigerator for two months.

Plain Rice Soup

This rice is used just like jasmine rice. It is great with relishes, Salted Duck Eggs (see this chapter), or Salted Shrimp Salad (see Chapter 4). You can make a bunch of different kinds of relishes and serve them with this rice soup.

INGREDIENTS | YIELDS 4 CUPS

4 cups water
1 cup uncooked jasmine rice
⅛ teaspoon salt

Boiling Uncooked Rice

Rice soup made with uncooked rice yields a more glutinous soup than when using cooked rice. The starch in the rice is released into the water, making the soup thicker.

Add water and rice to a medium saucepan. Bring to a boil and let simmer over low heat for 30 minutes until rice is soft and open. Stir regularly to prevent the rice from sticking to the bottom. If the mixture is too dry, add water as needed. The rice should be of a thick soup consistency with liquid 1" above the rice. When the rice is done, add salt and stir to mix. Turn off the heat.

CHAPTER 3

Relishes and Sauces

Chili Tamarind Relish

This version of tamarind relish uses tamarind paste or pulp rather than fresh tamarinds. Serve it with raw vegetables (cucumber slices, carrots, snake beans, celery, radishes, or turnips) or blanched vegetables (green beans, Asian eggplants, cabbage, broccoli, or cauliflower).

INGREDIENTS | SERVES 2

2 tablespoons palm sugar

1 tablespoon water

1½ cups tamarind pulp

12 dried long red Thai chilies or New Mexico chilies

1 teaspoon salt

2 tablespoons minced garlic

3 tablespoons dried shrimp

Dried Chilies

Sometimes long red Thai chilies are not readily available even at Asian grocery stores. New Mexico chilies are a great substitution. They are a little bit spicier and slightly larger.

1. Place palm sugar and 1 tablespoon water in a microwave-safe bowl. Melt palm sugar and water in the microwave for 45 seconds on high, or on the stovetop at very low heat until dissolved.

2. Work the tamarind pulp (can be purchased at Asian, Mediterranean, Mexican, or Indian grocery stores) to remove the pulp, leaving just the meat for use in the relish.

3. If using a mortar and pestle, add chilies and salt and pound until broken. Add garlic and dried shrimp and pound until incorporated. Add palm sugar and tamarind pulp and mix well.

4. Alternatively, add all ingredients in a food processor and pulse until incorporated.

5. Serve with fresh or blanched vegetables.

Northern-Style Relish with Pork (*Nam Prik Ong*)

This relish is a specialty in northern Thailand. Serve it with raw vegetables (cucumber slices, carrots, snake beans, celery, radishes, or turnips), blanched vegetables (green beans, Asian eggplants, cabbage, broccoli, or cauliflower), and crispy pork rind (chicharrón).

INGREDIENTS | YIELDS 2 CUPS

Paste

6 dried long red Thai chilies, soaked, drained, and deseeded

¼ teaspoon salt

2 teaspoons chopped galangal

1 tablespoon chopped lemongrass

4 tablespoons chopped shallot

2 tablespoons chopped garlic

1 teaspoon shrimp paste

1 cup chopped tomatoes (make sure they are not super-sweet)

Relish

3 tablespoons vegetable oil or lard

2 garlic cloves, peeled and minced

6 ounces ground pork

2 tablespoons fish sauce

Pinch of palm sugar

Pinch of salt

2–4 tablespoons chicken or pork stock if needed

1. Make the paste by pounding the chilies with the remaining paste ingredients, adding one by one into the mortar in the order given. Set aside.

2. Heat a fry pan over medium heat. Add oil and 2 cloves of minced garlic, and fry until fragrant and brown, about 15 seconds. Add paste and continue to fry over medium heat for several minutes until fragrant. Stir regularly.

3. Add minced pork and stir to break up the pork pieces. When pork is cooked, about 1–2 minutes, season with fish sauce, palm sugar, and salt. If the mixture is too dry, add pork or chicken stock as needed.

The Chili Infusion

Chilies are not indigenous to Asia. They arrived in Thailand from South America with Portuguese traders and missionaries. Today, the Thai people eat more chilies on average than any other country in the world.

Ham Relish

Ham is not a traditional Thai ingredient, but the way this relish is prepared is. Keep in mind that many different ingredients, like smoked salmon, can be swapped out for ham.

INGREDIENTS | SERVES 2

1 cup coconut milk

½ cup diced ham

¼ cup fermented rice (optional—can be found online or at some Asian grocery stores)

3 fresh long red chilies, sliced in rounds (any kind that is not too spicy will do)

2 tablespoons minced shallots

Pinch of salt

½ teaspoon palm sugar

2 tablespoons Tamarind Water (see Chapter 2)

1 tablespoon chopped cilantro

1. Bring coconut milk to a boil in a medium saucepan. Add ham and fermented rice (if using) and mix well.

2. Add the chilies, shallots, salt, sugar, and tamarind water and mix well. Bring to a boil and turn off the heat. Garnish with chopped cilantro. Serve with steamed or fresh vegetables of your choice.

Relish with Pork (*Lon Moo*)

This version of a cooked relish is great to share as a side dish or appetizer with fresh seasonal vegetables. Try serving with cucumbers, kohlrabi, or steamed daikon.

INGREDIENTS | SERVES 2

4 ounces ground pork

½ cup fermented rice

1 teaspoon salt

1 cup coconut milk

½ cup minced shallots

1 tablespoon palm sugar

4 red and green Serrano or jalapeño peppers

1. Marinate pork with fermented rice and salt for 2 hours in the refrigerator.

2. Heat coconut milk in a saucepan. Add marinated pork and stir to mix well.

3. Add all the shallots, sugar, and whole peppers to the saucepan. Bring to a boil, turn the heat off, and serve warm.

Green Mango Relish

This relish uses green mango, found in Asian grocery stores. Green mangoes from Mexico are often not sour enough to make this relish. If using a green mango from Mexico, try adding a little bit of tamarind water or lime juice to balance the flavor.

INGREDIENTS | SERVES 4

6 cloves garlic

10 fresh red Thai chilies

2 teaspoons shrimp paste

2 teaspoons palm sugar

1 tablespoon fish sauce

1 green mango, shredded

Combine all ingredients, except mango, in a food processor and blend until smooth. Add shredded mango and pulse until just chopped. Serve with steamed vegetables and Fried Fish with Turmeric (see Chapter 11).

Shrimp Paste Relish (*Nam Prik Kapi*)

This is probably the most common relish at a Thai dinner table. It is easy to make and you can adjust it to your preferred taste. It is best served with fried fish, such as Fried Fish with Turmeric (see Chapter 11), and fresh vegetables.

INGREDIENTS | YIELDS ½ CUP

5 cloves garlic

⅛ teaspoon salt

1 tablespoon shrimp paste, roasted

3–5 Thai chilies, red or green

2 teaspoons palm sugar

1 tablespoon lime juice

1 teaspoon fish sauce

1. Pound garlic, salt, and shrimp paste with a mortar and pestle. Add chilies and pound until chilies are bruised and broken into smaller pieces. Season with palm sugar, lime juice, and fish sauce.

2. Alternatively, add all ingredients to a small food processor. Grind until blended.

Stir-Fried Chili Relish with Dried Shrimp

This chili relish can be made to be very spicy or toned down to have equal parts sweet, salty, and spicy flavors. It's great with strong-flavored raw vegetables, like turnip or daikon (white Japanese radish), or Boiled Eggs (see Chapter 2).

INGREDIENTS | YIELDS 1 CUP

10–15 dried long red Thai chilies or New Mexico chilies

2 tablespoons chopped garlic

3 tablespoons chopped shallot

1 teaspoon salt

2 tablespoons Salted Shrimp (see Chapter 2) or store-bought salted shrimp

5 tablespoons pork fat or lard

2 teaspoons minced garlic

2 teaspoons sugar

2 tablespoons fish sauce

1. Make the paste by putting chilies, chopped garlic, shallot, salt, and dried shrimp in a food processor and processing until smooth. Alternatively, pound the ingredients with a mortar and pestle. Set aside.

2. Heat a fry pan until hot over medium heat. Add lard and wait for 10 seconds. Add minced garlic and fry until golden brown for 15 seconds

3. Add the paste to the pan and stir-fry until fragrant and the paste starts to turn a darker color, about 30 seconds.

4. Season with sugar and fish sauce. Taste and adjust to your preferred taste.

Sweet and Sour Sauce

This sauce is a base for other dipping sauces.
Used as is, this is a great sauce for Egg Rolls (see Chapter 5).

INGREDIENTS | YIELDS 1½ CUPS

½ cup water

1 cup sugar

½ cup white vinegar

1 teaspoon salt

1 tablespoon minced garlic

1 teaspoon Roasted Thai Chili Flakes (see Chapter 2)

1. In a small, heavy saucepan, combine the sugar, water, vinegar, and salt. Bring to a rolling boil over medium heat. Stir to dissolve the sugar and salt and reduce heat to low. Simmer until the liquid thickens slightly to a light syrup, about 20 minutes.

2. Add minced garlic and roasted chili flakes. Turn off the heat and cool to room temperature.

Storing the Sauce

Sweet and Sour Sauce can be stored at room temperature for a few weeks or indefinitely in the fridge.

Plum Sauce

This sauce is thick, sweet, sour, and a tad spicy. It's great for dipping fried foods like Shrimp Cakes (see Chapter 5). Preserved plum is available at Asian grocery stores.

INGREDIENTS | YIELDS 1 CUP

⅓ cup plum preserves
⅓ cup white vinegar
⅓ cup water
⅔ cup sugar
1 teaspoon minced red chilies

1. Place all the ingredients in a food processor or blender and process until smooth.

2. Transfer the mixture to a small saucepan and bring to a boil over medium heat; reduce heat to low and simmer until thick, about 20 minutes.

3. Allow mixture to cool to room temperature.

Sweet Pork (*Moo Waan*)

This dish is great as a side for relish or with Thai Fried Rice with Shrimp Paste (see Chapter 9).

INGREDIENTS | SERVES 2

2 tablespoons vegetable oil
1 tablespoon minced shallots
1 cup thinly sliced pork shoulder
2 tablespoons palm sugar
1 tablespoon fish sauce
1 teaspoon dark soy sauce
¼ cup water

1. Heat a medium sauté pan over medium-high heat, add oil, turn down the heat to medium, and sauté shallots until fragrant, about 15 seconds.

2. Add pork and stir-fry until pork is almost done.

3. Season with palm sugar, fish sauce, and dark soy sauce. Add water and sauté until water is reduced to a thick sauce. Turn off the heat.

Chili Jam (*Nam Prik Pao*)

*This sweet, tangy, and slightly spicy "jam" is great on its own,
with an omelet, or on top of your favorite vegetables.*

INGREDIENTS | YIELDS 4 CUPS

2 cups oil

2 cups sliced shallots

1 cup sliced garlic

¼ cup dried shrimp, rinsed

½ cup dried long red Thai chilies, deseeded and chopped (chilies from New Mexico are a good substitute)

5 slices galangal, about ⅛" thick

1 teaspoon shrimp paste, roasted

½ cup palm sugar

½ cup thick Tamarind Water (see Chapter 2—to make thick tamarind water, soak a Ping-Pong ball–sized scoop of deseeded tamarind paste in slightly warm water, squeeze out the liquid, and strain, saving the liquid for use. Add more water to the leftover solids if it doesn't make ½ cup)

1 tablespoon salt or 3 tablespoons fish sauce

Roasting Shrimp Paste

Place shrimp paste on a spoon and hold it over a flame on the stove for 1–2 minutes. Be careful as the spoon gets hot. You can also place shrimp paste in aluminum foil and heat it in a hot dry pan on the stove.

1. Heat oil in a wok or a cast-iron deep pan over medium heat. Deep-fry shallots, garlic, dried shrimp, chilies, and galangal separately, one by one, until golden. Drain on paper towels.

2. Blend them all in a food processor with shrimp paste. Add a little bit of frying oil, up to ½ cup, to moisten the mixture.

3. In a saucepan, bring the mixture to a boil and season with palm sugar, tamarind water, and salt or fish sauce. Simmer until quite thick, stirring regularly to prevent the paste from burning. The jam should be sweet, sour, and salty with a little bit of heat. If you would like it to be hotter, you can add fried dried small Thai chilies along with the dried big chilies.

Thick Sweet and Sour Sauce

This is a perfect sauce for any grilled meat, especially grilled chicken.
The sauce is thick, sweet, and sour, with a touch of spice.

INGREDIENTS | YIELDS ½ CUP

1 tablespoon minced fresh long red chili (Serrano, jalapeño, or finger pepper)

1 teaspoon minced garlic

½ teaspoon salt

1 tablespoon sugar

½ cup white vinegar

Combine all ingredients in a small saucepan. Bring to a boil over medium-high heat, then turn down to low heat and simmer until thickened, about 5–7 minutes. Remove from heat.

Spicy Thai Dressing

This dressing is great as a salad dressing or seafood dipping sauce.
The dressing will keep in the refrigerator for five days.

INGREDIENTS | YIELDS 1 CUP

8 fresh red or green Thai chilies, minced

8 cloves garlic, minced

6 tablespoons fish sauce

½ cup lime juice

2 teaspoons sugar

2 teaspoons honey

To make the dressing, crush the chilies and garlic with a mortar and pestle into a coarse paste. Add fish sauce, lime juice, sugar, and honey to the chili and garlic paste. Alternatively, put all ingredients in a food processor or blender and blend until chilies and garlic are chopped into small pieces, about 10 seconds.

Thai Dressings

Thai dressing revolves around the principle of balancing sour, spicy, sweet, salty, and bitter flavors. Different ingredients are used to bring in different flavors.

Roasted Chili Dipping Sauce with Shallots

*This sauce is especially great for grilled pork or beef,
and the roasted chilies add a delicious smoky flavor.*

INGREDIENTS | YIELDS ½ CUP

3 tablespoons lime juice

2 tablespoons fish sauce

1 teaspoon sugar

Large pinch of roasted chili flakes

1 shallot, finely sliced

1 tablespoon chopped coriander

Combine all ingredients and let sit for 15 minutes to allow for the shallots to marinate and to remove the strong, sharp taste.

Shallots

Shallots are in the onion and garlic family. They are mild when raw and cook down much faster than onions. Red onions are a great substitution for shallots.

Salted Egg Relish

This relish is great served with pineapple, green mango, or green apple. Raw and steamed vegetables will also complement the relish well.

INGREDIENTS | YIELDS 2 CUPS

2 Salted Duck Eggs (see Chapter 2), boiled
  for 8 minutes at low simmer

1 cup coconut milk

2 tablespoons minced pork

2 teaspoons fish sauce

½ cup chicken stock or water

1 teaspoon palm sugar

1 tablespoon Tamarind Water (see Chapter 2)

3 tablespoons minced shrimp

2 Serrano peppers, cut in rounds

1 tablespoon finely sliced lemongrass

2 kaffir lime leaves, thinly julienned

1 shallot, thinly sliced

1 tablespoon cilantro

1. Cut boiled duck eggs in half and scoop out the yolks. Chop yolks and whites into small pieces.

2. Heat coconut milk in a medium saucepan over medium heat; add pork and then fish sauce. Simmer until pork is almost cooked, about 1 minute. Add water or stock and season with palm sugar and tamarind water.

3. Add minced shrimp, peppers, and lemongrass and simmer until shrimp is done, about 3 minutes.

4. Finally, add chopped eggs, lime leaves, shallots, and cilantro and turn off the heat.

Roast Chili Sauce

Using this sauce or paste is a great way to spice up any dish. It is a great condiment to always have in the fridge. The flavor of this sauce adds a great depth to any dish, more so than just dried chilies.

INGREDIENTS | YIELDS 2 CUPS

2 cups vegetable oil
4 shallots, chopped
4 garlic cloves, chopped
10 small dried Thai chilies
½ teaspoon salt
1 teaspoon palm sugar

1. In a deep frying pan, fry shallot and garlic in oil that has been heated to 350°F until golden brown, about 2 minutes. Drain.

2. Fry chilies in the same oil until fragrant, about 1 minute. Drain.

3. Put shallots, garlic, and chilies in a food processor, add salt, sugar, and 2 tablespoons of frying oil and blend until smooth. If the mixture is too dry and becomes hard to mix, add more oil.

Spicy Yellow Bean Sauce

This sauce is great with noodle soups or as a salad dressing.
Dilute with more water for dressing.

INGREDIENTS | YIELDS 1 CUP

1 tablespoon minced cilantro stems
2 teaspoons chopped garlic
1 tablespoon chopped ginger
3 tablespoons soybean paste or yellow bean sauce
1 long red chili (Serrano or finger pepper)
1 teaspoon palm sugar
1 tablespoon white vinegar

Combine all ingredients in a blender and blend until smooth. Alternatively, pound all ingredients using a mortar and pestle until smooth, adding vinegar at the end.

Yellow Bean Paste

Thais call soybeans yellow beans. Because of this, yellow bean sauce or paste is the same as salted soybean or soybean paste.

Sweet Fish Sauce (*Nam Pal Waan*)

This is a great dipping sauce for fruits that are on the tart side like pineapples and green mangoes.

INGREDIENTS | SERVES 4

4 Thai chilies, sliced

3 teaspoons fish sauce

⅓ cup palm sugar

2 thinly sliced shallots

½ teaspoon shrimp paste (optional)

2 tablespoons Tamarind Water (see Chapter 2)

1 tablespoon Salted Shrimp (see Chapter 2)

¼ cup water

In a saucepan, combine all ingredients and bring to a boil. Let simmer over low heat until slightly thickened. Serve with whatever sweet and sour fresh fruit you can find.

Banana Pepper Relish (*Nam Prik Noom*)

This relish is a northern-style dish. Make sure the banana pepper that you use is spicy.

INGREDIENTS | YIELDS 1 CUP

5 shallots, unpeeled and grilled

3 garlic cloves, unpeeled and grilled

4 medium banana chilies, grilled

1 tablespoon shrimp paste

¼ teaspoon salt

1 teaspoon palm sugar

1 tablespoon chopped green onion

1 tablespoon chopped cilantro

Raw vegetables of your choice

1. Grill shallots, garlic, and chilies over medium flame until they are charred, about 1–2 minutes. Alternatively, place shallots, garlic, and chilies in heavy cast-iron pan over medium-high heat, and dry roast until charred, about 3–5 minutes. Remove from heat and let cool. When they are cool to touch, peel off the charred skin.

2. Roast shrimp paste by wrapping in a banana leaf or aluminum foil and put on a hot, heavy pan or roast over flame.

3. Add roasted shrimp paste, shallot, garlic, chilies, salt, and sugar to a food processor and pulse until coarsely chopped. Sprinkle with green onions and cilantro to serve. Serve with raw vegetables.

CHAPTER 4

Salads and Pickles

Beef Salad (*Yum Nuer*)

This is a classic street food usually served with sticky rice.
This dressing recipe is great for any type of grilled meat.

INGREDIENTS | SERVES 4

Salad

1 pound rump roast

2 tablespoons soy sauce

3 cups mixed green salad or romaine
   lettuce

½ cup sliced pickling cucumber

½ cup cherry tomatoes

Handful of chopped cilantro

Dressing

4 fresh red or green Thai chilies, minced

4 cloves garlic, minced

3 tablespoons fish sauce

4 tablespoons lime juice

1 teaspoon honey

1 teaspoon sugar

1. Marinate beef with soy sauce and let sit for 30 minutes.

2. Grill to desired doneness. Slice beef and put in a salad bowl. Throw in the rest of the salad ingredients.

3. To make the dressing, crush the chilies and garlic with a mortar and pestle to a coarse paste. Add fish sauce, lime juice, honey, and sugar to the chili and garlic paste. Alternatively, put all ingredients in a food processor or blender and blend until chilies and garlic are chopped into small pieces, about 10 seconds.

4. Add the salad dressing and toss well.

Thai Salads

Most Thai salads are spicy. The dressings almost always have a perfect balance of salty, sweet, sour, spicy, and bitter.

Prawn Salad (*Pla Kung*)

The addition of lemongrass in this recipe helps balance the strong seafood flavor of the shrimp.

INGREDIENTS | SERVES 4

½ cup water
1 pound peeled and deveined large prawns
1 stalk thinly sliced lemongrass
2 thinly sliced shallots
½ cup mint leaves
2 thinly sliced kaffir lime leaves
1 tablespoon fish sauce
1 tablespoon lime juice
5 Thai chilies, minced
1 wedge of green or purple cabbage

1. Bring ½ cup water to a boil in a sauté pan.

2. Add prawns and sauté over medium heat until they are just cooked, about 2 minutes. Be careful not to overcook the prawns. Transfer to a mixing bowl.

3. Add the remaining ingredients except cabbage to the bowl and mix well. Taste and adjust the sour, spicy, and salty to your preferred taste.

4. Serve on pieces of cabbage.

Thai Shrimp Ceviche

This is a famous restaurant dish. Make sure to buy fresh shrimp from a store you can trust. Only saltwater shrimp can be used.

INGREDIENTS | SERVES 4

6 fresh red or green Thai chilies, minced
4 cloves garlic, minced
3 tablespoons fish sauce
4 tablespoons lime juice
2 tablespoons chopped cilantro
1 pound medium-sized shrimp, peeled and deveined

1. Mix all ingredients, except shrimp, in a small bowl. Adjust ingredients to achieve the desired balance of salty, sweet, and sour.

2. Lay shrimp on a deep plate; pour the dressing over the shrimp. Place in the freezer for 20 minutes. Serve.

Thai Ceviche

This dish is simply raw. As the shrimp sits in the lime juice, the protein is denatured. The shrimp appears cooked after being exposed to the high acidity.

Pickled Cabbage

This is a great side dish to serve with curries or spicy relishes.

INGREDIENTS | SERVES 6

1 tablespoon chopped dried long red chili (or jalapeño, Serrano, or finger pepper)

Salt to taste

1 tablespoon chopped shallot

1 tablespoon chopped garlic

½ cup vegetable oil

1 cup coconut water (fresh or canned)

1 cup white vinegar

1 cup water

1 cup cauliflower, cut into bite-sized pieces

1 cup diced cucumber

1 cup shredded cabbage

1 cup corn kernels

1 tablespoon white sugar

1 teaspoon toasted sesame seeds

1. Make a smooth paste by pounding the chili, pinch of salt, shallot, and garlic with a mortar and pestle.

2. In a large fry pan, heat the oil over medium heat until hot. Add the paste and fry until fragrant, about 30 seconds. Add the coconut water, vinegar, and water, and bring to a boil.

3. Add the cauliflower, cucumber, cabbage, and corn and sauté for 1 minute, until wilted (be careful not to overcook them).

4. Add the sugar and mix well. Taste and adjust, adding more salt if needed. Sprinkle with sesame seeds. This is best used on the same day, but will keep in a sealed container in the refrigerator for up to two weeks.

Pickled Mustard Greens

Any hardy greens like collard greens, kale, or Swiss chard can be used in this recipe.
Pickled Chinese mustard greens can be purchased at most Asian grocery stores.

INGREDIENTS | YIELDS 4 CUPS

1 teaspoon plus 1 tablespoon salt, divided

4 cups water

2 bunches mustard greens

4–6 cups rice-rinsing water (the water reserved from rinsing the rice before cooking)

2 tablespoons palm sugar

1 tablespoon white sugar

1. Dissolve 1 teaspoon salt in water. Wash the mustard greens and separate the leaves. Cut the leaves into 2"-long pieces and soak them in the salt water overnight (this helps remove their peppery taste).

2. Discard the water and dry the leaves completely by laying them on the counter near the window or in the sun, if possible, until completely dry—usually about 24 hours.

3. In a large mixing bowl, mix 1 tablespoon salt, rice-rinsing water, and sugars together, making sure the sugar is dissolved.

4. Place the greens in a large, lidded jar and pour the liquid over them. Let ferment at room temperature in a cool, dry place for 1–2 weeks, then refrigerate. Greens will keep for a few months in the refrigerator.

Cucumber Salad

This easy dish is great as a side for several meals,
especially dishes that contain dried spices like yellow curry or satay.

INGREDIENTS | YIELDS 4 CUPS

Dressing

⅓ cup white vinegar
⅓ cup sugar
½ cup water
1 teaspoon salt

Salad

3 pickling cucumbers
1 whole Serrano pepper
1 thinly sliced shallot
1 teaspoon minced ginger
¼ cup chopped cilantro

1. In a medium saucepan, bring white vinegar, sugar, water, and salt to a boil to dissolve the sugar. Turn off heat and let cool.

2. Quarter the cucumber lengthwise and slice it thinly. In a mixing bowl, combine all the ingredients and toss well with dressing. Let the salad rest for 20 minutes.

Pickled Limes

Pickled limes can be purchased at the store, but making your own is a very easy process. In addition, pickled limes will keep for up to a year in the refrigerator. Use pickled limes whole because cutting them will release the bitterness and overpower the dish that they are in.

INGREDIENTS | YIELDS 5 PICKLED LIMES

5 small Mexican limes
1½ cups water
1 tablespoon salt
⅓ cup sugar
3 tablespoons white vinegar

1. Prick limes all over with a fork and steam for 1 hour. Leave them to dry in the sun or by a window for 24 hours.

2. In a medium saucepan, bring water, salt, sugar, and white vinegar to a boil to dissolve sugar. Pour over limes in a clean jar, cool, and cover.

3. Keep pickled limes at room temperature for up to six months.

Mango Salad

*Green mangoes are the best for this salad. They can be purchased at an
Asian grocery store from April to September. Carrots or cucumbers can be used for this recipe,
and green apples make an excellent substitution for mangoes if necessary.*

INGREDIENTS | YIELDS 3 CUPS

2 cups julienned green mangoes, 4" long

¼ cup thinly sliced shallot or red onion

¼ cup any kind of chopped, toasted, or fried nuts

2 tablespoons chopped cilantro

3 tablespoons lime juice (more if using cucumbers or carrots)

3 tablespoons fish sauce

2 minced Thai chilies

1 teaspoon sugar

Place everything in a bowl and toss. Adjust to desired taste.

Waterfall Beef (*Nam Tok*)

The beef is grilled until it is medium-rare and then sliced. This salad is similar to larb. *Pork is a good
alternative to beef, although other chewy meats might be a good substitute.*

INGREDIENTS | SERVES 2

2 tablespoons uncooked sticky rice

5 ounces beef sirloin

3 thinly sliced shallots

⅓ cup coarsely chopped spearmint and cilantro, mixed

1 teaspoon sugar

3 tablespoons lime juice

3 tablespoons fish sauce

½ teaspoon roasted Thai chili flakes

1. Dry-roast sticky rice in a frying pan over medium heat. Stir until golden brown, about 10–15 minutes. Grind roasted rice in a coffee grinder and set aside.

2. Grill beef to preferred doneness (usually Thais grill it medium-rare). Let the meat rest for 10 minutes.

3. Slice beef and combine all the ingredients in a mixing bowl. Mix well.

Southern Salad (*Salad Kaek*)

This dressing will be good on any kind of salad.
The combination of homemade potato chips and boiled eggs creates an amazing blend of texture.

INGREDIENTS | SERVES 4

Dressing

2 dried long red chilies

2 cups coconut milk

2 boiled egg yolks

¼ cup chopped shallots

½ cup roasted peanuts

1 teaspoon curry powder

¼ teaspoon salt

⅓ cup sugar

3 tablespoons fish sauce

¼ cup Tamarind Water (see Chapter 2)

Salad

1 small potato, sliced and fried

3 hard-boiled eggs

½ cup fried tofu, sliced

2 cups green leaf lettuce

1 cup blanched bean sprouts

5 small pickling cucumbers, halved
   lengthwise and sliced

1 onion, sliced

2 tomatoes, sliced

1. Make the dressing by combining all ingredients in a blender and blending until smooth.

2. Place all other ingredients in a mixing bowl and mix well. Drizzle with the dressing and serve.

Indian Influence on Thai Food

Thai cuisine has been strongly influenced by Indian food. For example, adding dried spices like curry powder adds a punch to Thai foods.

Fresh Pork Sausage and Fried Rice Ball Salad (*Yum Noon Sen*)

This northern-style salad is crunchy, spicy, sour, sweet, and salty all at once!

INGREDIENTS | SERVES 2

Crispy Rice Ball

1 tablespoon galangal, finely chopped

2 dried long red chilies, soaked in warm water for 5 minutes, seeded, and finely chopped

3 tablespoons finely chopped lemongrass

1 tablespoon finely chopped shallots

1 tablespoon finely chopped garlic

1 cup cooked Jasmine Rice (see Chapter 2)

1 tablespoon fish sauce

3 cups vegetable oil for deep-frying

Sausage

1 cup ground pork

½ cup chicken stock or water

½ cup boiled pork skin, shredded

¼ cup julienned ginger

¼ cup thinly sliced shallot

1 tablespoon minced garlic

¼ cup chopped cilantro

¼ cup chopped green onion

5 small chilies, fried and dried

1 teaspoon salt

3–4 tablespoons fish sauce

Frying Dried Chilies

Add 1 cup of oil to fry pan and let heat to 350°F. Add ½ cup chilies to hot oil and fry for 1 minute. Transfer to a paper towel on a plate to absorb the oil. Let cool. Alternatively, heat up a frying pan and add a little bit of oil to just coat the pan. Add chilies to the pan and stir until fragrant and chilies begin to change color.

1. Make rice balls by first making the paste. Pound the galangal, chilies, lemongrass, shallots, and garlic using a mortar and pestle.

2. Mix the paste with rice and fish sauce until incorporated.

3. Roll the rice into golf ball–sized balls. If the rice is too dry to stick, moisten with warm water.

4. Heat 3 cups of oil in a medium, heavy pot to 350°F.

5. Deep-fry the rice balls until golden and crispy, about 4 minutes. Let cool. Drain on paper towels.

6. Sauté pork with water or stock until pork is thoroughly cooked, about 2 minutes.

7. Break up rice ball into small pieces.

8. Mix cooked pork and the rest of the ingredients in a mixing bowl. Toss well and serve with cabbage or over fresh vegetables of your choice.

Bean Thread Noodle Salad (*Yum Woon Sen*)

This is a simple and flavorful salad. It is served at room temperature and will keep well at room temperature for a few hours unrefrigerated. Other meat or seafood can be substituted for shrimp and pork in this recipe.

INGREDIENTS | SERVES 2

Dressing

Pinch of salt

2 Thai chilies

1 teaspoon white sugar

2 teaspoons palm sugar

¼ cup lime juice

¼ cup fish sauce (or soy sauce and fermented soybean paste for a vegetarian option)

Salad

2 tablespoons vegetable oil

2 cloves garlic, minced

⅛ pound shrimp, minced

⅛ pound pork, minced

1 tablespoon soy sauce

2 ounces dried bean thread or cellophane noodles, boiled for 1½ minutes and drained

2 medium tomatoes, chopped

3 tablespoons chopped cilantro

2 thinly sliced shallots

2 tablespoons chopped green onions

1. Make dressing by pounding all the ingredients in a mortar and pestle or in a food chopper/processor.

2. Heat sauté pan over medium heat, add oil and 15 seconds later, add garlic. Fry until fragrant and golden, about 10 seconds.

3. Add minced shrimp and pork and stir-fry until cooked, about 2 minutes. Add soy sauce to taste.

4. Mix all remaining ingredients and the cooked meat in a mixing bowl.

5. Pour dressing on top and mix well.

Cilantro Roots

Thais use all the parts of a cilantro or coriander plant, including the roots, which are used in curry pastes, marinades, and dressings. The roots are not available in most places unless you grow your own cilantro plants. If you don't have roots, use the end of cilantro stems by cutting about 1" off the end of the cilantro bunch.

Green Bean Salad

Winged beans, which are from the tropical legume family, are not widely available in the United States. Green beans are a great substitution.

INGREDIENTS | SERVES 4

⅔ pound green beans

1 teaspoon dried roasted chili flakes

3 cloves garlic, roasted and chopped

2 roasted shallots, chopped

1 tablespoon sugar

2 tablespoons fish sauce

2 tablespoons lime juice

½ cup cooked sliced pork

½ cup coconut milk, boiled for 15 seconds, divided in half

2 tablespoons fried shallot (bought at store)

2 tablespoons chopped roasted peanuts

5 small chilies, fried and dried

Roasted Fresh Spices

To roast fresh shallots or garlic, place over an open flame until fragrant, about 1–2 minutes. Alternatively, place garlic or shallots in a hot wok with a little bit of water. Roast until water is evaporated.

1. Cut green beans on an angle, about 1" long. Blanch green beans by putting them in boiling water for 45 seconds. Place blanched green beans in cold water to stop cooking.

2. Make a paste by pounding roasted chili flakes, roasted garlic, and roasted shallot using a mortar and pestle. Mix in sugar, fish sauce, and lime juice with the paste and stir until sugar is dissolved. Reserve the mixture for dressing.

3. In a mixing bowl, mix blanched green beans, cooked pork, half of the coconut milk, fried shallots, roasted peanuts, and the dressing. Toss until well mixed.

4. Place the mixed salad on a plate and top with the rest of the coconut milk and roasted dried chilies.

Seafood Salad

Any combination of seafood like mussels, calamari, shrimp,
scallops, and fish can be used in this dish.

INGREDIENTS | SERVES 4

Dressing

3 Thai chilies, minced

2 tablespoons minced garlic

¼ cup lime juice

3–4 tablespoons fish sauce

Salad

12 ounces mixed seafood

3 tablespoons chopped scallions

¼ cup thinly sliced shallots

¼ cup thinly julienned ginger

¼ cup thinly sliced lemongrass, about 1 stalk

¼ cup spearmint leaves

1. Make the dressing by pounding Thai chilies and garlic using a mortar and pestle. Add lime juice and fish sauce to the paste.

2. Blanch seafood separately until just cooked and place it in a mixing bowl.

3. Add all other salad ingredients and the dressing to the blanched seafood and mix well.

Chicken Larb

Other meats aside from chicken can be used for this dish.
You can buy preground meat from the store or grind your own meat using a food processor.

INGREDIENTS | SERVES 2

2 tablespoons uncooked sticky rice

1 teaspoon minced garlic

Salt, divided

5 ounces ground chicken

3 tablespoons chicken stock

1 teaspoon white sugar

3 tablespoons lime juice

1 teaspoon Roasted Thai Chili Flakes (see Chapter 2)

1 tablespoon fish sauce

2 thinly sliced shallots

½ cup mixed mint and cilantro leaves

1. Dry-roast sticky rice in a frying pan over medium heat. Stir until golden brown, about 10–15 minutes. Grind roasted rice in a coffee grinder and set aside.

2. Add minced garlic and a pinch of salt to the ground chicken.

3. Heat stock or water in a sauté pan over medium-high heat, and season with salt to taste and sugar. Add chicken and simmer, stirring often, until just cooked, about 2–3 minutes.

4. Season with lime juice, chili flakes, and fish sauce. Mix in shallots, herbs, and ground roasted rice. Taste for seasoning before serving.

Green Papaya Salad (*Som Tum*)

This salad is the number one street food in Thailand. This is the simplest version of the salad, but you can dress it up by adding a few grilled shrimp to the mix. In Thailand, fermented fish or salted crab is often added.

INGREDIENTS | SERVES 2

3 garlic cloves, peeled

Pinch of salt

4–6 Thai chilies (less or more according to your spice preference)

2 tablespoons dried shrimp

1 tablespoon coarsely chopped roasted peanuts

4 cherry tomatoes, halved

2 snake beans (optional)

2 tablespoons palm sugar

1 tablespoon water

2–3 cups shredded green papaya

1 tablespoon lime juice

1 tablespoon Tamarind Water (see Chapter 2)

1–2 tablespoons fish sauce

1. Pound garlic, salt, and chilies using a mortar and pestle. Add dried shrimp, and pound until dried shrimp is broken.

2. Add peanuts, tomatoes, snake beans (if using), and the paste to a medium bowl and mix well. Set aside.

3. Place sugar in a microwave-safe bowl with 1 tablespoon water. Heat for 45 seconds to make a syrup. Set aside.

4. Place shredded green papaya in the bowl with the shrimp paste/peanut mixture. Add palm sugar syrup, lime juice, tamarind water, and fish sauce. Toss to coat papaya and serve.

Green Papaya

Green papayas are picked when they are young and green. Shred papaya using a mandoline or a small handheld shredder that you can purchase at Asian grocery stores.

Mixed Fruit Salad

This great salad combines different sweet and sour fruits mixed in with fish sauce and dried shrimp. It is a play on Green Papaya Salad (see this chapter).

INGREDIENTS | SERVES 4

3 garlic cloves, peeled

Pinch of salt

4–6 Thai chilies (less or more according to your spice preference)

2 tablespoons dried shrimp

2 tablespoons palm sugar

1 tablespoon water

1 tablespoon lime juice

1–2 tablespoons fish sauce

1 tablespoon Tamarind Water (see Chapter 2)

2–3 cups mixed fruits (fig, apples, guava, and berries) cut into bite-sized pieces

1 tablespoon coarsely chopped roasted peanuts

1. Pound garlic, salt, and chilies using a mortar and pestle. Add dried shrimp, and pound until dried shrimp is broken.

2. In a microwave-safe bowl, mix palm sugar with 1 tablespoon water. Heat for 45 seconds on high to make a syrup.

3. Mix the syrup with the paste, lime juice, fish sauce, and tamarind water to make dressing. In a mixing bowl, add cut fruits, dressing, and peanuts and toss.

Spicy Cucumber Salad

Another popular version of Green Papaya Salad (see this chapter) made when cucumbers are abundant in the summer.

INGREDIENTS | SERVES 2

3 garlic cloves, peeled

Pinch of salt

4–6 Thai chilies (less or more according to your preference)

2 tablespoons dried shrimp

2 tablespoons palm sugar

1 tablespoon water

1 tablespoon lime juice

1 tablespoon Tamarind Water (see Chapter 2)

1–2 tablespoons fish sauce

2–3 cups julienned pickling cucumbers

1 tablespoon roasted peanuts, coarsely chopped

1. Pound garlic, salt, and chilies using a mortar and pestle. Add dried shrimp, and pound until dried shrimp is broken.

2. In a microwave-safe bowl, mix palm sugar with 1 tablespoon water. Heat for 45 seconds on high to make a syrup.

3. Mix the syrup with the paste, lime juice, tamarind water, and fish sauce to make dressing. In a mixing bowl, add cucumber, dressing, and peanuts and toss.

Pickled Garlic

Larger garlic cloves or whole heads of small spring garlic can be used in this recipe. Pickled garlic is available at Asian grocery stores, but making your own is easy and it will keep for up to six months in the refrigerator.

INGREDIENTS | YIELDS 2 CUPS

20 cloves garlic

Water for soaking

Salt for soaking

2 cups water

1 cup white vinegar or coconut vinegar

2 tablespoons salt

1 cup white sugar

1. Peel garlic and soak in salted water overnight. (One part salt to four parts water.) This amount of salt water should cover the garlic.

2. Mix 2 cups water, vinegar, 2 tablespoons salt, and sugar in a saucepan. Bring to a boil over high heat to dissolve sugar.

3. Let cool. Place garlic in a jar, pour the syrup over the garlic, and seal the jar. Leave in the sun or a warm dry place like a windowsill for fifteen to twenty days.

Boiled Egg Salad

A low-fat, flavorful salad, this can be eaten on its own or on the side with other main entrées.

INGREDIENTS | SERVES 2

2–4 minced Thai chilies

2 tablespoons chopped pickled garlic

3 tablespoons lime juice

1 teaspoon salt

5 Boiled Eggs (see Chapter 2), sliced lengthwise

2 thinly sliced shallots, about ¼ cup

¼ cup julienned green apple

¼ cup spearmint

1 green onion, chopped into 2"-long pieces (use both white and green parts)

1. Make dressing by mixing Thai chilies, pickled garlic, lime juice, and salt in a bowl.

2. Lay pieces of sliced boiled eggs on a platter. Top with shallots, green apple, spearmint, and green onion.

3. Drizzle the dressing on top of the salad and serve at room temperature.

Sardine Salad

This recipe calls for sardines in tomato sauce, which you can buy in cans at the grocery store from brands like Chicken of the Sea.

INGREDIENTS | SERVES 4

1 tablespoon chopped green onions, about ¼" long, divided

1 (15-ounce) can sardines in tomato sauce

¼ cup sliced shallots

¼ cup spearmint leaves

1 teaspoon sliced Thai chilies (about 2 chilies)

3 tablespoons lime juice

1–2 tablespoons fish sauce

1. Put half of the chopped green onions and the remaining ingredients in a mixing bowl. Mix well.

2. Garnish with the rest of the green onions.

Hot Dog Salad

In Thailand, hot dogs are not as salty as the ones you find in an American supermarket. If less salty hot dogs are not available, smoked sausage can be used.

INGREDIENTS | SERVES 2

Dressing

2 tablespoons Chili Jam (see Chapter 3)

½ teaspoon salt

3 tablespoons Tamarind Water (see Chapter 2)

1 tablespoon lime juice

Salad

12 ounces low-salt frankfurter or smoked sausage

1 small red onion, sliced

1 tablespoon finely sliced green onions

½ cup toasted unsalted cashew nuts

Fresh lettuce to serve

1. Make the dressing by combining dressing ingredients, except lime juice, in a small saucepan. Bring to a boil and turn off the heat. Add lime juice and stir. Let cool.

2. Blanch sausages and slice on an angle about ⅛" thick. Combine sausages, red onions, green onions, cashew nuts, and the dressing and toss. Serve with fresh lettuce on the side.

Pickled Cucumbers with Cloves

Pickled cucumbers go great with curries. They can also be used to substitute Western-style pickled cucumbers in sandwiches. Sliced jalapeños or Serrano peppers can be added to add some heat.

INGREDIENTS | YIELDS 4 CUPS

1 pound pickling cucumbers
2 teaspoons salt
½ cup water
½ cup sugar
1 cup white vinegar
6 cloves

1. Quarter cucumbers lengthwise and rub with salt. Let sit overnight at room temperature.

2. In a saucepan, bring water, sugar, and vinegar to a boil. Add cloves and simmer at low heat for about 5 minutes. Cool overnight, leaving cloves in the pickle juice.

3. The next day, strain cloves from the juice. Place cucumber pieces in a glass jar, pour over the juice, and pickle for three weeks in a warm, dry place. Refrigerate after three weeks. Pickled cucumbers will keep for one year in the fridge.

Three Friend Salad

In this dish, the three friends refer to three kinds of meat, usually chicken, pork, and shrimp. The dressing has a deep flavor from the Chili Jam (Chapter 3).

INGREDIENTS | SERVES 4

Dressing
2 tablespoons Chili Jam (see Chapter 3)
1 teaspoon sugar
3 tablespoons fish sauce
¼ cup lime juice
2 tablespoons Tamarind Water (see Chapter 2)

Salad
1 cup boiled sliced pork
1 cup boiled sliced chicken breast
1 cup boiled shrimp
½ cup roasted cashew nuts or peanuts
½ cup shredded carrots
½ cup shredded cabbage

1. Make dressing by combining dressing ingredients, except lime juice, in a small saucepan. Bring to a boil to dissolve sugar. Turn the heat off and add lime juice. Stir to mix. Let cool.

2. Combine all other ingredients in a bowl. Toss with the dressing until incorporated.

Grilled Eggplant Salad

Small, long, green or purple Asian eggplants are used for this recipe.
Grill eggplants over charcoal, a gas grill, or over a flame on the stovetop.

INGREDIENTS | SERVES 4

5 small Thai chilies, finely chopped

¼ cup lime juice

3 tablespoons fish sauce

2 teaspoons sugar

½ cup water

¼ pound small fresh shrimp, shelled and butterflied

Pinch of salt

4 long Asian eggplants

4 poblano peppers

2 shallots, thinly sliced

1 hard-boiled egg, sliced lengthwise into 4 or 5 pieces

⅓ cup chopped cilantro

Eggplants

Asian eggplants are skinny, long eggplants that grow well in hotter climates. They have a thinner skin and are sweeter than those Italian or American varieties when cooked. If you are not using the eggplants immediately after cutting, cut eggplants should be soaked in water with a few drops of lemon or lime juice until they are used. This prevents the eggplants from turning brown.

1. Make a dressing by combining minced Thai chilies, lime juice, fish sauce, and sugar. Let sit.

2. Blanch shrimp by placing ½ cup water and shrimp in a small sauté pan with a pinch of salt. Sauté shrimp with water until cooked, about 1–2 minutes.

3. Grill the eggplants and peppers whole, turning occasionally until they are slightly charred on the outside and have softened.

4. Wrap eggplants and peppers with aluminum foil to further steam the eggplants. When cool enough to handle, peel off the charred skin.

5. Quarter the eggplants lengthwise and cut into 1½"-long pieces.

6. Cut the peppers into small strips. Lay eggplants and peppers on a plate. Top with sliced shallots, sliced boiled eggs, and shrimp. Poor over the dressing. Garnish with cilantro.

Grilled Chicken Salad

The dressing for this recipe can also be used as a dipping sauce for grilled meat.
In addition, pork loin can also be used.

INGREDIENTS | SERVES 4

Dressing

1 tablespoon finely minced long red chilies like Serrano, jalapeños, cayenne, or finger pepper

Pinch of salt

1 tablespoon sugar

2 tablespoons fish sauce

2 tablespoons lime juice

2 tablespoons white vinegar

1 tablespoon chopped roasted peanuts

Salad

2 cups chopped romaine lettuce

2 small tomatoes, sliced

2 grilled chicken breasts sliced into bite-sized pieces

1 cup chopped green onions, about 1½"-long pieces

1. Make the dressing by combining all dressing ingredients, except peanuts, in a small saucepan. Bring to a boil and simmer on low heat for 5 minutes, until reduced. Add chopped peanuts and let cool.

2. Place lettuce and tomatoes on a platter. Top with pieces of chicken. Drizzle with the dressing and garnish with green onions.

Salted Shrimp Salad

This is a great salad as accompaniment to curries or
eaten with Plain Rice Soup (see Chapter 2).

INGREDIENTS | SERVES 2

½ cup Salted Shrimp (see Chapter 2)

½ teaspoon fish sauce

1 teaspoon white sugar

2 tablespoons lime juice

1 clove garlic, thinly sliced

3 small Thai chilies, sliced

Combine all ingredients and serve.

Roasted Pork Salad

You can use leftover roasted chicken, BBQ, or even roasted turkey for this salad.

INGREDIENTS | SERVES 4

Pork

1 pound pork tenderloin

1 tablespoon soy sauce

1 tablespoon whiskey

1 teaspoon ground black pepper

Dressing

7 Thai chilies

5 cloves garlic

Pinch of salt

1 teaspoon sugar

1 tablespoon fish sauce

¼ cup lime juice

Salad

2 stalks lemongrass, finely sliced

2 thinly sliced shallots

½ cup spearmint leaves

3 thinly sliced kaffir lime leaves

3 tablespoons chopped scallions or green onions

3 tablespoons chopped cilantro

5 small chilies, fried and dried

1. Marinate pork with soy sauce, whiskey, and pepper for 30 minutes. Roast in the oven at 450°F until the inner temperature is 165°F, about 15 minutes. Let the pork rest for 15 minutes.

2. Make the dressing by combining all dressing ingredients. Stir until sugar is all dissolved.

3. Slice pork into ¼"-thick pieces. Mix all ingredients, except fried chilies, with the dressing and toss until incorporated. Garnish with fried chilies.

Mussel Salad

This dish is best enjoyed when mussels are boiled right before cooking. Mussels lose their flavor once cooked, so do not use frozen mussel meat for this recipe.

INGREDIENTS | SERVES 2

1 pound boiled mussels

1 shallot, thinly sliced

¼ cup julienned ginger

1 tablespoon chopped cilantro

1 tablespoon chopped green onions or scallions

1 teaspoon minced fresh Thai chilies

3 tablespoons fish sauce

2 tablespoons lime juice

2 tablespoons Tamarind Water (see Chapter 2)

1 teaspoon sugar

1 teaspoon thinly sliced kaffir lime leaves

Mix all ingredients in a mixing bowl. Adjust seasoning to preferred taste.

Tempeh Salad

Tempeh is a traditional soy product originally from Indonesia. It is made using a natural culturing and controlled fermentation process that binds soybeans into cake form.

INGREDIENTS | SERVES 4

Dressing

3 Thai chilies

3 tablespoons fish sauce or soy sauce

¼ cup lime juice

1 tablespoon sugar

Salad

8 ounces fresh tempeh, cubed and deep-fried

1 pickling cucumber, quartered lengthwise and sliced

1 medium tomato, chopped

¼ cup chopped cilantro

¼ cup chopped green onions

1. Make the dressing by combining all dressing ingredients in a small bowl. Stir until sugar is dissolved.

2. Combine all other ingredients with the dressing and toss.

Wild Mushroom Salad

Any kind of mushroom such as shitake, oyster, chanterelle, or regular button mushrooms will work in this salad. Substitute soy sauce for fish sauce and use vegetable stock to make this dish vegetarian.

INGREDIENTS | SERVES 2

2 tablespoons uncooked sticky rice

1 clove garlic, minced

1 pound mixed mushrooms

3 tablespoons chicken stock

1 teaspoon salt

1 teaspoon white sugar

3 tablespoons lime juice

1 teaspoon roasted Thai chili flakes

1 tablespoon fish sauce

2 thinly sliced shallots

½ cup of mixed mint and cilantro leaves

1. Dry-roast sticky rice in a frying pan over medium heat. Stir until golden brown, about 10–15 minutes. Grind roasted rice in a coffee grinder and set aside.

2. In a mixing bowl, add minced garlic to mushrooms.

3. Heat stock or water in a sauté pan over medium-high heat and season with salt and sugar. Add mushrooms and sauté, stirring often, until just cooked, about 5 minutes.

4. Season with lime juice, chili flakes, and fish sauce. Mix in shallots, herbs, and rice. Taste for seasoning.

Scallop Salad

The scallops are blanched briefly to retain the juicy texture. Lemongrass and mint play important roles in this dish.

INGREDIENTS | SERVES 2

½ cup water

4 ounces bay or sea scallops

3 tablespoons lime juice

Pinch of salt

1 tablespoon fish sauce

1 teaspoon minced Thai chilies

2 shallots, thinly sliced

1 stalk lemongrass, finely sliced

4 kaffir lime leaves, shredded

½ cup of chopped mixed spearmint and cilantro leaves

1. Blanch scallops by bringing ½ cup of water to a boil in a sauté pan. Add scallops and sauté in water over medium-high heat until cooked, about 2–3 minutes. Strain and set aside. In a mixing bowl, add lime juice, salt, and scallops. Mix well with a spatula and let sit for a few minutes.

2. Add fish sauce and Thai chilies. Taste and adjust. Add the rest of the ingredients and combine. Serve immediately.

CHAPTER 5

Appetizers

Egg Rolls (*Po Pia Tod*)

Egg rolls can be made with or without meat. Once made, the rolls can be frozen for up to six months. When you are ready to fry them, drop the frozen egg rolls into hot oil without thawing.

INGREDIENTS | YIELDS 30 EGG ROLLS

1 cup cabbage, shredded

1 cup thinly sliced celery

1 cup dried fungus mushrooms, soaked

1 teaspoon ground pepper

3 tablespoons soy sauce

1 tablespoon sugar

2 cups bean thread noodles, soaked for 30 minutes

3 tablespoons plus 4 cups vegetable oil

1 tablespoon minced garlic

1 egg, lightly beaten

1 teaspoon tapioca flour

2 tablespoons water

30 egg roll wrappers

Sweet and Sour Sauce (see Chapter 3)

Egg Rolls with Meat

If you are making egg rolls with meat, add ½ cup raw ground chicken or pork after browning the garlic. Sauté until the meat is cooked, and then continue with the rest of the recipe.

1. In a mixing bowl, mix together cabbage, celery, soaked fungus mushrooms, ground pepper, soy sauce, sugar, and bean thread noodles. Set aside.

2. Heat 3 tablespoons of oil in a medium sauté pan over medium-high heat. Fry the garlic until aromatic, about 10 seconds, add the egg and fry until slightly firm, and then scramble. Add the noodle mixture and stir-fry until cooked and well seasoned, about 3–5 minutes. Remove from heat and let cool.

3. Mix the tapioca flour with 2 tablespoons water and heat in the microwave for 30–40 seconds to make a paste.

4. Lay a sheet of egg roll wrapper on a counter, with one of the corners pointing toward you. Place 2 tablespoons of the filling at the corner closest to you. Roll the filling up to halfway. Fold in the two corners on the side and roll up to meet with the top corner. Glue with tapioca paste.

5. Heat the 4 cups oil in a deep frying pan to 350°F. Deep-fry each egg roll for 4 minutes. Drain on paper towels.

6. Serve with Sweet and Sour Sauce.

Banana Rolls

This appetizer is also great as dessert. The rolls can be served with ice cream or served on their own, drizzled with powdered sugar.

INGREDIENTS | YIELDS 25 ROLLS

5 ripe bananas, peeled
1 teaspoon tapioca flour
2 tablespoons water
25 egg roll wrappers
4 cups vegetable oil

1. Mash bananas into a paste.

2. Mix the tapioca flour with 2 tablespoons water and heat in the microwave for 30–40 seconds to make a paste.

3. Lay a sheet of egg roll wrapper on a counter with one of the corners pointing toward you. Place 2 tablespoons of the mashed bananas at the corner closest to you. Roll the filling up to halfway. Fold in the two corners on the side and roll up to meet with the top corner. Glue with tapioca paste.

4. Heat the oil in a deep frying pan to 350°F. Deep-fry each roll for 4 minutes. Drain on paper towels.

Shrimp Cakes (*Tod Man Kung*)

Uncooked shrimp cakes rolled in bread crumbs can be frozen for later use. If the cakes are frozen when it is time to cook, do not thaw the cakes. Just deep-fry them and allow one more minute for them to cook through.

INGREDIENTS | SERVES 4

2 coriander roots or stems, chopped
Pinch of salt
3 garlic cloves, minced
1 slice ginger, minced
Large pinch of ground white pepper
6 ounces minced uncooked shrimp
3 cups panko bread crumbs, divided
Large pinch of palm sugar
2–3 tablespoons light soy sauce
4 cups vegetable oil
½ recipe of Plum Sauce (see Chapter 3)

1. Pound coriander roots, salt, garlic, ginger, and pepper into a paste. Combine with minced shrimp and 2 cups bread crumbs; mix well. Season with sugar and soy sauce.

2. Roll into 1" balls and flatten into cakes. Coat the cakes in remaining bread crumbs.

3. In a fry pan, deep-fry the cakes for 4 minutes in oil that has been heated to 350°F. Taste and adjust the seasoning as desired.

4. Serve with Plum Sauce.

Pork Cakes

Corn is optional in this recipe. Chopped carrots can be used instead.

INGREDIENTS | SERVES 4

1 pound ground pork

1 medium onion, diced

½ cup fresh or frozen corn kernels

2 eggs

1 tablespoon chopped coriander roots or stem

2 tablespoons light soy sauce

2 tablespoons fish sauce

1 tablespoon sugar

1 tablespoon rice flour

1 tablespoon tapioca flour

Pinch of salt

1 teaspoon black pepper

3 cups vegetable oil

1. Combine all the ingredients except vegetable oil in a mixing bowl. Mix well with hands or spatula.

2. Roll the mixture into balls and flatten.

3. In a fry pan, deep-fry the cakes for 4 minutes in vegetable oil that has been heated to 350°F. Remove and drain on paper towels.

Crispy Pork Wonton

On cold winter nights, these wrapped wontons can be boiled in chicken stock to make soup.

INGREDIENTS | SERVES 4

½ pound ground pork

1 minced shallot

3 cloves garlic, minced

1 tablespoon minced cilantro

1 egg

1 tablespoon soy sauce

1 teaspoon sugar

½ teaspoon salt

Pinch of freshly ground black pepper

1 packet, wonton wrappers (about 30 wrappers)

3 cups vegetable oil

1. In a mixing bowl, combine ground pork, shallot, garlic, cilantro, egg, soy sauce, sugar, salt, and black pepper. Mix well.

2. For each wonton, put 2 teaspoons of the mixture in the middle of a wonton wrapper and bring top and bottom corners together. Seal with water.

3. In a frying pan, deep-fry wontons for 2 minutes in oil that has been heated to 350°F, until wontons are golden brown and start to float to the top. Turn wontons halfway through so they are evenly browned. Drain on paper towels.

Spicy Rice Balls

Often called rice bombs at parties, these little bursts of flavor will make the guests come back for more.

INGREDIENTS | YIELDS 30 RICE BALLS

4 cups hot jasmine rice

2 tablespoons red curry paste

1 tablespoon soy sauce

1 tablespoon sugar

2 kaffir lime leaves, cut into thin strips

3 cups vegetable oil

1. Combine all ingredients, except for the oil, in a bowl and taste to see if the mixture needs the seasoning adjusted. If it is dry, add some water so it is easier to roll.

2. Roll 2 tablespoons of the mixture into a round ball. Wetting your hands before rolling will prevent the mixture from sticking to the fingers.

3. Heat the oil in a fry pan to 350°F, or use a deep-fryer. Fry until golden, about 2 minutes. Drain on paper towels.

Corn Fritters

Be careful when frying these fritters; corn will pop in the hot oil and may splatter.

INGREDIENTS | SERVES 4

2 cups corn kernels

1 egg

2 teaspoons minced garlic

2 tablespoons all-purpose or gluten-free flour

½ teaspoon ground white pepper

1 teaspoon salt

3 cups vegetable oil

Ketchup or Sriracha Sauce (see Chapter 2) to taste

1. Mix all ingredients, except for oil, in a mixing bowl. Roll 3 tablespoons of the mixture into a ball and flatten slightly.

2. Heat oil in a heavy, medium saucepan. Don't crowd the pot; only add four cakes at a time. Deep-fry corn cakes until golden brown and crispy, about 4 minutes. Turn the cakes halfway through to brown both sides evenly.

3. Serve with ketchup or Sriracha Sauce.

Chicken Satay with Peanut Sauce

This simple, savory snack originated in Indonesia. The meat is sliced very thin so it cooks quickly over an open flame. Serve these on skewers with Cucumber Salad (see Chapter 4).

INGREDIENTS | SERVES 4

Peanut Sauce

2 tablespoons vegetable oil

⅓ cup coarsely ground peanuts

1 tablespoon sugar

1 tablespoon red curry paste

1 cup coconut milk

½ teaspoon salt

1 tablespoon Tamarind Water (see Chapter 2) or lime juice

Chicken

8 ounces boneless, skinless chicken breast, cut into thin strips about 1" × 4"

¼ cup coconut milk

2 tablespoons chopped cilantro roots or stems

½ teaspoon curry powder

½ teaspoon turmeric powder

2 teaspoons sugar

1½ teaspoons fish sauce

2 tablespoons vegetable oil

Bamboo skewers

Satay

This appetizer or snack originated in Indonesia, but has been largely influenced by Indian cooking styles. A perfect harmony of dry spices, fresh cilantro roots, and a side of Cucumber Salad (see Chapter 4) make this dish irresistible. Marinated satay pieces can be frozen for later use.

1. To make the peanut sauce, heat a saucepan over medium heat, and add the oil. Add the peanuts, sugar, and curry paste when the oil is hot, and fry at medium-low heat until fragrant, being careful not to burn the curry, about 15 seconds. Add coconut milk and salt.

2. Bring the ingredients in the saucepan to a boil. Boil for a few minutes or until the sauce thickens slightly. Adjust the seasoning with tamarind water. The sauce should taste slightly sweet followed by a touch of tartness and saltiness. Cover to keep hot.

3. Marinate chicken pieces with coconut milk, cilantro roots or stems, curry powder, turmeric powder, sugar, fish sauce, and vegetable oil for 3 hours or overnight. Mix well with hand or spatula.

4. Soak bamboo skewers in water for 1 hour to prevent the skewers from burning.

5. Slide each slice of marinated chicken onto a bamboo skewer.

6. Grill the skewered chicken until done and still moist, about 1½ minutes on each side. Serve hot with peanut sauce for dipping.

Shrimp Toast with Sesame Seeds

Any type of bread, including gluten-free bread, can be used in this recipe.
Stale bread is ideal because it is already dry.

INGREDIENTS | SERVES 4

Sauce

¼ cup orange marmalade

¼ cup vinegar

¼ teaspoon salt

Toasts

8 slices whole wheat or white bread

1 teaspoon minced garlic

¼ teaspoon ground white pepper

¼ teaspoon salt

1 teaspoon minced cilantro roots or stems

4 ounces ground pork

12 ounces minced shrimp

2 teaspoons soy sauce

1 egg

2 tablespoons hulled white sesame seeds

3 cups vegetable oil for deep-frying

Cucumber slices

1. Make the sauce by bringing all the sauce ingredients to a boil in a saucepan and simmering at low heat until slightly thick, about 10 minutes. Set aside.

2. Cut off the edges of the pieces of bread and cut in half. On a baking sheet, toast in the oven at 350°F for 5 minutes. Toasting will prevent the bread from absorbing extra oil when frying.

3. Pound garlic, pepper, salt, and cilantro roots or stems using a mortar and pestle. Alternatively, mash the ingredients with a knife on the cutting board and mince them together.

4. Add pork, shrimp, soy sauce, egg, and the paste in a mixing bowl and mix well with your hands until incorporated.

5. Scoop 1 tablespoon of the filling onto a piece of bread and flatten slightly.

6. Drizzle sesame seeds on top of the filling.

7. In a fry pan, deep-fry for 4 minutes in oil that has been heated to 350°F, turning the pieces after 2 minutes to evenly brown both sides of the toasts.

8. Serve with the sauce and sliced cucumbers.

Crispy Vermicelli (*Mee Grob*)

This dish might have more steps than other Thai staples, but the flavor makes it all worth the effort.

INGREDIENTS | SERVES 4

6 ounces dried vermicelli noodles, soaked in room temperature water for 15 minutes

3¼ cups vegetable oil, divided

2 teaspoons minced garlic

2 teaspoons minced shallots

¼ cup minced shrimp

¼ cup ground pork

1 tablespoon fish sauce

1 tablespoon salted/fermented soybeans

1 tablespoon white vinegar

4 tablespoons palm sugar

1 teaspoon ground white pepper

1 tablespoon lime juice

½ cup fried tofu, sliced into 1" × ½" pieces, ⅛" thick

5 cloves minced Pickled Garlic (see Chapter 4)

1 tablespoon thinly sliced kaffir lime leaves

1 tablespoon chopped cilantro

1 cup bean sprouts

½ cup chopped Chinese chives

Frying Garlic in Hot Oil

When frying garlic in recipes, first make sure your oil is hot at medium to medium-low heat. Add garlic and stir-fry until garlic is golden brown. It usually takes about 10–15 seconds. Constantly move the garlic around so it will not burn. Garlic needs to be browned before adding the next ingredients. The bitterness in garlic will be balanced out by the other flavors in the dish.

1. Drain the noodles in a colander and let sit for 10 minutes.

2. Heat 3 cups oil in a medium saucepan over medium-high heat. Deep-fry a handful of noodles at a time until golden brown, about 1–2 minutes. Drain on paper towels.

3. Heat a medium sauté pan over medium-high heat. Turn heat to medium, add ¼ cup oil, and fry garlic and shallots until brown, about 10 seconds. Add shrimp and pork and sauté for about 1 minute. Add fish sauce, salted soybeans, vinegar, sugar, and white pepper and stir-fry until the sauce is reduced and thickened, about 2 minutes. Add lime juice and taste. Adjust seasonings if needed. The sauce should be sweet, sour, and a little salty.

4. Reduce heat to low and add fried vermicelli noodles. Fold the sauce over the noodles. Add fried tofu pieces and mix.

5. Garnish with minced pickled garlic, kaffir lime leaves, and cilantro. Serve with a side of fresh sprouts and chives.

Fried Banana (*Kluay Tod*)

This appetizer is served hot immediately after frying.

INGREDIENTS | SERVES 8

¾ cup rice flour

¼ cup tapioca flour

2 tablespoons sugar

1 teaspoon salt

¼ cup white sesame seeds

½ cup shredded coconut, dried or frozen

¾–1 cup water

8 bananas, ripe but firm

3 cups vegetable oil

1. Mix both of the flours, sugar, salt, sesame seeds, and shredded coconut in a mixing bowl. Add water slowly until mixture is thick enough to coat the bananas, about the consistency of pancake batter.

2. Cut bananas in half crosswise, then slice those pieces lengthwise into 2–3 pieces. Heat oil in a fry pan over medium heat to reach 350°F. Dip banana pieces in the batter and fry for about 5 minutes (or until golden) in the oil that has been heated to 350°F. Turn banana pieces halfway to evenly brown the pieces.

Fish Cakes (*Tod Man Pla*)

It is possible to blend the mixture in a food processor and pulse it until it slightly thickens instead of slapping it to the bowl. Be careful not to overmix because the cakes will be very chewy.

INGREDIENTS | SERVES 4

8 ounces ground fish like cod or snapper

4 tablespoons red curry paste

1½ tablespoons fish sauce

1 teaspoon sugar

1 egg

5 kaffir lime leaves, thinly sliced

2 tablespoons finely chopped green beans

3 cups vegetable oil

Cucumber Salad (see Chapter 4)

1. Combine fish, curry paste, fish sauce, sugar, and egg in a stainless steel or sturdy mixing bowl. Mix thoroughly. Gather the mixture into a ball and throw it back to the side of the bowl. Continue slapping the mixture to the side of the bowl until the mixture is thick and sticky.

2. Mix in lime leaves and green beans.

3. Heat oil in a fry pan over medium heat to reach 350°F. Roll the fish mixture into small discs and deep-fry. Drain on paper towels and serve with Cucumber Salad.

Chicken in Pandan Leaves

In Thailand, this dish is not often made at home. Instead, it is a welcome treat when you go out to eat at restaurants. The fragrance from pandan leaves adds flavor to the chicken while they are being deep-fried.

INGREDIENTS | YIELDS 12 PIECES

3 skinless, boneless chicken thighs (or chicken breasts if preferred)

1 teaspoon minced cilantro roots or stems

⅛ teaspoon salt

2 garlic cloves, minced

1 teaspoon minced ginger

1 whole star anise

1 teaspoon ground white pepper, or 10 whole peppercorns

½ cup Thai sweet, thick soy sauce

5 tablespoons palm sugar

2 tablespoons light soy sauce

3 tablespoons Chinese cooking wine

2 tablespoons sesame oil

3 tablespoons water

12 pandan leaves

3 cups vegetable oil for deep-frying

1 tablespoon toasted white sesame seeds

Pandan Leaves

Pandan is a tropical plant used in Southeast Asian cooking. It is used like vanilla in desserts to add flavor and aroma. It is also used in many savory dishes or used to make specialty drinks.

1. Cut chicken into bite-sized pieces, about 3 or 4 pieces from one chicken thigh and about double that amount for chicken breasts.

2. Make a paste from cilantro roots or stems, salt, garlic, ginger, star anise, and ground pepper or peppercorns using a mortar and pestle.

3. In a mixing bowl, mix sweet soy sauce, palm sugar, light soy sauce, Chinese cooking wine, and sesame oil. In a separate bowl, mix half of the sauce with all of the paste. Marinate chicken pieces with the paste and half of the sauce for at least 3 hours or better yet, overnight in the refrigerator.

4. Make a dipping sauce by combining the other half of the sauce with about 3 tablespoons of water.

5. Wrap each chicken piece in each pandan leaf by placing chicken pieces toward the end of the leaf, leaving 2" of open space below the chicken. Grab the top of the leaf and start folding it around the chicken until about 5" is left and then slide it under one of the wrapped leaf sections to lock it in place.

6. Deep-fry in the oil that has been heated to 350°F and garnish with sesame seeds.

Chicken Cakes

This recipe is an adaptation of Fish Cakes (see this chapter). The chicken cakes will have almost the same texture as fish cakes once they are fried. Serve with Cucumber Salad (see Chapter 4).

INGREDIENTS | SERVES 4

8 ounces ground chicken breast

4 tablespoons red curry paste

1½ tablespoons fish sauce

1 teaspoon sugar

1 egg

5 kaffir lime leaves, thinly sliced

2 tablespoons finely chopped green beans

3 cups vegetable oil

1. Combine ground chicken, curry paste, fish sauce, sugar, and egg in a stainless steel or sturdy mixing bowl. Mix thoroughly. Gather the mixture into a ball and throw back to the side of the bowl. Continue slapping the mixture to the side of the bowl until the mixture is slightly thick and sticky.

2. Mix in lime leaves and green beans.

3. Heat oil in a fry pan over medium-high heat. Roll into small discs and deep-fry at 350°F. Drain on paper towels and serve with Cucumber Salad.

Fried Tofu

This snack has to be served immediately after fried. It will only stay crispy for about 30 minutes.

INGREDIENTS | SERVES 4

Tofu

1 pound firm tofu

3 cups vegetable oil

Sauce

1 tablespoon crushed roasted peanuts

½ cup Sweet and Sour Sauce (see Chapter 3)

1. Take tofu out of the packet. Place a kitchen towel on a plate. Put tofu block on top and place another kitchen towel on top of the tofu. Put a heavy pot on top to help release water. This will help the oil to not splatter as much when frying.

2. Cut tofu in half diagonally into two triangles. Slice into ¼"-thick triangles.

3. In a fry pan, deep-fry tofu for 4 minutes in oil that has been heated to 350°F, turning halfway through to evenly brown both sides of the tofu pieces.

4. Add peanuts to Sweet and Sour Sauce and serve with tofu as dipping sauce. Slices of cucumbers are also great to serve on the side of fried tofu.

Grilled Pork (*Moo Ping*)

A fattier cut of pork is ideal for this recipe. Slice the pork thinly so it will cook quickly over an open flame. Serve with Sticky Rice (see Chapter 2).

INGREDIENTS | SERVES 4

Pork

1 pound pork butt or shoulder
4 tablespoons light soy sauce
1 tablespoon sugar
1 tablespoon salt
2 tablespoons vegetable oil
1 tablespoon cilantro stems
1 fresh, crushed black peppercorn
4 cloves garlic, minced
Bamboo skewers, soaked for 1 hour in
  water

Sauce

3 tablespoons lime juice
2 tablespoons fish sauce
1 teaspoon sugar
Large pinch of roasted chili flakes
1 shallot, finely sliced
1 tablespoon chopped coriander

Cutting Meat Thinly

It is best to slice meat thinly so it will cook faster. If the meat is too thick, it will take too long to cook and the spices can burn.

1. Slice pork into ⅛"-thick, 2" × 4" pieces. Marinate with soy sauce, sugar, salt, vegetable oil, cilantro stems, black peppercorn, and garlic for at least 3 hours or overnight in the refrigerator.

2. In a small bowl, mix together the sauce ingredients and set aside.

3. Thread pork pieces on the skewers and grill over charcoal, gas grill, or grill pan over stovetop. Remove from heat and serve with the sauce.

Chinese Pork and Shrimp Dumplings (*Kanom Jeeb*)

This appetizer also makes a great breakfast.
Serve it with spicy sauce with Plain Rice Soup (see Chapter 2)

INGREDIENTS | SERVES 6

Sauce

2 tablespoons light soy sauce

2 tablespoons dark sweet soy sauce

1 tablespoon white vinegar

¼ teaspoon chopped fresh chilies (or to taste)

¼ teaspoon salt

Dumplings

1 pound ground pork

2 shallots, minced

3 cloves garlic, minced

½ cup chopped cilantro

1 egg

1½ tablespoons soy sauce

½ teaspoon sugar

Pinch of salt

¼ cup shredded dried black fungus mushrooms, soaked for 30 minutes

Pinch freshly ground black pepper

Wonton wrappers

1. Make the sauce by combining all sauce ingredients in a small bowl. Set aside.

2. In a mixing bowl, combine ground pork, shallots, garlic, chopped cilantro, egg, soy sauce, sugar, salt, soaked fungus mushrooms, and black pepper. Mix well.

3. Put 1 tablespoon of the mixture in the middle of a wonton wrapper and bring the four corners together. Dab water on each corner and squeeze the four corners together to close. Continue until all the mixture is finished. Steam in a steamer until the meat is cooked, about 15–20 minutes. Serve with the sauce.

Dumplings

Dumplings are of Chinese origin. They are often served as part of a dim sum experience, which is a traditional Chinese style of serving small bite-size or individual portions of food.

Fried Sweet Potatoes

If you can find them in your grocery store, taro roots make a great substitute for sweet potatoes in this recipe.

INGREDIENTS | SERVES 4

¾ cup rice flour

¼ cup tapioca flour

2 tablespoons sugar

1 teaspoon salt

¼ cup white sesame seeds

½ cup shredded coconut, dried or frozen

¾–1 cup water

3 large sweet potatoes

3 cups vegetable oil

1. Mix both of the flours, sugar, salt, sesame seeds, and shredded coconut in a mixing bowl. Add water slowly until mixture is thick enough to coat the potatoes, about the consistency of pancake batter.

2. Peel sweet potatoes, cut in half crosswise, and then slice lengthwise into 2 or 3 pieces, about ¼" thick. Heat oil in fry pan over medium-high heat. Dip sweet potato pieces in the batter and fry in oil that has been heated to 350°F until golden, about 5 minutes. Turn the pieces halfway to evenly brown the sweet potatoes. Drain on paper towels.

Crab Cakes

Twice-cooked crab cakes will certainly make an impression on your guests, while steamed cakes rolled in bread crumbs can be frozen for later use. Serve with Plum Sauce (see Chapter 3) or on their own.

INGREDIENTS | SERVES 4

1 cup crab meat

1 cup ground pork

2 teaspoons minced cilantro roots or stems

1 teaspoon minced garlic

¼ teaspoon ground white pepper

1½ tablespoons light soy sauce

¼ teaspoon salt

2 eggs, divided

3 tablespoons panko bread crumbs

3 cups vegetable oil for deep-frying

1. In a mixing bowl, combine crab meat, ground pork, cilantro roots or stems, garlic, pepper, soy sauce, salt, and 1 egg. Mix well with hands.

2. Place ½ cup of the mixture in a small ramekin and steam in steamer for 10 minutes. Let cool.

3. Take the mixture out of the ramekins. Beat one egg and dip the cooked mixture in the egg to coat. Roll the wet patties in bread crumbs.

4. Heat oil in a heavy, medium frying pan to 350°F. Fry the patties for 2 minutes until bread crumbs are golden brown and crispy. Turn the patties halfway through frying to ensure even browning. Drain on paper towels.

Crispy Rice with Pork Relish

If crispy rice is not available, use firm, crispy vegetables like carrots or celery to serve this relish.

INGREDIENTS | SERVES 4

4 cups oil

12 crispy rice patties or cakes (purchased at an Asian grocery store) or 6 slices white or wheat bread, toasted and cut in half

1 tablespoon minced garlic

1 teaspoon minced cilantro roots or stems

¼ teaspoon ground white pepper

1 dried long red chili, soaked and seeded

1½ cups coconut cream

½ cup ground pork

½ cup minced shrimp

2 tablespoons sugar

1 tablespoon fish sauce

¼ cup ground roasted peanuts

1 tablespoon minced shallots

2 tablespoons chopped cilantro

1. Heat oil in a fry pan to 350°F. Deep-fry rice patties in hot oil. Let rest on paper towels to absorb excess oil. (If using toasted bread, skip this step.)

2. Make a paste of garlic, cilantro roots or stems, white pepper, and chili using a mortar and pestle.

3. In a saucepan, bring coconut cream to a boil and let simmer for 2 minutes until there is some oil on the surface. Add the paste and simmer until fragrant, about 1 minute. Add ground pork and shrimp and stir to mix. Simmer until shrimp and pork are cooked, about 2 minutes.

4. Season with sugar and fish sauce and stir to mix well. Add peanuts and shallots and stir to mix. Remove from heat and garnish with chopped cilantro to serve.

Green Wraps (*Miang Kam*)

This dish offers a great balance of flavor and texture. Just a small bite of this appetizer has everything: sweetness, spiciness, saltiness, sourness, and bitterness. When serving at a party, have the guests place each of the ingredients on top of the leaf, drizzle with a spoonful of sauce, wrap to close, and enjoy!

INGREDIENTS | SERVES 4

Sauce

¼ cup finely ground dried shrimp

½ cup roasted, shredded coconut

¼ cup chopped, unsalted, roasted peanuts

¼ cup palm sugar

2 tablespoons fish sauce

½ cup water

Wraps

15 betel or piper sarmentosum leaves (or Chinese broccoli leaves, collard greens, or kale)

½ cup unsalted roasted peanuts

¼ cup small dried shrimp

½ cup roasted unsweetened shredded coconut

⅓ cup diced ginger (about ¼"-sized piece)

⅓ cup diced shallots or onion

1 lime, cut into small cubes

6 Thai chilies, cut into thin rounds

1. Make the sauce by combining all sauce ingredients in a small saucepan. Bring to a boil and simmer over low heat until thick, about 5–7 minutes.

2. Arrange all the wrap ingredients on a platter separately and serve with the sauce.

Spicy Bite

What to do when you bite a too-hot Thai chili? Taking a pinch of salt and drinking hot tea is the best cure. Salt and hot tea or hot water will wash the oil on your tongue. It might hurt a little when drinking, but after that, it will cool off quickly.

Raw Oysters

Thai food is known for combining all the major flavors (salty, sweet, sour, spicy, and bitter) into every bite. This succulent raw oysters dish is no exception.

INGREDIENTS | SERVES 4

Sauce

4 fresh red or green Thai chilies, minced

4 cloves garlic, minced

3 tablespoons fish sauce

4 tablespoons lime juice

1 teaspoon sugar

1 teaspoon honey

Oysters

12 raw oyster on shells

3 tablespoons fried shallots

3 tablespoons cilantro

1. Make the sauce by combining all sauce ingredients in a blender and blend until finely chopped but still chunky. Put aside.

2. On a serving plate, top the oysters with fried shallots, cilantro, and the sauce. Serve immediately.

Chinese Sausage Salad

This dish can also be served with Plain Rice Soup (see Chapter 2) or with plain cooked Jasmine Rice (see Chapter 2).

INGREDIENTS | SERVES 4

2 tablespoons vegetable oil

4 links Chinese sausage, sliced diagonally into ⅛" pieces

2 pickling cucumbers, halved and sliced on an angle

2 shallots, thinly sliced

3 fresh Thai chilies, thinly sliced

½ cup chopped, loosely packed fresh cilantro leaves

¼ cup lime juice

3 tablespoons fish sauce

1 teaspoon sugar

2 tablespoons chopped cilantro

2 tablespoons chopped green onions

1. Heat a deep sauté pan or wok over medium heat and add oil. Pan-fry sausage slices until crisp on the outside, about 2 minutes.

2. In a mixing bowl, combine fried sausage pieces and the rest of the ingredients. Toss and adjust seasoning. Serve immediately.

CHAPTER 6

Soups

Coconut Soup with Chicken (*Tom Kha Kai*)

This dish is the most popular soup in Thai restaurants throughout the world. It can be made with different meats or just vegetables, depending on your preference.

INGREDIENTS | SERVES 4

Sauce

3 tablespoons fish sauce or soy sauce

4 tablespoons lime juice

2 teaspoons minced Thai chilies (or more for spicier soup)

1 tablespoon cilantro leaves

Soup

1 stalk lemongrass, cut into 1½" pieces

1 shallot, cut in half and mashed

8 slices galangal

2 Thai chilies

1 can chicken or vegetable stock

1 (13.5 ounce) can coconut milk

3 kaffir lime leaves, torn in fourths

8 ounces chicken breast, cubed, or 1 cup fried tofu cubes

5 ounces oyster or button mushrooms

½–1 teaspoon salt

1 teaspoon palm sugar

1. Mix all sauce ingredients in a small bowl and set aside.

2. Slightly bruise lemongrass, shallot, galangal, and chilies using a pestle or meat tenderizer.

3. In a saucepan, combine stock with coconut milk. Bring to boil. Add lemongrass mixture and lime leaves to the boiling stock. Simmer over low heat for 3–4 minutes.

4. Add chicken, turn the heat back up, and bring back to simmer. One minute later add mushrooms. Turn down the heat and continue to simmer until chicken is cooked, about 4–5 minutes over low heat. Season with salt and sugar to taste. Turn off the heat.

5. Add the sauce to the hot soup and serve.

Coconut Soup with Salmon

Here is another version of the popular Thai coconut soup with a less common ingredient. Salmon is not a common fish in the Thai market, but the texture is perfect for this soup.

INGREDIENTS | SERVES 4

Sauce

3 tablespoons fish sauce or soy sauce

4 tablespoons lime juice

2 teaspoons minced Thai chilies (or more for a spicier soup)

1 tablespoon cilantro leaves

Soup

1 stalk lemongrass, cut into 1½" pieces

1 shallot, cut in half

8 slices galangal

2 Thai chilies

1 can chicken or vegetable stock

1 (13.5 ounce) can coconut milk

3 kaffir lime leaves, torn in fourths

6 ounces salmon, cubed into 1" pieces

5 ounces oyster or button mushrooms

½–1 teaspoon salt

1 teaspoon palm sugar

1. Mix all sauce ingredients in a small bowl and set aside.

2. Slightly bruise lemongrass, shallots, galangal, and chilies using a pestle or meat tenderizer.

3. In a saucepan, combine stock with coconut milk. Bring to boil. Add lemongrass mixture and lime leaves to boiling stock. Simmer for a few minutes on medium-low heat.

4. Add salmon, and 1 minute later add mushrooms. With the heat on low, continue to simmer until salmon is cooked, about 4–5 minutes. Season with salt and sugar to taste. Turn off the heat.

5. Add the sauce to the hot soup and serve.

Coconut Soup with Mixed Seafood

The flavor of the sauce and spices in this soup will stand up against any type of seafood you want to add, so experiment and have fun!

INGREDIENTS | SERVES 4

Sauce

3 tablespoons fish sauce or soy sauce

4 tablespoons lime juice

2 teaspoons minced Thai chilies (or more for spicier soup)

1 tablespoon cilantro leaves

Soup

1 stalk lemongrass, cut into 1½" pieces

1 shallot, cut in half

2 Thai chilies

8 slices galangal

1 can chicken or vegetable stock

1 (13.5 ounce) can coconut milk

3 kaffir lime leaves, torn in fourths

6 ounces shrimp, scallops, and clams

5 ounces oyster or button mushrooms

½–1 teaspoon salt

1 teaspoon palm sugar

1. Mix all sauce ingredients in a small bowl.

2. Slightly bruise lemongrass, shallots, galangal, and chilies using a pestle or meat tenderizer.

3. In a saucepan, combine stock with coconut milk. Bring to boil. Add lemongrass mixture and lime leaves to boiling stock. Simmer for a few minutes on low heat.

4. Add seafood, and 1 minute later add mushrooms. With heat on low, continue to simmer until clam shells open. Season with salt and sugar to taste. Turn off the heat.

5. Add the sauce to the hot soup and serve.

Lemongrass Soup with Chicken (*Tom Yum Kai*)

Bright and light, this soup tends to be a little spicier than coconut soup.

INGREDIENTS | SERVES 4

Sauce

4 tablespoons lime juice

2 teaspoons minced Thai chilies

3 tablespoons fish sauce

½ teaspoon sugar

Handful of cilantro

Soup

4 cups chicken stock

1 stalk lemongrass, chopped into 1½" pieces and bruised

6 slices galangal, sliced and bruised

4 kaffir lime leaves, torn

1 tablespoon fish sauce

6 ounces sliced chicken breast or chicken thigh

¾ cup shitake, oyster, or other wild mushrooms

Large pinch of salt

1. Mix all sauce ingredients in a small bowl and set aside.

2. Bring stock to a boil in a medium saucepan. Add lemongrass, galangal, and kaffir lime leaves to the stock. Simmer for 3–5 minutes. Season with fish sauce.

3. Add chicken, and 1 minute later add mushrooms. Simmer over low heat until the chicken and mushrooms are cooked, about 4 minutes. Season with salt.

4. Add the sauce to the hot soup and serve.

Cutting Lemongrass

The entire lemongrass stalk can be used when cooking; only the leafy part is tossed. If you'd rather keep them, the leaves are great for making lemongrass tea. Cut lemongrass into short stalks and bruise each piece with a pestle or meat tenderizer.

Lemongrass Soup with Shrimp (*Tom Yum Kung*)

Sometimes milk is added to this soup to make it thicker.
Chili Jam (see Chapter 3) can also be added for more a complex flavor and color.

INGREDIENTS | SERVES 4

Sauce

4 tablespoons lime juice

2 or 3 Thai chilies, minced (about 1–2 teaspoons of minced chilies)

3 tablespoons fish sauce

½ teaspoon of sugar

Handful of cilantro

Soup

10 uncooked medium shrimp, unpeeled

4 cups water

1 stalk lemongrass, chopped and bruised

6 slices galangal, sliced and bruised

4 kaffir lime leaves, torn

1 tablespoon fish sauce

¾ cup shitake, oyster, and other wild mushrooms

⅓ cup chopped tomatoes

1. Mix all sauce ingredients in a small bowl.

2. Peel and devein the shrimp. Save the shells to make stock. Bring water to boil and add shrimp shells. Boil for about 3 minutes and strain the stock. Add lemongrass, galangal, and kaffir lime leaves to the stock and bring it back to boil. Season with fish sauce.

3. Add mushrooms, and 3–4 minutes later, add shrimp and simmer over low heat until shrimp just change color, about 2–3 minutes. Add tomatoes and simmer for another minute.

4. Add the sauce to the hot soup and check seasoning. It should be salty, sour, and spicy.

Ingredients for Life

A study by Thailand's Kasetsart University and Japan's Kyoto and Kinki Universities shows that the ingredients like galangal, lemongrass, and lime leaves in lemongrass soup and coconut soup are 100 times more effective in inhibiting cancerous tumor growth than any other foods.

Clear Soup with Bean Thread Noodles, Pork, and Shrimp (*Kaeng Jued*)

Although the Thai name means "curry," this dish is more of a soup. Adding vegetables like summer squash or daikon is a great way to change up the flavors.

INGREDIENTS | SERVES 4

3 cloves garlic

1 teaspoon minced cilantro roots or stems

2 tablespoons vegetable oil

1 cup ground pork

6 peeled medium shrimp

3 tablespoons soy sauce, divided

3 cups chicken or pork stock

1 cup soaked bean thread noodles (about 4 ounces dried noodles)

½ cup soaked fungus mushrooms

2 tablespoons chopped green onions

1. Pound garlic and minced cilantro roots or stems using a mortar and pestle. Heat a medium saucepan and add oil. Fry garlic and cilantro stem paste over medium heat until fragrant, about 10–15 seconds. Add pork and shrimp and stir-fry until pork and shrimp are halfway done, about 1 minute. Season with 1 tablespoon of soy sauce.

2. Add ½ cup stock to moisten the mixture. Add the noodles and fungus mushrooms and mix well. Stir-fry for another minute.

3. Add the rest of the stock and bring to a boil. Season with the rest of the soy sauce and turn off the heat. Garnish with chopped green onions.

Liang Soup (*Kaeng Liang*)

This soup is rich enough to be an entrée or you can enjoy it in smaller portions as an appetizer.

INGREDIENTS | SERVES 4

Paste

10 black peppercorns

½ cup ground dried shrimp

5 shallots, sliced

1 tablespoon shrimp paste

Soup

12 ounces medium shrimp

4–6 cups chicken stock

1 cup sweet potatoes or pumpkin, cubed

1 cup mushrooms (any kind)

1 cup summer squash, cubed

2–3 tablespoons fish sauce

1 cup basil (not Thai basil)

Soup or Curry?

Some curries are thin and not very spicy, but if there is paste involved in a recipe, it is categorized as curry. For example, in Thailand, this soup is called Kaeng Liang or Liang Curry rather than Liang Soup. It is so light that it can often go either way.

1. Make the paste by pounding all the paste ingredients using a mortar and pestle, starting with only peppercorn. Add dried shrimp and pound until dried shrimp is broken into small pieces. Add shallots and shrimp paste and continue to pound until it becomes a coarse paste.

2. Add shrimp to the paste and slightly break up the shrimp with the pestle. If using a food processor to make the paste, break up fresh shrimp with a knife and mix in with the paste. Use a spatula to mix.

3. In a saucepan over medium-high heat, bring stock to a boil, add the paste with shrimp and stir. Add all the vegetables starting with sweet potatoes, then mushrooms, and squash at the end. Cook each vegetable for about 1 minute before adding the next. Add fish sauce and bring to a boil. Add basil and turn off the heat. Serve.

Soup with Tofu and Seafood

There are several different ways to make this soup; using seaweed is just one of the combinations. It adds an earthy taste to the dish.

INGREDIENTS | SERVES 4

4 ounces ground pork

4 tablespoons light soy sauce, divided

½ teaspoon white sugar

2 pinches ground white pepper, divided

4–6 cups chicken stock

6 ounces silken tofu, cut into 2" cubes

1 ounce dried seaweed, broken into bite-size pieces and soaked until softened

¼ teaspoon salt

1 green onion, chopped into 1" pieces

2 tablespoons chopped cilantro

1 teaspoon Deep-Fried Minced Garlic (see Chapter 2)

1. Mix the pork, 2 tablespoons soy sauce, sugar, and a pinch of white pepper together in a mixing bowl.

2. In a saucepan, bring the stock to a boil over high heat; turn the heat down to low and simmer. Roll pork mixture into small dumplings, the size of your thumb, and add to the stock. Simmer for 1 minute, and then add the tofu and seaweed.

3. Season the soup with 2 tablespoons soy sauce and salt. Remove from heat and adjust to your desired taste.

4. Garnish with green onions, chopped cilantro, 1 pinch white pepper, and fried garlic.

Hot and Sour Soup

*This is a very popular Chinese soup. Pork can be omitted for a
just-as-delicious vegetarian version of the soup.*

INGREDIENTS | SERVES 6

2 tablespoons vegetable oil

1 teaspoon chopped garlic

3 ounces ground pork

1½ cup chopped straw mushrooms

1 tablespoon Chinese chili sauce or
Sriracha Sauce (see Chapter 2)

1–2 tablespoons soy sauce

1 teaspoon salt

6 cups stock or water

8 ounces soft or silken tofu, cut into ½"
cubes and deep-fried, or fresh

1 tablespoon tapioca flour

2 tablespoons water

1 tablespoon chopped green onion

1 teaspoon sesame oil

1. Heat 2 tablespoons of oil in a saucepan over medium heat. Add chopped garlic and fry until fragrant, about 10 seconds. Add pork and sauté for 1 minute, breaking up the pork.

2. Add mushrooms and stir-fry for 30 seconds. Add Sriracha or Chinese chili sauce, soy sauce, salt, stock, and tofu and bring to a boil. Boil for 2 minutes.

3. Meanwhile, in a mixing bowl, add tapioca flour to 2 tablespoons water and stir to mix well. Add the tapioca mixture to the soup and stir well. Adjust seasoning to taste. Add more water if needed. Serve sprinkled with green onions and sesame oil.

Wonton Soup

Blanched egg noodles or rice noodles can be added to this soup to turn it into a more substantial meal.

INGREDIENTS | SERVES 4

1 pound ground pork

2 shallots, minced

3 cloves garlic, minced

½ cup chopped cilantro, divided

1 egg

1½–2 tablespoons soy sauce

Pinch of sugar

Pinch of salt

2 pinches freshly ground white pepper,
divided

Wonton wrappers

2 cups chicken stock

2–4 tablespoons light soy sauce

1. In a mixing bowl, combine the ground pork, shallots, garlic, half of chopped cilantro (leave half for garnishing), egg, soy sauce, sugar, salt, and 1 pinch pepper. Mix well.

2. Put 1 tablespoon of the mixture in the middle of each wonton wrapper and bring the four corners together, squeezing the four corners to close. Continue until all the mixture is finished.

3. Heat the stock in a medium saucepan and bring to boil over high heat. Drop wontons in the stock and let simmer over medium-low heat until wontons float to the surface. Add some water or stock if there is not enough stock. Season with soy sauce. Serve hot and sprinkle with ground pepper and cilantro.

Pork Cabbage Wrap Soup

This dish is also a "curry" from the Thai perspective. It is called Kang Jued, *or bland curry. It may not sound very appetizing when translated, but it's packed with flavor!*

INGREDIENTS | SERVES 4

8 cabbage leaves

8 cilantro stems (pick off the leaves for garnish)

2 tablespoons vegetable oil

¼ cup minced garlic

4 ounces ground pork

8 ounces silken tofu, cut into ½" cubes

4 tablespoons soy sauce, divided

2 tablespoons sugar, divided

1 egg

3 cups chicken stock

1 tablespoon corn flour

4 tablespoons water

1. Blanch cabbage in boiling water until softened, about 20 seconds. Let drain in a colander. Blanch cilantro stems for about 10 seconds and let rest.

2. Heat a sauté pan over medium heat and add oil. Fry garlic until fragrant, about 10 seconds. Add pork and sauté for 1 minute, breaking up the meat as you sauté. Add tofu and continue to stir-fry for another minute. Add 1 tablespoon soy sauce and 1 tablespoon sugar and mix well. Add egg and scramble together with pork and tofu.

3. Lay the pork and tofu mixture on cabbage leaves. Wrap cabbage around the filling and tie with blanched cilantro stems.

4. Add stock to a medium soup pot. Lay wrapped pork in the pot and bring to a boil. Add the remaining soy sauce and sugar. Lower heat to low and simmer for 15 minutes.

5. In a mixing bowl, mix 1 tablespoon corn flour with 4 tablespoons water. Add to the soup and continue to simmer until it thickens slightly. Garnish with cilantro leaves and serve.

Coconut Beef Soup

This version of coconut soup has no vegetables and is served with a side of blanched vegetables of your choosing.

INGREDIENTS | SERVES 4

1 pound sirloin

2 (13.5-ounce cans) coconut milk

10 slices galangal roots

2 tablespoons thinly sliced lemongrass

2 tablespoons sugar

4 tablespoons fish sauce

4 tablespoons Tamarind Water (see Chapter 2)

1 teaspoon thinly julienned kaffir lime leaves

3 bruised Thai chilies

1. Depending on your cooking preference, grill or pan-sear beef until the outside is just brown, but not cooked all the way (about 2 minutes per side on a grill or on the stove over medium heat). Slice beef into small bite-size pieces.

2. In a saucepan, bring coconut milk to a boil. Add beef, galangal, and lemongrass and simmer on low heat for 20 minutes.

3. Season with sugar, fish sauce, and tamarind water, and garnish with kaffir lime leaves and bruised chilies.

Egg Noodle with Roast Duck Soup

Roast duck can easily be purchased at many Chinese restaurants. If you can't find egg noodles, rice noodles can also be used for this soup.

INGREDIENTS | SERVES 2

2 cups chicken stock

½ teaspoon salt

1 teaspoon sugar

2 teaspoons oyster sauce

4 ounces egg noodles

2 stalks bok choy, chopped

3 ounces roast duck, sliced

2 teaspoons Chinese preserved cabbage (purchase at Asian grocery store)

1 tablespoon chopped green onions

1 tablespoon chopped cilantro

1 teaspoon Deep-Fried Minced Garlic (see Chapter 2)

Pinch of ground white pepper

1. In a saucepan, bring stock to a boil and season with salt, sugar, and oyster sauce. Blanch noodles and bok choy in boiling water, about 10 seconds for each.

2. Place noodles and bok choy in a bowl and top with pieces of roast duck. Pour seasoned stock over and sprinkle with preserved cabbage, green onions, cilantro, fried garlic, and white pepper.

Beef Noodle Soup

Any kind of rice noodles can be used to make this soup,
but egg noodles or fresh angel hair pasta are also great choices.

INGREDIENTS | SERVES 4

Stock

Pinch of salt

1 (3-pound) bone-in beef roast

8 cups water

2 tablespoons dark soy sauce

2 tablespoons light soy sauce

2 tablespoons sugar

5 slices galangal

1 stalk lemongrass

Handful of cilantro stalks

1 star anise

1 piece dried orange peel or 1 teaspoon
   ground orange peel

2 pandan leaves

1 teaspoon cracked pepper, white or
   black

Soup

½ cup chopped celery

3 cups blanched bean sprouts

8 ounces dried rice noodles, blanched

1. Put all stock ingredients in a large saucepan and bring to the boil. Lower heat to low and simmer for 2 hours. Remove the beef from the stock. Strain stock and check seasoning. Add more water if needed. Slice beef shank thinly

2. Bring stock back to boil, and add sliced beef back to the pot. Add celery and turn off the heat. Place bean sprouts and noodles in a bowl and pour over the soup.

Curried Egg Noodle Soup with Beef (*Kao Soi Nuer*)

This is a northern Thai dish that was influenced by Burmese cuisine.

INGREDIENTS | SERVES 4

Paste

4 dried long red Thai or New Mexican chilis

3 shallots, chopped

4 cloves garlic, chopped

1 tablespoon chopped turmeric, fresh or dried roots

2 tablespoons finely chopped ginger

¼ teaspoon salt

2 teaspoons minced cilantro stems

Soup

⅓ cup coconut cream

4 ounces sliced beef sirloin

1 tablespoon palm sugar

2 tablespoons light soy sauce

2 cups chicken stock or water

1 cup fresh egg noodles

1 tablespoon chopped green onions

1 tablespoon chopped cilantro

Lime wedges

2 tablespoons deep-fried shallots, bought at the store

1. Make the paste by roasting the chilies, shallots, garlic, turmeric, and ginger, one at time, in a dry pan over low heat for 1–2 minutes each. Allow to cool, and pound the ingredients together with salt and cilantro stems using a mortar and pestle until smooth.

2. In a fry pan, simmer coconut cream over low heat until it is thick and shiny on the surface, about 2 minutes. Add the paste and let simmer at low heat until fragrant, about 4 minutes. Add beef slices and simmer until beef is just cooked, about 3 minutes.

3. Season with palm sugar and soy sauce. Add stock and continue to simmer until beef is tender, about 25 minutes. Add more stock or water if needed.

4. Blanch egg noodles in water for about 15 seconds and place in a bowl. Ladle the beef curry on top. Garnish with chopped onions, chopped cilantro, wedges of lime, and fried shallots.

Pork Noodle Soup (*Kuay Tiew Moo*)

This is a hearty, easy-to-make soup with very few, simple ingredients.

INGREDIENTS | SERVES 2

1 clove minced garlic

2 cilantro stems, minced

5 ounces ground pork

4 cups chicken stock

1 teaspoon sugar

1 tablespoon soy sauce

Pinch of salt

6 ounces dried rice noodles (usually labeled rice stick on the package), soaked for 1 hour

1 cup bean sprouts

1 tablespoon chopped cilantro

1 tablespoon chopped green onions

2 tablespoons Deep-Fried Minced Garlic (see Chapter 2)

Ground white pepper to taste

1. In a mixing bowl, mix the minced garlic and cilantro stems with pork.

2. In a saucepan, bring stock to a boil. Turn the heat to medium, add pork, and break up the pork with a spoon. Season with sugar, soy sauce, and salt and simmer for 2–3 minutes until the pork is cooked.

3. Boil water in a saucepan. Blanch the noodles and bean sprouts in boiling water for about 10 seconds, and put in a bowl. Pour the stock with pork over the blanched noodles and sprouts. Garnish with cilantro and green onions. Top with fried garlic and ground pepper.

Noodles to Use in Thai Soups

Any rice or egg noodles can be used in any of the noodle soups, including bean thread noodles. Most rice noodles in the United States come in dried form. You can buy fresh flat noodles at an Asian grocery store. They are ready to be used without soaking. Egg noodles are usually frozen or refrigerated and are ready to be cooked like fresh pasta. There are also dried egg noodles, which are often used for stir-fried noodles.

Seafood Hot Pot (*Po Taek*)

This seafood hot pot is mostly served at restaurants or on the streets.
The hot soup is served over flame as part of the meal with rice.

INGREDIENTS | SERVES 4

5 cups water or chicken stock

5 bruised cilantro roots or 10 bruised cilantro stems

2 bunches Chinese celery or 2 stalks celery, chopped

8 slices galangal

1 crab in shell, quartered

7 ounces medium shrimp, peeled and deveined

3 ounces squid, cut into 1" × ½" pieces

1 pound mussels with shells on

1 cup holy basil or sweet Thai basil

1 teaspoon ground white pepper

5 tablespoons fish sauce

5 Thai chilies, bruised

1. In a saucepan, bring water or stock to a boil. Add cilantro roots or stems, celery, and galangal. Let boil for 3 minutes.

2. Add seafood, basil, white pepper, fish sauce, and Thai chilies. Bring back to boil. Cook for 3–5 minutes over medium heat.

Daikon Soup

Daikon is white Japanese radish. It is sweet and tender when cooked.

INGREDIENTS | SERVES 4

6 ounces ground pork

4–5 cups chicken stock

1 large daikon or 2 small ones, quartered lengthwise and cut into 1½" pieces

2 tablespoons light soy sauce

½ cup chopped green onions

1 tablespoon chopped cilantro

½ teaspoon ground pepper

Pork Seasoning

2 cilantro stems, minced

3 garlic cloves, minced

1 teaspoon ground white pepper

2 teaspoons light soy sauce

1 teaspoon palm or white sugar

1. Combine pork and pork seasonings in a bowl. Mix well. Roll pork into small dumplings, about 1" balls.

2. In a large saucepan, bring stock to a boil, add pork dumplings, and let cook for 1 minute over medium heat. Add daikon and light soy sauce; let simmer until daikon is cooked, about 20 minutes. Add more stock if needed. Check seasoning and add more soy sauce if needed. Turn off the heat and garnish with green onions, cilantro, and ground pepper.

Stuffed Bitter Melon Soup

Bitter melons are, well, bitter. Once fully cooked, they have sweet undertones.
Bitter melons are an acquired taste.

INGREDIENTS | SERVES 4

1 bitter melon, available at Asian
  grocery stores
1 clove minced garlic
½ teaspoon salt
1 pinch ground pepper
½ cup ground pork
5 cups chicken stock
2 tablespoons soy sauce
1 recipe cooked Jasmine Rice (see
  Chapter 2)

1. Cut both ends off from the bitter melon and slice it into 3 or 4 sections. Scoop out the seeds. Be careful not to break the pieces.

2. Combine minced garlic, salt, and pepper with ground pork. Mix well. Stuff each section of the bitter melon with the pork mixture. Do not overstuff the melon.

3. Add stock into a medium saucepan. Add the stuffed bitter melon and soy sauce. Let simmer for 30 minutes over medium-low heat. The melon will turn a yellow/green color. It should be fork-tender. Serve with cooked Jasmine Rice.

Hot and Sour Pork Rib Soup

This soup is a great dish on its own or over cooked Jasmine Rice (see Chapter 2). The flavor of the hot and sour sauce and the simmered ribs is robust and complex.

INGREDIENTS | SERVES 6

4 cups water
1 stalk lemongrass, chopped and bruised
6 slices galangal, sliced and bruised
4 kaffir lime leaves, torn
1 tablespoon fish sauce
2 pounds pork ribs, cut into 2" pieces
  (ask your butcher to do it)

Sauce

4 tablespoons lime juice
3 tablespoons fish sauce
2 or 3 Thai chilies, minced (about 1–2
  teaspoons of minced chilies)
½ teaspoon of sugar
¼ cup of chopped cilantro

1. In a saucepan, bring water to a boil. Add lemongrass, galangal, and kaffir lime leaves to the stock and simmer over medium-low heat for 1 minute. Season with fish sauce.

2. Add pork ribs and simmer the ribs for 1 hour. Turn off the heat.

3. In a bowl, mix lime juice, fish sauce, chilies, sugar, and cilantro. Add the sauce to the soup and serve.

Lemongrass Soup with Shrimp and Chili Jam

The addition of Chili Jam (see Chapter 3) makes this soup more complex.
Sometimes milk is added to thicken the soup slightly.

INGREDIENTS | SERVES 6

10 uncooked medium shrimp, unpeeled

4 cups water

1 stalk lemongrass, chopped and
bruised

6 slices galangal, sliced and bruised

4 kaffir lime leaves, torn

1 tablespoon fish sauce

¾ cup oyster mushrooms

2 tablespoons Chili Jam (see Chapter 3)

Sauce

4 tablespoons lime juice

3 tablespoons fish sauce

2 or 3 Thai chilies, minced (about 1–2
teaspoons of minced chilies)

½ teaspoon sugar

2 tablespoons chopped cilantro

1. Peel and devein the shrimp. Save the shells to make stock. Bring water to boil in a large saucepan and add shrimp shells. Simmer for about 3 minutes over medium heat and strain the stock. Add lemongrass, galangal, and kaffir lime leaves to the stock and bring it back to boil. Season with fish sauce.

2. Add mushrooms, and 3 minutes later, add shrimp. Simmer until shrimp just changes color, about 2 minutes. Turn off the heat.

3. In a bowl, mix lime juice, fish sauce, chilies, sugar, and cilantro. Ladle the soup and check seasoning. It should be salty, sour, and spicy.

4. Add sauce and Chili Jam to the soup and stir to mix. Serve immediately.

Growing Lemongrass

Lemongrass is easy to grow in warmer climates. Place stalks of lemongrass in water for 2 weeks, until they sprout roots. Bury in the soil 2" deep in full sun. When harvesting, cut the stalks as close to the soil as possible from the center of the bush. Be careful, as the leaves are very sharp; wear protective clothing.

CHAPTER 7

Curries

Green Curry with Beef and Bamboo Shoots

Green curry is one of the spiciest curries. The texture of the bamboo shoots will stand up against the beef in this dish.

INGREDIENTS | SERVES 4

2 (13.5-ounce) cans coconut milk

½ cup Green Curry Paste (see Chapter 2)

1 pound beef sirloin, sliced ⅛" thick, 1" × 1½" pieces

½ cup water

2 cups bamboo shoots

3–4 tablespoons fish sauce

2 teaspoons sugar

3 kaffir lime leaves, torn

1 cup Thai basil leaves, whole

Thai Curries

Thai curries consist of a curry paste and a combination of protein or vegetables mixed with coconut milk, stock, or water. It is a method of making food rather than one single ingredient or dish.

1. Do not shake the coconut milk. Scoop the cream off the top of coconut milk cans, about halfway down. In a large fry pan, bring the cream to a boil over medium heat. Stir in curry paste and turn down the heat to low. Simmer on low heat, without stirring, until fragrant and coconut cream starts to release some oil, about 3–5 minutes.

2. Add beef to the mixture and simmer for 2 minutes, stirring occasionally. Add the rest of coconut milk and water and bring it back a boil. Simmer the beef for 30 minutes at low heat.

3. Add bamboo shoots and bring back to boil, then let simmer for 3 minutes over low heat. Season with fish sauce and sugar. Taste for seasoning. Add Thai basil and kaffir lime leaves and turn the heat off.

Green Curry with Chicken and Butternut Squash

Butternut squash adds a creamy texture to the curry. If you have trouble finding butternut squash, any winter squash makes an excellent substitution.

INGREDIENTS | SERVES 4

2 (13.5-ounce) cans coconut milk

½ cup Green Curry Paste (see Chapter 2)

1 pound boneless chicken breast or chicken thighs, sliced into bite-size pieces

½ cup water

2 cups butternut squash, cut to 1" cubes

3–4 tablespoons fish sauce

2 teaspoons sugar

3 kaffir lime leaves, torn

1 cup Thai basil, whole

Light Coconut Milk

Light coconut milk is simply coconut milk with more water. Buy regular coconut milk so there is enough cream on top to fry the paste. Add less coconut milk and more water to reduce the fat content in coconut milk–based curries.

1. Do not shake the coconut milk. Scoop the cream on top of coconut milk cans, about halfway down. In a large fry pan, bring the cream to a boil over medium heat. Stir in curry paste and turn down the heat to low. Simmer on low heat, without stirring, until fragrant and coconut cream starts to release some oil, about 3–5 minutes.

2. Add chicken to the mixture and simmer for 2 minutes, stirring occasionally. Add the rest of coconut milk and water.

3. Add butternut squash and bring back to boil. Season with fish sauce and sugar. Taste for seasoning. Add Thai basil and kaffir lime leaves and turn the heat off.

Red Curry with Pork and Pumpkin

Pumpkin or kabocha are great additions for this curry.
When using, partially peel the pumpkin and cut it into 2" cubes.

INGREDIENTS | SERVES 4

2 (13.5-ounce) cans coconut milk

½ cup Red Curry Paste (see Chapter 2)

1 pound pork loin, sliced ⅛" thick, 1" × 1½" size

½ cup water

2 cups cubed pumpkin

3–4 tablespoons fish sauce

2 teaspoons sugar

3 kaffir lime leaves, torn

1 cup Thai basil, whole

Coconut Fat

Coconut fat is a medium-chain fatty acid. Although it is considered a saturated fat, your body will break it down faster than the saturated fat found in meat.

1. Do not shake the coconut milk. Scoop the cream on top of coconut milk cans, about halfway down. In a large fry pan, bring the cream to a boil over medium heat. Stir in curry paste and turn down the heat to low. Simmer over low heat, without stirring, until fragrant and coconut cream starts to release some oil, about 3–5 minutes.

2. Add pork to the mixture and simmer for 2 minutes, stirring occasionally. Add the rest of coconut milk and water and bring it back to boil. Simmer the pork for 20 minutes at low heat.

3. Add pumpkin and bring back to boil. Let simmer for 5 minutes. Season with fish sauce and sugar. Taste for seasoning. Add Thai basil and kaffir lime leaves and turn the heat off.

Red Curry with Pork and Pineapple

Pineapple adds sweetness and tartness to this curry.
When preparing, no extra water is added to the curry. The juice released from the simmering pineapple will act as a substitute for the extra water needed in the curry.

INGREDIENTS | SERVES 4

2 (13.5-ounce) cans coconut milk

½ cup Red Curry Paste (see Chapter 2)

1 pound pork loin, sliced ⅛" thick, 1" × 1½" pieces

4 cups minced pineapple

3–4 tablespoons fish sauce

2 teaspoons sugar

3 kaffir lime leaves, torn

1 tablespoon cracked white peppercorn

Curing Curries

Curries are best when they are allowed to sit for 2 hours before serving. The sauce gets a chance to penetrate and soak into the meat and vegetables, and the curry becomes thicker and more flavorful.

1. Do not shake the coconut milk. Scoop the cream on top of coconut milk cans, about halfway down. In a large fry pan, bring it to a boil over medium heat. Stir in curry paste and turn down the heat to low. Simmer over low heat, without stirring, until fragrant and coconut cream starts to release some oil, about 3–5 minutes.

2. Add pork to the mixture and simmer for 2 minutes, stirring occasionally. Add the rest of coconut milk and bring it back to boil. Simmer the pork for 5 minutes at low heat.

3. Add pineapple and bring back to boil. Let simmer for 15 minutes over low heat. Season with fish sauce and sugar. Taste for seasoning. Add kaffir lime leaves and white pepper, and turn the heat off.

Red Curry with Wild Mushrooms

Any types of wild mushrooms that are available at the supermarket are great for this dish. In the absence of meat, the different kinds of mushrooms add texture and flavor to the curry.

INGREDIENTS | SERVES 4

2 (13.5-ounce) cans coconut milk

½ cup Red Curry Paste (see Chapter 2)

6 cups mixed wild mushrooms, chopped and sliced into bite-size pieces

3–4 tablespoons fish sauce or light soy sauce

2 teaspoons sugar

3 kaffir lime leaves, torn

1 cup Thai basil

1. Do not shake the coconut milk. Scoop the cream on top of coconut milk cans, about halfway down. In a large fry pan, bring to a boil over medium heat. Stir in curry paste and turn down the heat to low. Simmer at low heat, without stirring, until fragrant and coconut cream starts to release some oil, about 3–5 minutes.

2. Add the rest of coconut milk and bring it back to boil.

3. Add mushrooms and bring back to boil. Simmer for 5 minutes over low heat. Season with fish sauce or soy sauce and sugar. Taste for seasoning. Add kaffir lime leaves and Thai basil leaves and turn the heat off.

Panang Curry with Beef

One of the classic ways to make Panang is to let the beef slowly simmer in the curry until it is tender.

INGREDIENTS | SERVES 4

2 (13.5-ounce) cans coconut milk

½ cup Panang Curry Paste (see Chapter 2)

2 pounds sliced beef sirloin

2 tablespoons fish sauce

2 tablespoons sugar

6 torn kaffir lime leaves

1 cup Thai basil

1. Do not shake the coconut milk. Scoop the cream on top of coconut milk cans, about halfway down. In a large fry pan, bring the cream to a boil over medium heat. Stir in curry paste and turn down the heat to low. Simmer over low heat, without stirring, until fragrant and coconut cream starts to release some oil, about 3–5 minutes.

2. Add beef to the mixture and simmer for 2 minutes, stirring occasionally. Add the rest of coconut milk and bring it back to boil. Simmer the beef for 30 minutes at low heat.

3. Season with fish sauce and sugar. Taste for seasoning. Add kaffir lime and Thai basil leaves and turn the heat off.

Massaman Curry with Goat and Sweet Potatoes

This curry is largely influenced by Malaysian and Indonesian curries. Chewier meats can stand up against some of the more flavorful dried spices in the paste.

INGREDIENTS | SERVES 4

2 (13.5-ounce) cans coconut milk

1½ pound goat shank, cut into 2" cubes

½ cup Southern (or Massaman) Curry Paste (see Chapter 2)

2 tablespoons roasted peanuts

2 tablespoons sugar

2 tablespoons fish sauce

2 tablespoons Tamarind Water (see Chapter 2)

2 cups cubed sweet potatoes

1 medium onion, chopped into bite-size pieces

2 bay leaves

1 cinnamon stick, broken

4 white cardamom pods

1. Do not shake the coconut milk. Scoop the cream on top of coconut milk cans, about halfway down, into a medium saucepan. Bring the other half of coconut milk to a boil in another saucepan, add goat cubes, and simmer for 45 minutes over medium-low heat.

2. Bring coconut cream that was scooped out to a boil over medium heat. Stir in curry paste and turn down the heat to low. Simmer over low heat, without stirring, until fragrant and coconut cream starts to release some oil, about 3–5 minutes.

3. Add goat and stock from other saucepan, along with peanuts, to the fried paste and bring to a boil. Season with sugar, fish sauce, and tamarind water.

4. Add sweet potatoes, onions, bay leaves, cinnamon stick, and cardamom and simmer for 10 minutes. Taste and adjust as needed. Serve.

Massaman Curry with Chicken and Potatoes

Bone-in chicken takes a while to cook, but once it is ready, it is irresistible.
The meat just falls off the bone!

INGREDIENTS | SERVES 4

2 (13.5-ounce) cans coconut milk

12 pieces bone-in chicken thighs and/or drumsticks

½ cup Southern (or Massaman) Curry Paste (see Chapter 2)

2 tablespoons roasted peanuts

2 tablespoons sugar

2 tablespoons fish sauce

2 tablespoons Tamarind Water (see Chapter 2)

2 cups 2"-cubed sweet potatoes

1 medium onion, chopped into bite-size pieces

2 bay leaves

1 cinnamon stick, broken

4 white cardamom pods

1. Do not shake the coconut milk. Scoop the cream on top of coconut milk cans, about halfway down, into a medium saucepan. In another saucepan, bring the other half of coconut milk to a boil, add chicken pieces, and simmer for 45 minutes over low heat.

2. Bring coconut cream that was scooped out to a boil over medium heat. Stir in curry paste and turn down the heat to low. Simmer at low heat, without stirring, until fragrant and coconut cream starts to release some oil, about 3–5 minutes.

3. Add chicken and the stock from the other saucepan, along with the peanuts, to the fried paste, and bring to a boil over medium heat. Season with sugar, fish sauce, and tamarind water.

4. Add sweet potatoes, onions, bay leaves, cinnamon stick, and cardamom and simmer for 10 minutes. Taste and adjust as needed. Serve.

Yellow Curry with Beef and Potatoes

Yellow curry combines fresh Thai spices with Indian curry powder, which is a mixture of different spices. This curry is often served with pickled vegetables such as pickled cucumbers.

INGREDIENTS | SERVES 4

2 (13.5-ounce) cans coconut milk

1½ pounds beef shanks, cut into 2" cubes

½ cup Yellow Curry Paste (see Chapter 2)

1 teaspoon sugar

2 tablespoons fish sauce

2 cups cubed potatoes

1 medium onion, chopped into bite-size pieces

1. Do not shake the coconut milk. Scoop the cream on top of coconut milk of both cans, about halfway down, into a medium saucepan. In another saucepan, bring the other half of coconut milk to a boil. Add beef cubes and simmer for 45 minutes over medium-low heat.

2. Bring coconut cream that was scooped out to a boil over medium heat. Stir in curry paste and turn down the heat. Simmer at low heat, without stirring, until fragrant and coconut cream starts to release some oil, about 3–5 minutes.

3. Add beef and the stock from the other saucepan to the fried paste, and bring to a boil. Season with sugar and fish sauce.

4. Add potatoes and onions and simmer for 10 minutes. Taste and adjust as needed.

Yellow Curry with Shrimp and Tomatoes

This is a different version of yellow curry that omits the potatoes and onions and instead adds tomatoes for extra acidity and sweetness.

INGREDIENTS | SERVES 4

1 (13.5-ounce) can coconut milk

3 tablespoons Yellow Curry Paste (see Chapter 2)

1½ pounds medium shrimp, peeled and deveined

1 teaspoon sugar

1–2 tablespoons fish sauce

2 cups chopped tomatoes

1. Do not shake the coconut milk. Scoop the cream on top of coconut milk can, about halfway down, into a medium saucepan. Bring coconut cream to a boil over medium heat. Stir in curry paste and turn down the heat to low. Simmer over low heat, without stirring, until fragrant and coconut cream starts to release some oil, about 3–5 minutes.

2. Add shrimp to the fried paste and bring to a boil. Simmer over medium-low heat for 1 minute, and then add the coconut milk from the can to the pot. Bring back to a boil. Season with sugar and fish sauce.

3. Add tomatoes and simmer for 1 minute. Taste and adjust as needed.

Chu Chee with Shrimp

Chu Chee curry is red curry–based, and it is thicker and spicier, using less liquid than other curries. Finely shredded kaffir lime leaves are the key to this dish. This is a great curry for seafood like clams, fish, or lobster.

INGREDIENTS | SERVES 4

1 (13.5-ounce) can coconut milk

⅓ cup Red Curry Paste (see Chapter 2)

1½ pounds large or medium shrimp, peeled and deveined

2 tablespoons palm sugar

3 tablespoons fish sauce

2 kaffir lime leaves, finely julienned

1. Do not shake the coconut milk. Scoop the cream on top of coconut milk can, about halfway down, into a medium saucepan. Bring the coconut cream to a boil over medium heat. Stir in curry paste and turn down the heat to low. Simmer over low heat, without stirring, until fragrant and coconut cream starts to release some oil, about 3–5 minutes.

2. Add shrimp to the fried paste and simmer for 2 minutes. Season with sugar and fish sauce. Add the rest of coconut milk to the pot and bring to a boil.

3. Add kaffir lime leaves and turn the heat off. Taste and adjust seasoning as needed.

Chu Chee with Fried Snapper

Frying fish before adding it to the curry adds a different texture to this dish than if you were to cook the fish with the curry. Any fish like cod or mackerel is great for this recipe.

INGREDIENTS | SERVES 4

1 (13.5-ounce) can coconut milk

⅓ cup Red Curry Paste (see Chapter 2)

2 pounds snapper fillet, deep- or pan-fried

2 tablespoons palm sugar

3 tablespoons fish sauce

2 kaffir lime leaves, finely julienned

How to Find the Freshest Seafood

The best source for fresh fish is a great fishmonger, someone who will steer you toward the best fish he or she has to offer. If you are on your own, follow your nose. Fresh fish should not smell fishy. Instead it should smell clean, and if it is an ocean fish, like the sea. If there is any fishy smell at all, don't buy it. In addition, check the skin: it should be slippery and moist; press the fish: it should feel firm; and look at the eyes: they should be plump and clear.

1. Do not shake the coconut milk. Scoop the cream on top of coconut milk can, about halfway down, into a medium saucepan. Bring coconut cream to a boil over medium heat. Stir in curry paste and turn down the heat to low. Simmer over low heat, without stirring, until fragrant and coconut cream starts to release some oil, about 3–5 minutes.

2. Add fried fish to the fried paste and simmer for 1 minute. Season with sugar and fish sauce. Add the rest of coconut milk to the pot and bring to a boil.

3. Add kaffir lime leaves and turn the heat off. Taste and adjust seasoning as needed.

Southern Dried Red Curry with Chicken

Dairy is not common in Thai food. It is usually only used in foods that are influenced by Malaysian or Indonesian cuisines.

INGREDIENTS | SERVES 4

3 tablespoons Red Curry Paste (see Chapter 2)

1 teaspoon curry powder

3 cups vegetable oil for frying

½ cup salted butter

4 bone-in chicken thighs

2 (13.5-ounce) cans coconut milk

3 tablespoons fish sauce

3 tablespoons lime juice

2 tablespoons palm sugar

1. Combine red curry paste with curry powder and set aside. Heat oil and butter in a heavy, medium saucepan. Fry chicken thighs until golden, but not all the way done, about 7 minutes. Reserve frying oil.

2. Transfer fried chicken thighs to a large saucepan, add coconut milk, and simmer for 30 minutes until chicken is cooked and tender.

3. In a different saucepan, heat ½ cup of oil used to deep-fry the chicken. Add the curry paste and fry over low heat until fragrant. Add chicken thighs and coconut milk and season with fish sauce, lime juice, and palm sugar. Simmer until reduced, about 20 minutes. Taste and adjust seasoning if desired. Remove from heat and serve.

Steamed Fish Curry

Traditionally, banana leaves are folded into little ramekins and used as containers to steam the fish curry.

INGREDIENTS | SERVES 4

1 (13.5-ounce) can coconut milk

2 teaspoons rice flour

¼ cup Red Curry Paste (see Chapter 2)

1 pound red snapper or catfish, sliced into 1" pieces

1 egg

3 tablespoons fish sauce

2 cups Thai basil

2 tablespoons finely julienned kaffir lime leaves

Steaming

The best way to steam most Asian dishes is in a large steamer that will fit a whole fish. Large aluminum steamers are available at most Asian grocery stores. It takes up space, but it is well worth it.

1. Shake coconut milk can, open, and combine ½ cup coconut milk with rice flour in a frying pan. Bring the mixture to a simmer and stir constantly until rice flour is cooked, about 1 minute.

2. Combine curry paste and 1 cup of coconut milk in a mixing bowl, stirring until well mixed. Add fish, egg, and fish sauce and stir to combine. Slowly add the rest of coconut milk, stirring at the same time. Stir slowly with wooden spatula for another 20 minutes in order for the mixture to thicken.

3. Add ½ cup of Thai basil and kaffir lime, and stir to mix.

4. Line five ½-cup ramekins with the rest of the Thai basil. Scoop out fish mixture, and fill each ramekin with fish mixture until the mixture is all gone.

5. Steam fish curry in a large steamer (you can purchase a large steamer at Asian grocery store. If large steamer is not available, any steamer with flat steaming trays will work. You might only be able to steam two ramekins at a time) over high heat for 15 minutes. Top the ramekins with the coconut milk and rice flour mixture and continue to steam for 1 minute. Turn off the heat and let cool.

Sour Curry with Fish and Watermelon Rind

This is a stock-based curry with a coarse paste. The paste can easily be made in a small food chopper thanks to all the wet ingredients.

INGREDIENTS | SERVES 4

Paste

7–9 dried long red Thai chilies

½ teaspoon salt

2 red shallots, chopped

2 garlic cloves

1 teaspoon shrimp paste

Curry

3 cups water

5 ounces catfish, sliced into bite-size pieces

2 cups bite-size pieces watermelon rind

2 tablespoons Tamarind Water (see Chapter 2)

1–2 tablespoons fish sauce

2 teaspoons palm sugar

Watermelon Rind

Thai watermelon has a thicker rind and a flavor that is not as bitter as ones found in the United States. However, the ones found here are still suitable to make this sour curry. When gathering your ingredients, be sure to pick a larger watermelon with seeds (those watermelons have a thicker rind). To prepare, chop the rind into 2" squares and peel off the skin. Leave some watermelon meat attached to the rind to balance the bitter taste.

1. Make the paste by grinding all paste ingredients with a mortar and pestle. For this paste, a small food chopper will do the job.

2. In a saucepan, bring the water to a boil, add the paste and fish, and simmer for 3 minutes until the fish is cooked. Remove fish.

3. Add watermelon rind to saucepan. When the rinds are cooked, about 20 minutes, add tamarind water, fish sauce, and palm sugar. Add fish pieces back to the pot and simmer for another 2 minutes. Adjust seasoning to taste.

Sour Curry with Shrimp and Cauliflower

One teaspoon of fresh turmeric can be added to this paste to give it a brighter color and flavor.

INGREDIENTS | SERVES 4

Paste

7–9 dried long red Thai chilies

½ teaspoon salt

2 red shallots, chopped

2 garlic cloves

1 teaspoon shrimp paste

Curry

5 ounces medium shrimp, peeled and deveined

3 cups water

2 cups chopped cauliflower

2 tablespoons Tamarind Water (see Chapter 2)

1–2 tablespoons fish sauce

2 teaspoons palm sugar

Curry Pastes

Curry pastes are the foundation of most Thai preparations and are essentially concentrated flavors meant to add complexity and depth to the dish. They are usually a relatively moist paste of chili peppers, garlic, shallots, and other herbs and spices. Typically, curry pastes are mixed with either broth or coconut milk to create a sauce or cooking liquid. Curry pastes can be kept in the refrigerator for one month.

1. Make the paste by grinding all paste ingredients using a mortar and pestle. For this paste, a small food chopper will do the job. Add shrimp to the paste and bruise the shrimp into the paste with the pestle. Do not mash the shrimp, only softly bruise them. If using food processor, pulse a few times to break the shrimp up a little bit.

2. In a saucepan, bring water to a boil, add the paste and shrimp to the boiling water, wait 1 minute until the shrimp is cooked, and take the shrimp out and place in serving dish.

3. Add cauliflower and simmer for 3–4 minutes. Add tamarind water, fish sauce, and palm sugar. Add shrimp back to the pot; adjust the seasoning to taste.

Jungle Curry with Beef

*This curry is one of the spiciest. It is stock-based and the paste
is fried with oil instead of coconut cream.*

INGREDIENTS | 4 SERVINGS

2 tablespoons vegetable oil

⅓ cup Northern (or Jungle) Curry Paste
(see Chapter 2)

8 ounces thinly sliced beef

3–4 tablespoons fish sauce

4–6 cups stock or water

3 cups green beans

2 tablespoons shredded grachai (wild
ginger)

10 kaffir lime leaves, torn

1 tablespoon pickled green peppercorns

Handful of basil leaves

1. Heat oil in a sauté pan over medium-low heat, add curry paste, and fry until fragrant, about 15 seconds. Add beef and stir-fry over medium heat until beef is almost cooked, about 2 minutes.

2. Add fish sauce and then stock. Bring stock back to a boil. Add vegetables and simmer over medium-low heat until cooked, about 3 minutes. Add the rest of the ingredients and stir to mix. Taste and adjust seasoning. Remove from heat and serve.

Panang Curry with Scallops

*Scallops are light and are perfect for Panang.
The delicate paste will allow the scallops to really shine in the thick curry sauce.*

INGREDIENTS | SERVES 4

1 (13.5-ounce) can coconut milk

3 tablespoons Panang Curry Paste (see
Chapter 2)

1 pound bay or sea scallop

1 tablespoon fish sauce

1 tablespoon sugar

½ cup Thai basil

3 torn kaffir lime leaves

1. Do not shake the coconut milk. Scoop the cream on top of coconut milk can, about halfway down, into a small saucepan. Bring cream to a boil over medium heat. Stir in curry paste and reduce heat to low. Simmer, without stirring, until fragrant and coconut cream starts to release some oil, about 3–5 minutes.

2. Add scallops to the mixture and simmer for 2 minutes, stirring occasionally. Add the remaining coconut milk. Turn heat up to medium-high, add fish sauce and sugar, and bring mixture to a boil.

3. Add Thai basil and kaffir lime leaves, stir, and remove from heat.

Red Curry with Roast Duck and Tomatoes

You can purchase roast duck at a Chinese restaurant.
This curry can also be made with leftover grilled chicken.

INGREDIENTS | SERVES 4

2 pounds roast duck (can be purchased at a Chinese restaurant)

2 (13.5-ounce) cans coconut milk

½ cup Red Curry Paste (see Chapter 2)

2 cups cherry tomatoes, halved

3 tablespoons fish sauce

2 teaspoons sugar

3 kaffir lime leaves, torn

½ cup Thai basil leaves

Red Curry Paste Applications

Red curry paste is often treated as a general-purpose paste that can be added to almost any Thai recipe. Add in a few dried spices, and it becomes Panang curry. It is used in stir-fries and as a seasoning ingredient.

1. De-bone the duck and slice the meat into 1½" strips.

2. Do not shake the coconut milk. Scoop the cream on top of coconut milk can, about halfway down, into a small saucepan. Bring cream to a boil over medium heat. Stir in curry paste and reduce heat to low. Simmer, without stirring, until fragrant and coconut cream starts to release some oil, about 3–5 minutes.

3. Add roast duck to the mixture and simmer for 2 minutes, stirring occasionally. Add the rest of coconut milk and bring it back to boil over medium-high heat. Reduce heat to low and simmer for 5 minutes.

4. Add tomatoes, increase heat to medium-high, and bring mixture to a boil. Reduce heat to low and let simmer for 2 minutes. Season with fish sauce and sugar and taste. Finish with lime leaves and Thai basil and turn off the heat.

Green Curry with Trout Dumplings and Apple Eggplants

*Other types of fish can be used to make good dumplings,
but trout have a chewier texture that is just perfect for them.*

INGREDIENTS | SERVES 4

1½ pounds minced trout fillet
3 tablespoons tapioca flour
3 teaspoons salt, divided
½ teaspoon ground white pepper
4 cups water
2 (13.5-ounce) cans coconut milk
½ cup Green Curry Paste (see Chapter 2)
2 cups apple eggplant, quartered
3 tablespoons fish sauce
2 teaspoons sugar
1 cup whole Thai basil
3 kaffir lime leaves, torn

1. Make dumplings by combining minced trout, tapioca flour, 2 teaspoons salt, and ground pepper in a mixing bowl. Roll the mixture into a ball and slap to the side of the bowl. Continue slapping until the ball becomes thick and firm. Roll the mixture into small dumplings, about 1" size.

2. Heat water and remaining salt in a large saucepan or Dutch oven over high heat until boiling. Poach the dumplings until they float, about 2–3 minutes. Drain and set aside.

3. Do not shake the coconut milk. Scoop the cream on top of coconut milk cans, about halfway down, into a small saucepan. Reserve remaining coconut milk for another use. Bring cream to a boil over medium heat. Stir in curry paste and reduce heat to low. Simmer, without stirring, until fragrant and coconut cream starts to release some oil, about 3–5 minutes.

4. Add fish dumplings to the mixture and simmer for 2 minutes.

5. Add eggplant and bring back to boil over medium-high heat. Reduce heat to low and simmer for 5 minutes until eggplant is soft. Season with fish sauce and sugar. Add Thai basil and kaffir lime leaves and turn the heat off. Serve hot.

Pad Thai Shrimp with Bean Thread Noodles (Chapter 8)

Strawberry Tapioca Pudding (Chapter 14)

Spicy Cucumber Salad (Chapter 4)

Penne Pasta with Garden Tomatoes (Chapter 13)

Coconut Soup with Chicken (*Tom Kha Kai*) (Chapter 6)

Stir-Fried Mixed Vegetables with Chicken (*Pak Kai*) (Chapter 10)

Salty and Sweet Chicken (Chapter 10)

Basil Fried Rice with Beef (Chapter 9)

Spicy Rice Balls (Chapter 5)

Pad See Ew with Chicken (Chapter 8)

Green Papaya Salad (*Som Tum*) (Chapter 4)

Drunken Noodles with Beef
(*Pad Kee Mao Nuer*) (Chapter 8)

Spinach with Soybean Paste (Chapter 10)

Egg Rolls (*Po Pia Tod*) (Chapter 5)

Chicken Satay Sandwich (Chapter 13)

Dried Noodles with Ground Pork and
Soy Sauce (*Kuay Tiew Haeng*) (Chapter 8)

Ice Cream Dog (Chapter 14)

Green Curry with Trout Dumplings and Apple Eggplants (Chapter 7)

Beef Salad (*Yum Nuer*) (Chapter 4)

Bean Thread Noodle Salad (*Yum Woon Sen*)
(Chapter 4)

Thai Basil Lime Sparkler (Chapter 14)

Butternut Squash Soup (Chapter 13)

Thai Iced Tea (*Cha Yen*) (Chapter 14)

Cucumber Salad (Chapter 4)

Red Curry with Salmon and Green Peppercorn

Other fish like halibut or cod can be used for this thick curry.

INGREDIENTS | SERVES 4

1 (13.5-ounce) can coconut milk
¼ cup Red Curry Paste (Chapter 2)
2 salmon steaks, about 6–8 ounces each
3 sprigs green peppercorn
1–2 tablespoons fish sauce
2 teaspoons sugar
3 kaffir lime leaves, torn
½ cup Thai basil leaves

1. Do not shake the coconut milk. Scoop the cream on top of coconut milk can, about halfway down, into a sauté pan. Bring it to a boil over medium heat. Stir in curry paste and turn down the heat to low. Simmer over low heat, without stirring, until fragrant and coconut cream starts to release some oil, about 3–5 minutes.

2. Add salmon to the mixture and simmer for 2 minutes. Flip the steaks and cook for another 2 minutes on the other side. Add the rest of coconut milk and bring it back to boil.

3. Add green peppercorn and season with fish sauce and sugar and taste. Add kaffir lime leaves and Thai basil and fold them in. Turn the heat off and serve.

Noodle Dishes

Pad Thai Shrimp

This is the most famous Thai food of all time. It is probably easier to find someone selling Pad Thai in the United States than in Thailand.

INGREDIENTS | SERVES 2

Sauce

2 tablespoons palm sugar

1 tablespoon white sugar

2 tablespoons Tamarind Water (see Chapter 2)

2 tablespoons fish sauce

Noodles

6 ounces dried, thin rice stick noodles (soaked in cold water for 1 hour)

2 teaspoons vegetable oil

1 shallot, minced

8 medium shrimp, peeled and deveined

2 eggs

¼ cup Fried Tofu (see Chapter 5)

Pinch of Roasted Thai Chili Flakes (see Chapter 2)

2 teaspoons Salted Shrimp (see Chapter 2)

1 teaspoon salted radish

2 cups bean sprouts

1 cup sliced Chinese chives or scallions, cut into 2" pieces

Crushed roasted peanuts for garnish

Lime wedges

1. Make the sauce by mixing palm sugar, white sugar, tamarind water, and fish sauce in a saucepan; simmer over low heat until sugar is dissolved.

2. Drain the noodles.

3. Heat a wok or large sauté pan over medium heat, add oil, and fry shallots until fragrant and colored, about 10 seconds.

4. Add shrimp and sauté for about 1 minute. Remove shrimp from the pan and set aside.

5. Crack eggs into the pan and break the yolk. Let eggs fry for 2 minutes without stirring, and then break up the eggs. Mix in tofu, chili flakes, dried shrimp, and radish. Stir-fry until the tofu is thoroughly heated up, about 1 minute, and then add noodles.

6. Turn up the heat to high, then stir-fry for 3–5 minutes, turning the noodles until they are soft and become translucent and brown in color. Add the prepared sauce. Stir for a few moments until the sauce is mostly absorbed. Add shrimp back to the pan.

7. Add most of the bean sprouts and Chinese chives (keep some for garnish) and cook for another 30 seconds. The noodles should be a little sweet, sour, and salty.

8. Serve topped with crushed peanut, fresh Chinese chives, bean sprouts, and a wedge or two of lime.

Pad See Ew with Chicken

Pad See Ew can be purchased almost anywhere in Thailand. It is largely influenced by Chinese cooking.

INGREDIENTS | SERVES 2

6 ounces dried wide rice noodles

3–4 tablespoons vegetable oil

3 cloves chopped garlic

4 ounces chicken, sliced into bite-size pieces

2–4 teaspoons light soy sauce

2–3 tablespoons dark soy sauce

½ cup chicken stock or water, if needed

2 eggs

2 cups Chinese broccoli, chopped

2–3 tablespoons sugar

Pinch ground white pepper

Chilies in Vinegar (see Chapter 2)

Thai Noodles

There are three main types of noodles in Thai cooking: rice, mung bean (bean thread), and egg noodles. Thai rice stick noodles have a transparent appearance, a slightly chewy texture, and almost no flavor, which makes them great for absorbing dressings and sauces. Rice noodles are most common, and are soaked before they are added to a dish.

1. Soak noodles in hot water for 15 minutes, drain, and run under cold water.

2. Heat a deep pan or a wok over medium heat. Add oil and sauté the chopped garlic in the oil for 10–15 seconds, until fragrant and brown. Add the chicken and stir until the meat is cooked, about 2 minutes.

3. Toss in the noodles along with light soy sauce and dark soy sauce. Stir and spread out over heated surface of the wok. Let noodles pan-fry for about 1 minute, stirring the entire time, until noodles are softened and have absorbed all the sauces. If noodles are taking a while to cook, add some chicken stock or water.

4. Make a well and add eggs in the middle of the pan, crack the yolks, and let fry for 1 minute. When the eggs are partially cooked, mix in with the noodles.

5. Add the broccoli. Stir and fold in the broccoli until wilted, about 1 minute. Sprinkle with sugar. Stir and mix well. Serve warm topped with white pepper and Chilies in Vinegar (see Chapter 2).

Drunken Noodles with Beef (*Pad Kee Mao Nuer*)

There are many different versions of this dish. Some are made with rice noodles and some are made with spaghetti noodles. Different vegetables can be used for this dish. It is the spiciest noodle dish around, so be sure to drink lots of water!

INGREDIENTS | SERVES 4

4 ounces beef sirloin, sliced thinly into bite-size pieces

1 tablespoon oyster sauce

6 ounces dried, flat rice noodles

3–5 Thai chilies

1 shallot

4 cloves garlic

¼ cup vegetable oil

¼ cup chopped yellow onions

2 tablespoons fish sauce

3–4 tablespoons dark soy sauce

2 teaspoons sugar

½ cup chicken stock or water if needed

2 handfuls Thai basil

Hot Soaking Noodles

Flat rice noodles are the only noodles that should be soaked in hot water. They are larger in size, which makes them harder to cook on home stovetops. Soaking them in hot water first will help you cook the noodles faster. Make sure to rinse the noodles with cold water to stop them from cooking so they don't get mushy when stir-frying.

1. Marinate beef with oyster sauce for 15 minutes.

2. Soak noodles in hot tap water for 15 minutes and rinse with cold water.

3. Make a paste by combining the chilies, shallot, and garlic using a mortar and pestle or food processor. You can also mince the ingredients well and mix them together.

4. Heat a wok or a deep fry pan over medium heat. Add oil and fry the paste for 10 seconds, until fragrant. Add beef and stir-fry until beef is mostly cooked, about 1 minute.

5. Add yellow onions and sauté until translucent, about 1 minute. Add noodles and season with fish sauce, soy sauce, and sugar. If the noodles are still hard, add a little stock or water to the stir-fry and stir until cooked. Add basil at the very end and stir for another 30 seconds until basil is wilted. Remove from heat and serve hot.

Coconut Vermicelli (*Mee Kati*)

*This is a creamy noodle dish that mainly uses the oil from coconut milk.
It is sweet, sour, and salty, without the heat.*

INGREDIENTS | SERVES 2

2 tablespoons vegetable oil

1 tablespoon minced shallots

2 teaspoons minced cilantro stem

½ cup Fried Tofu (see Chapter 5)

1 cup coconut milk

2 tablespoons ketchup

2 tablespoons Tamarind Water (see Chapter 2)

1 tablespoon palm sugar

1–2 tablespoons fish sauce

2 teaspoons soybean paste

4 ounces dried vermicelli noodles (Wai Wai brand), soaked for 20 minutes

½ cup Chinese chives

½ cup bean sprouts

1. Heat a sauté pan or large wok over medium heat and add oil. When the oil is hot, add shallot and cilantro stem and fry until fragrant, about 10 seconds. Add tofu and stir-fry for 1 minute.

2. Add coconut milk, ketchup, tamarind water, palm sugar, fish sauce, and soybean paste and mix well. Add noodles and mix. Stir-fry until the sauce is absorbed by the noodles.

3. Fold in chives and bean sprouts. Remove from heat and serve.

Pad Thai with Pork

Beef is not used to make Pad Thai because the strong flavor overpowers the mildness of the sauce. Pork, on the other hand, is a perfect addition to the traditional dish.

INGREDIENTS | SERVES 2

Sauce

2 tablespoons palm sugar

1 tablespoon white sugar

2 tablespoons Tamarind Water (see Chapter 2)

2 tablespoons fish sauce

Noodles

8 ounces dried, thin rice stick noodles (soaked in cold water for 1 hour)

2 teaspoons vegetable oil

1 shallot, minced

4 ounces ground pork or thinly sliced pork

2 eggs

¼ cup Fried Tofu (see Chapter 5)

Pinch of Roasted Thai Chili Flakes (see Chapter 2)

2 teaspoons Salted Shrimp (see Chapter 2)

1 teaspoon salted radish

1 cup Chinese chives or scallions, cut into 2" pieces

2 cups bean sprouts

Crushed roasted peanuts for garnish

Lime wedges

1. Drain the noodles.

2. Make the sauce by mixing palm sugar, white sugar, tamarind water, and fish sauce in a saucepan, and simmer over low heat until sugar is dissolved.

3. Heat a wok or large sauté pan over medium heat, add oil, and fry shallots until fragrant and colored, about 10 seconds.

4. Add pork and sauté for about 2 minutes.

5. Crack the eggs into the pan and break the yolks. Let eggs fry for 2 minutes without stirring, then mix in with pork. Mix in tofu, chili flakes, salted shrimp, and radish. Stir-fry until the tofu is thoroughly heated, about 1 minute, and then add noodles.

6. Turn up the heat to high and then stir-fry for 3–5 minutes, stirring the noodles the whole time until they are soft and become translucent and brown in color. Add the prepared sauce. Stir for about 1–2 minutes, until the sauce is mostly absorbed. Finally, add most of the Chinese chives and bean sprouts (save some for garnish), and cook for another 30 seconds. The noodles should be a little sweet, sour, and salty.

7. Serve topped with crushed peanuts, fresh Chinese chives, bean sprouts, and a wedge or two of lime.

Dried Noodles with Ground Pork and Soy Sauce (*Kuay Tiew Haeng*)

Extra dried red chilies can be added to this dish to make it spicier if you'd like. Since these noodles are dried, they are often served with a side of seasoned stock.

INGREDIENTS | SERVES 3

6 ounces minced pork

3 tablespoons water or chicken stock

6 cups water for blanching noodles

6 ounces dried rice stick noodles, soaked for 1 hour

1 cup bean sprouts

1 teaspoon Deep-Fried Minced Garlic (see Chapter 2)

2 tablespoons light soy sauce

2 tablespoons chopped roasted peanuts

1 tablespoon sugar

Large pinch of Roasted Thai Chili Flakes (see Chapter 2)

1 tablespoon chopped cilantro

2 or 3 wedges of lime

Seasoned Stock

Seasoned plain stock is often served as a side with dried noodle dishes or dried egg noodles with pork and seafood. It is also served with Chicken and Rice (Chapter 9). To make seasoned chicken stock, combine one part stock and one part water. Add soy sauce to season. Add one tablespoon at a time and taste. Garnish with chopped green onions and chopped cilantro.

1. In a large sauté pan or wok, cook pork with 3 tablespoons water or chicken stock over medium heat until all the way done, about 2–3 minutes. Set aside.

2. Bring 6 cups of water to a boil in a large saucepan or soup pot. Blanch noodles and bean sprouts, about 10 seconds, and place them in a bowl.

3. Top the noodles with pork, fried garlic, soy sauce, peanuts, sugar, chili flakes, and cilantro. Squeeze lime on top and mix all ingredients with the noodles.

Flat Noodles with Thick Gravy and Beef (*Raat Na Nuer*)

This noodle dish falls somewhere between soup and stir-fried noodles.
It's served with pickled jalapeños and Roasted Thai Chili Flakes (see Chapter 2).

INGREDIENTS | SERVES 2

6 ounces dried flat rice noodles

3 ounces sliced beef

2 teaspoons oyster sauce or light soy sauce

2 tablespoons dark soy sauce

4 tablespoons vegetable oil, divided

2 teaspoons minced garlic

1 cup chicken stock

1 cup chopped Chinese broccoli

1 tablespoon dark soy sauce

1 tablespoon light soy sauce

1 tablespoon salted soybean or soybean paste

1 tablespoon tapioca flour

1 tablespoon water

1. Soak noodles in hot tap water for 15 minutes and then rinse with cold water.

2. Marinate pork with oyster sauce or light soy sauce.

3. Rub noodles with 2 tablespoons dark soy sauce and let sit for 3–5 minutes.

4. Heat a wok or deep sauté pan over medium heat, and add 2 tablespoons oil. Stir-fry the noodles with oil at medium heat until noodles are wilted, about 1–2 minutes. Set aside.

5. Heat another wok or sauté pan over medium heat, add the other 2 tablespoons of oil, and fry garlic until brown, about 10 seconds. Add beef and stir-fry until it is halfway done, about 1–2 minutes. Add stock and bring the mixture to a boil. Add broccoli and season with dark soy sauce, light soy sauce, and soybean paste. Simmer for 3 minutes.

6. In the meantime, mix tapioca flour with water in a mixing bowl and stir. Add the mixture to the simmering stock and stir. Pour sauce over noodles to serve.

Pad See Ew with Vermicelli Noodles and Shrimp

*Vermicelli adds a different texture to this popular stir-fry dish,
so much so that it almost feels like a different dish altogether!*

INGREDIENTS | SERVES 3

4 ounces dried vermicelli noodles

3–4 tablespoons vegetable oil

3 cloves chopped garlic

4 ounces medium shrimp, peeled and deveined

2–3 tablespoons black soy sauce

2–4 teaspoons light soy sauce

½ cup chicken stock or water

2 eggs

2 cups Chinese broccoli, chopped

2–3 tablespoons sugar

Pinch ground white pepper

Chilies in Vinegar (see Chapter 2)

1. Soak noodles in cold tap water for 30 minutes; drain.

2. Heat a deep pan or a wok over medium heat. Add oil and sauté the chopped garlic for 10 seconds, until fragrant and brown. Add the shrimp and stir until cooked, about 2 minutes. Remove the shrimp and set aside.

3. Toss in the noodles along with black soy sauce and light soy sauce in a mixing bowl. Stir and spread out over heated surface of the wok. Let noodles pan-fry for about 1 minute, sautéing the whole time until noodles are soft and have absorbed all the sauce. If noodles are taking a long time to cook, add some chicken stock or water.

4. Make a well in the noodles and add eggs in the middle of the pan. Crack the yolks and let them fry for a minute. When the eggs are partially cooked, mix in with the noodles.

5. Add the broccoli. Stir and fold in the broccoli until wilted, about 1–2 minutes. Sprinkle with sugar. Stir and mix well. Serve warm garnished with white pepper and chilies in vinegar.

Crispy Egg Noodles and Shrimp with Thick Gravy

This is one of the prettiest noodle dishes to serve. The color and shape of the noodles, and the bright green Chinese broccoli, make this dish very appetizing.

INGREDIENTS | SERVES 2

4 ounces fresh egg noodles

3 cups plus 2 tablespoons vegetable oil, divided

2 teaspoons minced garlic

3 ounces shrimp, peeled and deveined

1 cup chicken stock

1 cup chopped Chinese broccoli

1 tablespoon extra-black soy sauce

1 tablespoon light soy sauce

1 tablespoon salted soybean or soybean paste

1 tablespoon tapioca flour

1 tablespoon water

1. In a deep sauté pan or wok, deep-fry egg noodles over medium heat at 350°F in 3 cups oil until crispy and golden, about 2–3 minutes.

2. Heat another wok or sauté pan over medium heat and add 2 tablespoons oil. Fry garlic until brown, about 10 seconds. Add shrimp and stir-fry until halfway done, about 1 minute. Add stock and bring the mixture to a boil. Add broccoli and season with extra-black soy sauce, light soy sauce, and soybean paste. Simmer for 3 minutes on medium-low heat.

3. In the meantime, mix tapioca flour with water in a mixing bowl and stir. Add the mixture to the simmering stock and stir. Pour sauce over noodles to serve.

Pad Thai Tofu

Fish sauce is often used as a base for Pad Thai. This vegetarian version uses soy sauce for the base and omits the dried shrimp that is also a typical Pad Thai ingredient.

INGREDIENTS | SERVES 2

Vegetarian Sauce

5 tablespoons palm sugar

2 teaspoons white sugar

4½ tablespoons Tamarind Water (see Chapter 2)

½ teaspoon salt

2 tablespoons soy sauce

Noodles

8 ounces dried, thin rice stick noodles (soaked in cold water for 1 hour)

2 teaspoons vegetable oil

1 shallot, minced

⅔ cup Fried Tofu (see Chapter 5)

2 eggs

Pinch of Roasted Thai Chili Flakes (see Chapter 2)

1 teaspoon salted radish, store bought

2 cups bean sprouts

1 cup Chinese chives or scallions, cut into 2" pieces

Crushed roasted peanuts for garnish

Lime wedges

1. Drain the noodles.

2. Make the sauce by mixing palm sugar, white sugar, tamarind water, salt, and soy sauce in a saucepan, and simmer over low heat until sugar is dissolved.

3. Heat a wok or large sauté pan over medium heat, add oil, and fry shallots until fragrant and colored, about 10 seconds.

4. Add fried tofu and sauté for about 1 minute until tofu is heated.

5. Crack eggs into pan and break the yolks. Let eggs fry for 2 minutes, without stirring, and then mix in with tofu. Add chili flakesand salted radish.

6. Add noodles, turn up the heat to medium-high, and then stir-fry for 3–5 minutes, stirring the noodles the entire time until they are soft and become translucent and brown in color.

7. Add the prepared sauce. Stir for 30 seconds, until the sauce is mostly absorbed. Finally, add most of the bean sprouts and Chinese chives (save some for garnish) and cook for another 30 seconds. The noodles should be a little sweet, sour, and salty.

8. Serve topped with crushed peanuts, fresh Chinese chives, bean sprouts, and a wedge or two of lime.

Noodle Soup with Lemongrass and Shrimp

This recipe takes traditional lemongrass soup to a whole other level by adding noodles.

INGREDIENTS | SERVES 4

Sauce

4 tablespoons lime juice

3 tablespoons fish sauce

2 or 3 Thai chilies, minced (about 1–2 teaspoons of minced chilies)

½ teaspoon sugar

¼ cup chopped cilantro

Soup

10 uncooked medium shrimp, unpeeled

10 cups water, divided

1 stalk lemongrass, chopped and bruised

6 slices galangal, bruised

4 kaffir lime leaves, torn

1 tablespoon fish sauce

¾ cup shitake, oyster, and other wild mushrooms

⅓ cup chopped tomatoes

8 ounces dried rice stick noodles, soaked for 1 hour

1. Peel and devein the shrimp. Save the shells to make stock.

2. In a large saucepan, bring 4 cups water to a boil and add shrimp shells. Boil for about 3 minutes and strain the stock. Add lemongrass, galangal, and kaffir lime leaves to the stock and bring it back to boil. Season with fish sauce.

3. Add mushrooms, and 3–5 minutes later, add shrimp and simmer until shrimp just change color, about 1–2 minutes. Add tomatoes and boil for 30 seconds, turn the heat off.

4. In a small bowl, mix the sauce by combining lime juice, fish sauce, chilies, sugar, and cilantro. Ladle the sauce into the soup and check seasoning. It should be salty, sour, and spicy.

5. Bring 6 cups of water to a boil in a large saucepan. Blanch noodles for 15 seconds and place noodles in a bowl. Ladle the soup over and serve.

Flat Noodles with Pickled Radish and Chicken

The flavor of this Chinese-style late-night dish can be enhanced if a carbon steel wok is used.

INGREDIENTS | SERVES 2

10 ounces dried, flat rice noodles

5 ounces chicken breast, sliced into bite-size pieces

4–5 tablespoons light soy sauce, divided

3 tablespoons vegetable oil, divided

2 garlic cloves, minced

2 teaspoons Chinese pickled radish

¼ cup chopped green onions

¼ cup chopped Chinese or regular celery

2 teaspoons dark soy sauce

2 eggs

1 cup green leaf lettuce, chopped in big pieces

1 teaspoon Deep-Fried Minced Garlic (see Chapter 2)

Pinch of white pepper

2 tablespoons chopped cilantro

1. Soak noodles in hot tap water for 20 minutes and rinse with cold water.

2. Marinate chicken with 2 teaspoons soy sauce for 15 minutes.

3. Heat a wok or deep pan, and add 2 tablespoons of oil. When the oil is hot, add chicken and fry until chicken is halfway done, about 4 minutes. Add garlic and Chinese pickled radish, and half of green onions and celery, and sauté for 1 minute.

4. Add noodles and follow with dark soy sauce and remainder of light soy sauce. Stir-fry until all the sauce is absorbed and noodles are brown and dry, about 5–7 minutes.

5. Make a well in the middle of the noodles, add the remaining tablespoon of oil, and crack eggs into pan. Break the yolks and fry for 1 minute. Fold eggs in with the noodles. Add the remaining green onions and celery, and green leaf lettuce. Fold in the vegetables and turn off the heat. Serve garnished with fried garlic, white pepper, and cilantro.

Stir-Fried Bean Thread Noodles (*Pad Woon Sen*)

This noodle dish is great on its own, but most Thais serve it as an entrée with rice on the side.
This is one of the few times that noodles are served with rice.

INGREDIENTS | SERVES 4

4 ounces sliced chicken breast

4 teaspoons light soy sauce, divided

3 tablespoons vegetable oil

1 teaspoon minced garlic

1 teaspoon minced shallots

2 eggs

8 ounces dried bean thread noodles, soaked for 15 minutes

2 teaspoons sugar

2 teaspoons black soy sauce

½ cup chopped Chinese celery or thinly sliced regular celery

½ cup chopped green onions

1 cup bean sprouts

2 tablespoons coarsely chopped cilantro

1. Marinate chicken with 2 teaspoons light soy sauce for 15 minutes.

2. Heat a wok or deep sauté pan over medium heat. When the pan is hot, add oil and fry garlic and shallots until golden brown, 10 seconds.

3. Add chicken and stir, turning the chicken pieces as you stir, until the outside of the chicken is completely cooked, about 1–2 minutes. Crack eggs on the side of chicken and break the yolks; let them fry for 2 minutes without stirring.

4. Add noodles, sugar, remaining light soy sauce and black soy sauce, and stir-fry until the noodles are wilted and the sauce is mostly absorbed, about 2 minutes.

5. Add celery, green onions, and bean sprouts, and fold the vegetables in until they are wilted, about 1 minute. Garnish with cilantro and serve.

Curried Noodles with Beef

Curry powder adds extra punch to this noodle dish. It is not overly spicy and has a good balance of salty and sweet.

INGREDIENTS | SERVES 4

8 ounces flat dried rice noodles
3 tablespoons dark soy sauce, divided
4 tablespoons vegetable oil, divided
2 cloves minced garlic
½ pound ground beef
3 tablespoons diced onions
1 teaspoon curry powder
1 cup chicken stock
3 tablespoons light soy sauce
1 tablespoon fish sauce
2 tablespoons oyster sauce
Pinch of sugar
2 tablespoons peas and diced carrots
2 tablespoons chopped celery
2 tomatoes, chopped
2 tablespoons pickled radish
2 tablespoons water
2 tablespoons tapioca flour
½ leaf green leaf lettuce
Pinch ground white pepper
2 tablespoons chopped cilantro

Curry Powder

Store-bought curry powder is a mixture of dried spices. Thais rarely use dried spices in their cooking. Therefore, mild curry powder is a better choice for Thai dishes. When buying curry powder, buy the mild curry powder. Homemade curry powder is usually milder than many of the store-bought versions. Old or stale curry powder can be dry-roasted in a pan to revive the flavors.

1. Soak noodles in hot tap water for 15 minutes and rinse with cold water.

2. Rub noodles with 2 tablespoons dark soy sauce and let sit for a few minutes. Heat a wok or deep sauté pan over medium heat and add 2 tablespoons oil. Stir-fry the noodles over medium heat until noodles are wilted, about 1–2 minutes.

3. Heat another sauté pan or wok over medium heat. When hot, add remaining 2 tablespoons oil and then garlic, and fry until fragrant, about 10 seconds. Add ground beef and stir-fry to brown the beef, about 1 minute. Add onions and curry powder and stir-fry until onions are translucent, about 30 seconds. Add stock and bring to boil. Follow with light soy sauce, fish sauce, oyster sauce, sugar, peas and carrots, celery, tomatoes, and radish. Taste and adjust seasoning.

4. In a small mixing bowl, mix 2 tablespoons water with tapioca flour. Pour into the simmering stock and stir until thickened. Turn off the heat.

5. Lay lettuce on a plate and put noodles on top. Top noodles with the beef sauce, and sprinkle with some ground pepper and garnish with cilantro.

Drunken Spaghetti with Chicken

Drunken noodles can be made with many different types of pasta. Thais have been making drunken noodles with spaghetti for a long time and it doesn't make the dish any less Thai.

INGREDIENTS | SERVES 4

Drunken Noodle Paste Mix
3–5 Thai chilies
1 shallot
4 cloves garlic

Other Ingredients
4 ounces chicken, sliced into bite-size pieces
2 teaspoons light soy sauce
8 cups water to boil spaghetti
6 ounces dried spaghetti
¼ cup vegetable oil
¼ cup chopped yellow onions
2 tablespoons fish sauce
3–4 tablespoons dark soy sauce
2 teaspoons sugar
½ cup chicken stock or water if needed
1 cup Thai basil

History of Drunken Noodles
There are two schools of thought regarding the origin of the dish. The first involves a bunch of guys who were drinking and looking to make something to eat that would go with their drinks. According to the story, they go into the kitchen and come up with this recipe. In the second story, the guys were drinking at a restaurant and would not leave, so the cook made these super spicy noodles to make them go. The dish became a hit and they stayed on to drink more.

1. Marinate chicken with 2 teaspoons light soy sauce.

2. In a large saucepan, bring 8 cups water to a boil. Drop in spaghetti and let boil for 8–10 minutes, stirring occasionally. Once done, run the noodles under cold water and set aside.

3. Make the paste using a mortar and pestle, a food processor, or mince it well and mix chilies, shallot, and garlic together.

4. Heat oil in a wok or a deep sauté pan over medium heat. Fry the paste for 10 seconds until fragrant. Add chicken and stir-fry until chicken is mostly cooked, about 1 minutes. Add yellow onions and sauté until translucent, about 30 seconds

5. Add noodles and season with fish sauce, soy sauce, and sugar. If the noodles are not cooked or still hard, add a little stock or water and stir until cooked. Add basil at the very end and stir for another 30 seconds until basil is wilted. Remove from heat and serve.

Pad Thai Shrimp with Bean Thread Noodles

Bean thread noodles are a good substitute to use when making Pad Thai.

INGREDIENTS | SERVES 2

Sauce

2 tablespoons palm sugar

1 tablespoon white sugar

2 tablespoons Tamarind Water (see Chapter 2)

2 tablespoons fish sauce

Noodles

6 ounces dried bean thread noodles, soaked for 20 minutes

2 teaspoons vegetable oil

1 shallot, minced

8 shrimp, peeled and deveined

2 eggs

¼ cup Fried Tofu (see Chapter 5)

Pinch of Roasted Thai Chili Flakes (see Chapter 2)

2 teaspoons Salted Shrimp (see Chapter 2)

1 teaspoon salted radish

2 cups bean sprouts

1 cup Chinese chives or scallions, cut into 2" pieces

Crushed roasted peanuts for garnish

Lime wedges

¼ teaspoon chili powder (optional)

Bean Thread Noodles

Bean thread noodles are made from mung bean flour. They become clear once cooked, hence the name clear or glass noodles. Don't confuse them with vermicelli noodles, as they look almost identical when dry. Read the label and make sure they are made from mung beans.

1. Drain the noodles.

2. Make the sauce by mixing palm sugar, white sugar, tamarind water, and fish sauce in a saucepan and simmer on low heat until sugar is dissolved.

3. Heat a wok or large sauté pan over medium heat, add oil, and fry shallots until fragrant and colored, about 10 seconds.

4. Add shrimp and sauté for about 1 minute. Remove shrimp from the pan and set aside.

5. Crack the eggs into the pan and break the yolks. Let eggs fry for 2 minutes without stirring, and then break up the eggs. Mix in tofu, chili flakes, salted shrimp, and radish. Stir-fry until the tofu is thoroughly heated up, about 1 minute, and then add noodles.

6. Turn up the heat to medium-high and then stir-fry for 3–5 minutes, stirring and turning the noodles the whole time until they are soft and become translucent and brown in color. Add the prepared sauce. Stir for 30 seconds until the sauce is mostly absorbed. Add shrimp back to the pan.

7. Add most of the bean sprouts and Chinese chives (save some for garnish) and cook for another 30 seconds. The noodles should be a little sweet, sour, and salty.

8. Serve topped with crushed peanut, fresh Chinese chives, bean sprouts, and a wedge or two of lime. Add chili powder if you'd like this dish to be a little hotter.

Noodles with Pork Meatballs

Frozen meatballs can be purchased at any Asian grocery store, but homemade meatballs taste so much better and are free of preservatives.

INGREDIENTS | SERVES 4

6 ounces ground pork

1 teaspoon minced garlic

¼ teaspoon and 1 pinch salt, divided

2 cilantro stems, minced

2 pinches ground white pepper, divided

¼ cup crushed ice

4 cups chicken stock

1 teaspoon sugar

1 tablespoon soy sauce

6 ounces dried rice stick noodles, soaked for 1 hour

1 cup bean sprouts

1 tablespoon chopped cilantro

1 tablespoon chopped green onions

2 tablespoons Deep-Fried Minced Garlic (see Chapter 2)

Chicken Stock

It is always a good idea to have some chicken stock stored and ready to use if a recipe calls for it. When making a big pot of stock, split it in smaller containers and freeze for later use.

1. Make pork meatballs by mixing pork, garlic, ¼ teaspoon salt, minced cilantro stems, and 1 pinch pepper. Place in food processor and pulse in 5-second increments until well mixed. Add ice slowly and continue to pulse until the mixture thickens slightly. Remove from processor and roll the mixture into small balls.

2. In a large stockpot, bring stock to a boil. Add pork meatballs to stock. Season with sugar, soy sauce, and salt. Simmer for 3 minutes over medium-low heat.

3. Set up another large saucepan with boiling water. Blanch the noodles and bean sprouts in boiling water, about 10 seconds, and put in a large bowl. Pour the stock with pork over the noodles. Garnish with cilantro and green onion. Topped with fried garlic and ground pepper.

Drunken Pasta with Chicken

This is a great way to use up leftover pasta. The chewy texture of pasta noodles and the combination of spices really brings this dish up a notch.

INGREDIENTS | SERVES 3

Paste

8 Thai chilies
3 shallots
6 cloves garlic
2 teaspoons shrimp paste

Noodles

8 ounces penne pasta
¼ cup plus 1 tablespoon vegetable oil
6 ounces sliced chicken breast
¼ cup sliced carrots
1 cup asparagus, cut into 1" pieces
1 cup sliced mushroom
½ cup chopped red and green bell pepper
1–2 tablespoons fish sauce
1 tablespoon palm sugar
1 cup Thai basil

1. Make the paste with a mortar and pestle or mince all paste ingredients separately and mix them together.

2. Bring a large saucepan of water to a boil. Add penne pasta and boil for 7–9 minutes. Run under cold water, and when cooled off rub with 1 tablespoon vegetable oil.

3. Heat a wok or deep sauté pan over medium heat, add ¼ cup vegetable oil and fry the paste until fragrant, about 10 seconds. Add chicken and stir-fry until chicken is mostly done, about 1 minute. Add carrots and stir for 1 minute. Add the rest of the vegetables and stir-fry for another minute. Add fish sauce and palm sugar to season.

4. Add pasta to the pan. Taste and adjust the seasoning with fish sauce or sugar if needed. If the noodles are not done, add a little water. Fold basil in until wilted, about 30 seconds. Turn off the heat and serve.

Spaghetti with Salted Fish

Spaghetti has the convenience of a longer shelf life than Chinese fresh egg noodles. It is also firm so it will stand up to the vigorous stirring that Thai dishes require.

INGREDIENTS | SERVES 3

½ pound dried spaghetti

¼ cup plus 1 tablespoon vegetable oil

4 dried long red chilies, chopped into thirds

1 tablespoon minced garlic

¼ cup sun-dried tomatoes, sliced lengthwise into thin strips

3 ounces salted fish or anchovies

½ cup chopped Chinese broccoli

¼ cup shredded Parmesan (optional)

1 cup holy basil or Thai sweet basil

1 teaspoon freshly ground black pepper

Lime wedges

Cheese

There is really no dairy in Thai cooking. When traveling south, you will see more margarine or butter added to curries or roti, fried dough.

1. Bring water to a boil in a large saucepan. Boil spaghetti for 7–9 minutes until done. Rinse under cold water and rub with 1 tablespoon vegetable oil when cooled off. Put aside.

2. Heat a deep sauté pan or wok over medium heat and add ¼ cup oil. Fry dried chilies until fragrant, about 30 seconds, and remove from the pan.

3. Turn down the heat to low, add garlic and sun-dried tomatoes, and sauté for 1 minute, until fragrant.

4. Add spaghetti and salted fish or anchovies and stir to mix. The noodles should be salty enough without adding any more salt. Add Chinese broccoli and fold in for 30 seconds. Add Parmesan cheese and mix in. If omitting cheese, more salted fish might be needed.

5. Add basil and black pepper and fold until basil is wilted. Serve with wedges of limes.

Kanom Jeen with Shrimp

This dish comes with a variety of sauces or curries on it. In Thailand the noodles are made fresh and can be purchased at the markets; in the United States, these noodles are not readily available. Bun noodles will work as a perfect substitution.

INGREDIENTS | SERVES 2

1 (13.5-ounce) package Vietnamese bun noodles (thick noodles that come in separate sticks instead of folded)

8 ounces medium shrimp, peeled and deveined

½ cup chopped tomatoes

4 shallots, peeled

5–7 long red or green chilies (finger peppers or long Thai chilies)

4 banana peppers

¼ cup water

¼ cup fish sauce

3 tablespoons lime juice

2 tablespoons sugar

1–2 teaspoons minced Thai chilies (optional)

1. In a saucepan, bring water to a boil. Cook bun noodles until soft, about 5–7 minutes. Try the noodles and if not done, boil a little longer. Rinse under cold water.

2. Grill the shrimp over medium heat and chop into smaller pieces, about 1" long.

3. Grill tomatoes, shallots, long chilies, and banana peppers and peel off the charred skin. Chop into ½" pieces. If a grill is not available, heat up a heavy pan on the stove and dry pan-fry all ingredients, moving them around occasionally.

4. Put all ingredients in a mixing bowl, add water, fish sauce, lime juice, and sugar, and mix well. If the mixture is too dry, add a little more water.

5. Lay noodles on a plate, top with the shrimp mixture and some minced chilies if desired, and serve.

Dry Egg Noodles with Pork and Seafood

There are different versions of this dish using different kinds of noodles and protein.
Try different ingredients at home.

INGREDIENTS | SERVES 2

½ cup chicken stock

3 ounces pork loin, sliced thinly into 1"
strips

3 ounces mixed seafood (clams, shrimp,
squid)

3 leaves green leaf lettuce

6 cups water for blanching the noodles

4 ounces fresh egg noodles or fresh
angel hair pasta

1–2 tablespoons soy sauce

2 teaspoons sugar

1 tablespoon Deep-Fried Minced Garlic
(see Chapter 2)

2 teaspoons preserved cabbage

2 tablespoons chopped green onions

1 tablespoon chopped cilantro

Pinch of ground white pepper

Chilies in Vinegar (see Chapter 2)

¼ teaspoon Roasted Thai Chili Flakes
(see Chapter 2), optional

Egg Noodles and Pasta

Egg noodles and pasta have the same
ingredients and can be substituted for one
another accordingly. Using fresh egg noodles or fresh pasta is a much better choice
than using the dried versions.

1. In a saucepan, bring stock to a boil and cook pork over medium heat until done, 2 minutes. Remove pork from stock and set aside. Put seafood in the stock and simmer to cook, about 1 minute. Clams should be all open. Discard closed shells.

2. Line the bottoms of two noodle bowls with lettuce. Bring 6 cups of water to a boil in a saucepan. Untangle the fresh egg noodles and blanch noodles for about 30 seconds and split them into two bowls. Season the noodles with soy sauce, sugar, fried garlic, preserved cabbage, green onions, and cilantro (set some aside to garnish). Use a fork to fluff noodles and mix well.

3. Top the noodles with pork and seafood. Garnish with cilantro. Serve with Chilies in Vinegar (see Chapter 2) and Roasted Thai Chili Flakes (see Chapter 2).

Noodles with Chili Jam

Chili Jam is a very versatile ingredient that can be added to soup, fried rice, or, in this case, stir-fried noodles.

INGREDIENTS | SERVES 4

¼ cup vegetable oil

1 tablespoon minced garlic

4 ounces chicken breast, sliced into bite-size pieces

6 tablespoons Chili Jam (see Chapter 3) or bottled store-bought chili jam

6 ounces vermicelli noodles (Wai Wai brand), soaked in cold water for 20 minutes

2–3 tablespoons white vinegar

1 tablespoon light soy sauce

1–2 tablespoons fish sauce

1–2 tablespoons sugar

1 cup bean sprouts

½ cup chopped green onions

1. Heat a wok or a deep sauté pan over medium heat, add oil, and fry garlic until fragrant and golden, about 10 seconds. Add chicken and fry until chicken is cooked, about 1 minute.

2. Add chili jam and stir-fry until fragrant, about 1 minute. Add noodles and the rest of the ingredients except bean sprouts and green onion. Stir-fry until incorporated. Taste and adjust seasoning. Add bean sprouts and green onions, and fold in the vegetables until wilted.

CHAPTER 9

Rice Dishes

Thai Fried Rice with Chicken (*Kao Pad Kai*)

There are many different versions of Thai fried rice. The key to this dish is a perfectly cooked egg.

INGREDIENTS | SERVES 4

4 ounces sliced chicken breast

2 tablespoons light soy sauce, divided

3 tablespoons vegetable oil

2 garlic cloves, minced

Pinch of salt

¼ cup sliced yellow onion

2 eggs

3 cups cooked Jasmine Rice (see Chapter 2)

2 tablespoons ketchup

Pinch of sugar

1 cup Chinese broccoli

2 tablespoons chopped green onions

1 tablespoon chopped cilantro

Pinch of ground white pepper

Cooking Rice for Fried Rice

Leftover rice is best for making perfect fried rice. If you are cooking rice to use for fried rice, use the ratio of one to one for water and jasmine rice. If using long-grain rice, add a little extra water after measuring.

1. Marinate chicken with ½ tablespoon soy sauce for 15 minutes.

2. Heat a deep sauté pan or a wok over medium heat. Add oil and fry garlic with salt over medium heat until fragrant and brown, about 10 seconds.

3. Add chicken and ½ tablespoon soy sauce and fry until chicken is cooked, about 1 minutes. Add onion and fry until translucent, about 30 seconds.

4. Add eggs, crack the yolk, and fry without stirring for 1 minute, until egg is cooked; do not scramble. Add rice, ketchup, remaining soy sauce, and sugar and stir-fry until rice is heated up and starts to turn a darker color, about 1 minute.

5. Add Chinese broccoli and stir-fry until broccoli is cooked, about 1 minute. Taste and adjust seasoning. Add green onion and cilantro and fold it in. Turn off the heat and serve sprinkled with ground white pepper.

Fried Rice with Pineapple and Shrimp (*Kao Pad Sapparos*)

If using fresh pineapple, cut pineapple in half lengthwise, scoop out the meat to use for the dish, and place fried rice back in the pineapple half to serve.

INGREDIENTS | SERVES 2

3 tablespoons oil

2 garlic cloves, peeled, chopped

1 tablespoon curry powder

¼ cup chopped yellow onion

8 medium uncooked shrimp, peeled and deveined

Pinch of salt

2 eggs

Large pinch of white sugar

1–2 tablespoons light soy sauce

½ cup minced pineapple

3 cups cooked Jasmine Rice (see Chapter 2) (the best rice is leftover rice from yesterday or days before—you can also cook rice the day before)

2 tablespoons chopped spring onion

1 tablespoon cilantro leaves

Curry Powder

When using curry powder, always make sure to fry it until it is fragrant. If more curry powder is needed in a dish, fry the powder in a separate pan and add it to the dish. Do not add curry powder directly to a dish without frying first. Curry powder should be fried with oil over low heat for 10 seconds.

1. Heat a deep sauté pan or wok over medium heat, add oil, and fry garlic until fragrant and just starting to color, about 10 seconds. Turn the heat down to low, add curry powder and onion, and when fragrant, after about 10 seconds, add the shrimp and salt.

2. Turn up the heat to medium and stir-fry until shrimp are almost cooked, about 1–2 minutes. Add the eggs and scramble slightly, let fry without stirring for 1 minute, and season with sugar and soy sauce.

3. Add pineapple and rice, mix, and toss. Add spring onions and fold. Serve sprinkled with cilantro.

Basil Fried Rice with Shrimp (*Kao Pad Ka Prow*)

Vegetables like green beans, mushrooms, and bell peppers can be added to this fried rice.
Add the veggies with the rice to allow for enough cooking time.

INGREDIENTS | SERVES 4

Drunken Noodle Paste Mix

3–5 Thai chilies

1 shallot

4 cloves garlic

Fried Rice

¼ cup vegetable oil

4 ounces shrimp, peeled and deveined

¼ cup chopped yellow onions

3 cups cooked Jasmine Rice (see Chapter 2) or leftover rice

1–2 tablespoons fish sauce

2 tablespoons dark soy sauce

2 teaspoons sugar

2 cups Thai holy basil or Thai sweet basil

Holy Basil, Thai Sweet Basil, and Lemon Basil

There are three main types of basil used in Thai cooking. Holy basil is used mostly in stir-fry dishes and occasionally in curries. Thai sweet basil is used mostly in curries and some stir-fries, and lemon basil is used in Liang Soup (see Chapter 6). You can substitute Thai sweet basil for holy basil if necessary.

1. Make the paste using a mortar and pestle, a food processor, or mince all of the paste ingredients well and mix together.

2. Heat a wok or deep sauté pan over medium heat. Add oil and fry the paste for 10 seconds until fragrant. Add shrimp and stir-fry until shrimp is mostly cooked, about 1 minute. Take the shrimp out and set aside.

3. Add yellow onions and sauté until translucent, about 30 seconds. Add rice and season with fish sauce, soy sauce, and palm sugar. Add cooked shrimp back to the pan and fold in. Add basil and stir for another 30 seconds, folding in the basil until wilted. Remove from heat and serve.

Thai Fried Rice with Shrimp Paste

This is an old dish made mostly for special events. The combination of different ingredients adds both texture and flavor to this simple dish.

INGREDIENTS | SERVES 3

4 tablespoons vegetable oil

1 tablespoon minced garlic

1 tablespoon shrimp paste, mixed with 1 tablespoon water

1 teaspoon sugar

1 tablespoon fish sauce

3 cups cooked Jasmine Rice (see Chapter 2) or leftover rice

2 tablespoons vegetable oil

1 egg, beaten

½ cup Sweet Pork (see Chapter 3)

3 tablespoons Salted Shrimp (see Chapter 2)

3 tablespoons thinly sliced shallot

2 tablespoons chopped cilantro

3 Thai chilies, sliced (optional)

1. Heat a wok or deep sauté pan over medium heat, add oil, and fry garlic until slightly brown, about 10 seconds. Add shrimp paste mixture and fry until fragrant, about 10 seconds. Add sugar and fish sauce to season, turn the heat down to low, and add rice. Stir to mix well. Turn off the heat.

2. Heat another fry pan over medium heat. Add 2 tablespoons oil and beaten egg. Make a thin omelet by swirling the egg around the pan. When egg is cooked and cooled off, roll omelet and slice into thin strips.

3. Plate up the fried rice and top with omelet strips, Sweet Pork, Salted Shrimp, and sliced shallots. Garnish with cilantro and sliced Thai chilies, if using.

Fried Rice with Chinese Sausage (*Kao Pad Kun Chiang*)

Chinese sausage is readily available at Asian grocery stores or online. This sausage is dry-cured with Chinese spices, and can be frozen for later use.

INGREDIENTS | SERVES 2

3 dried shitake mushrooms

3 cups water for soaking mushrooms

2 cups uncooked jasmine rice

3 tablespoons vegetable oil

1 tablespoon minced garlic

¼ cup sliced ginger

2 Chinese sausages, sliced into ⅛" rounds

3 ounces sliced pork

6 ounces medium shrimp, peeled and deveined

2 tablespoons oyster sauce

2 tablespoons soy sauce

3 tablespoons sliced green onions, divided

1. Soak mushrooms for 30 minutes in 3 cups water; reserve the water. Slice mushrooms into thin strips. Wash rice and set aside.

2. Heat a wok or deep sauté pan over medium heat. Add oil and fry garlic and ginger until fragrant, about 10 seconds. Add sausage, pork, and shrimp and stir-fry until just halfway cooked, about 1 minute. Add shitake mushrooms and sauté to mix. Add rice, oyster sauce, and soy sauce and mix well.

3. Cook the rice mixture in a rice cooker or on the stovetop with mushroom soaking water. If using the stovetop, bring the rice to a boil, turn the heat down to very low, cover, and let cook for 15 minutes until all liquid is absorbed. If there is not 3 cups soaking water, add water to make 3 cups. Served garnished with green onions.

Stewed Pork over Rice and Broccoli (*Kao Kaa Moo*)

This dish was influenced by Chinese cooking, but the spicy sauce adds a touch of Thai cuisine. If you'd like, other greens can be used in place of Chinese broccoli.

INGREDIENTS | SERVES 8

2–3 pounds pork leg, skin on or off, depending on preference

6 cloves garlic, mashed

3 cilantro roots, or 6 cilantro stems

½ teaspoon five-spice powder

1 tablespoon dark soy sauce

2 tablespoons light soy sauce

2 tablespoons sugar

2 cups water or enough to cover the pork

6 cups cooked Jasmine Rice (see Chapter 2)

2 cups Chinese broccoli, chopped and blanched

Sauce

2 Serrano peppers

1 teaspoon minced cilantro stem

3 tablespoons minced garlic

¼ teaspoon salt

2 tablespoons white vinegar

1. Add all ingredients, except for the Chinese broccoli and those used to make the sauce, to a soup pot or large saucepan, and bring to a boil. Simmer on low heat for 4–6 hours. Alternatively, use a pressure cooker or a crock pot to cook the pork.

2. Make the sauce by combining all ingredients in a bowl. Let sit for 30 minutes.

3. Serve over rice with the sauce and blanched Chinese broccoli.

Chicken and Rice (*Kao Man Kai*)

This dish is influenced by Hunan-style chicken and rice. Singaporeans have their own version of this dish and it has become the Singaporean national dish. This is a Thai version with a spicier sauce.

INGREDIENTS | SERVES 8

1 whole (3-pound) chicken (or bone-in pieces of chicken)

Large pinch of salt

2 tablespoons soy sauce

5 or 6 slices of ginger

4 cloves garlic, smashed

6 cilantro stems

Enough water to just cover chicken

4 tablespoons vegetable oil

3 tablespoons finely chopped garlic

3 tablespoons finely minced ginger

1 tablespoon finely minced coriander stem

7 cups uncooked jasmine rice

9 cups chicken stock, divided

2 cups sliced cucumber

Cilantro leaves for garnish

Sauce

2 tablespoons ginger, peeled and finely chopped in a food processor

2 tablespoons garlic, finely chopped in a food processor

2 teaspoons Thai chili, finely chopped in a food processor

1⅓ cups light soy sauce

¼ cup dark Thai soy sauce

¼ cup soybean paste

¼ cup granulated sugar

¼ cup lime juice

¼ cup water

½ cup vinegar

1. Add chicken, salt, soy sauce, slices of ginger, garlic, and cilantro stems to a large stock pot. Add enough water to just cover chicken. Bring to boil and simmer with the lid on for about 20–25 minutes. Take the chicken out of the stock and let cool.

2. In a large, deep frying pan, heat oil and then add chopped garlic, minced ginger, and minced coriander stem. Fry until fragrant and golden brown, about 1 minute. Add rice and 1 cup of stock, and stir-fry until rice is golden brown, about 2 minutes. Add the rest of chicken stock to the rice. Bring to a boil and lower the heat to a very low simmer. Cover and simmer until the rice is cooked, about 15 minutes. Alternatively, cook the rice with stock in rice cooker.

3. Make the sauce by combining all the ingredients. Taste and adjust.

4. Slice cooked chicken. Put rice on serving dish and serve with sauce and sliced cucumbers. Garnish with fresh cilantro leaves.

Roast Duck over White Rice (*Kao Naa Ped*)

Roast duck is readily available at most Chinese restaurants. Oftentimes, the sauce that comes with it doesn't have much spice. This version of duck dipping sauce adds some kick to the dish.

INGREDIENTS | SERVES 4

3 cups cooked Jasmine Rice (see Chapter 2)

1 cup blanched bok choy

2 cups roast duck (from a Chinese restaurant)

1 tablespoon chopped cilantro

Sauce

4 tablespoons dark soy sauce

2 tablespoons white vinegar

1 long chili (Serrano or jalapeño), sliced

½ teaspoon light soy sauce

1. In a lightly oiled frying pan, heat rice thoroughly over low heat. Remove from heat and transfer to serving dish.

2. Make the sauce by combining all sauce ingredients in a mixing bowl. Set aside. In a saucepan, boil water and blanch bok choy for 30 seconds. Remove from water.

3. Top the rice with roast duck and a side of blanched bok choy. Garnish with cilantro.

4. Serve with the sauce.

Green Curry Fried Rice

This is a great dish to make with leftover curries. It is simple to prepare, and cooking the curry with the rice gives it a smokier flavor than just pouring the curry over the rice.

INGREDIENTS | SERVES 4

1 cup any style green curry from Chapter 7

3 cups cooked Jasmine Rice (see Chapter 2)

1–2 teaspoons fish sauce

½ cup Thai basil

Thai Chili and Fish Sauce (Chapter 2)

1. Heat up curry in a deep pan or a wok over medium-high heat. When the curry is boiling, add rice and stir-fry until the curry and rice are thoroughly mixed.

2. Season with fish sauce and fold in Thai basil. Serve curry with Thai Chili and Fish Sauce.

Braised Chicken and Turmeric Rice

This is a southern-style dish from India and Malaysia. Thai cardamom can be hard to find, so you can use white Indian cardamom pods as a substitute. The green cardamom pods are much stronger, so they are not recommended.

INGREDIENTS | SERVES 6

Paste

1 teaspoon roasted coriander seeds

2 teaspoons roasted cumin seeds

2 cloves, roasted

¾" piece cassia bark, roasted

1½ tablespoons chopped fresh turmeric, or ½ teaspoon dried turmeric

1½ tablespoons minced garlic

2 tablespoons chopped ginger

Chicken

2 half chickens, chopped into 5 large pieces

3 cups vegetable oil for deep-frying

5 red shallots, sliced

Pinch of salt, divided

4 cups uncooked jasmine rice

6 cups stock

1 piece cassia bark or cinnamon stick, roasted

2 bay leaves

2 or 3 Thai or Indian cardamom pods, roasted

Sweet Chili Sauce

2 long red chilies or Serrano peppers, deseeded and chopped

1 or 2 fresh Thai chilies

2 cilantro roots or end of the stems (about 5 stems cut 1" from the bottom)

Large pinch of salt

1 large garlic clove, minced

⅓ cup white sugar

⅓ cup vinegar

1. First make the paste. Pound the ingredients together using a mortar and pestle, adding each ingredient one by one. If you don't have a mortar and pestle, grind dried spices together in a coffee grinder, or put fresh spices in a small food chopper and blend until smooth. Add the dried spices and mix well.

2. Marinate chicken pieces with the paste rubbed on for 3–5 hours in the fridge.

3. Heat oil in a large, deep frying pan over medium heat, and deep-fry shallots at 300°F until golden, about 2 minutes. Remove shallots and deep-fry the chicken for 5 minutes. Combine shallots, pinch of salt, and chicken with rice and add stock, pinch of salt, cassia bark, bay leaves, and cardamom pods; bring to a boil. Turn down the heat to very low and cover the pot. When the rice is cooked, about 15 minutes, the chicken should also be done. Remove from heat and transfer to serving dish. The rice and chicken is served with sweet chili sauce.

4. To make the sauce, mince the chilies and cilantro stems. Combine all the sauce ingredients in a frying pan and bring to simmer over medium heat until it becomes a thick syrup, about 5 minutes. Let cool before serving.

Thai Fried Rice with Crabmeat

This is a classic restaurant dish for Thais. Crab fried rice is ordered for the table and everyone shares it as a main rice dish along with other entrées and steamed rice.

INGREDIENTS | SERVES 4

3 tablespoons vegetable oil

2 garlic cloves, minced

Pinch of salt

3 ounces crabmeat

1–2 tablespoons light soy sauce, divided

¼ cup sliced yellow onion

2 eggs

3 cups cooked Jasmine Rice (see Chapter 2)

2 teaspoons dark soy sauce

Pinch of sugar

2 tablespoons chopped green onions

1 tablespoon chopped cilantro

Pinch of ground white pepper

Eating Out

When eating out in Thailand, it is always family style. It doesn't matter who orders which dish—all dishes will be placed in the middle of the table in the order that it has been made for everyone to share.

1. Heat a deep sauté pan or a wok over medium heat. Add oil and fry garlic with salt over medium heat until fragrant and brown, about 10 seconds.

2. Add crabmeat and ½ tablespoon light soy sauce and fry until crabmeat is brown, about 30 seconds. Add onion and fry until translucent, about 30 second.

3. Add eggs and break yolks a bit. Fry without stirring for 1 minute, until egg is cooked; do not scramble. Add rice, dark soy sauce, remaining light soy sauce, and sugar and stir-fry until rice is heated up and starts to take on a darker color, about 1 minute. Taste and adjust seasoning. Add green onion and cilantro and fold in. Turn off the heat and serve sprinkled with ground white pepper.

Rice Soup with Pork (*Kao Tom Moo*)

This dish is a classic breakfast for Thais. Other meats like chicken, turkey, or seafood can be used in this dish instead of pork.

INGREDIENTS | SERVES 4

1 tablespoon vegetable oil

1 tablespoon minced garlic

6 ounces ground pork

6 cups chicken stock

1½ cups cooked Jasmine Rice (see Chapter 2)

3 tablespoons light soy sauce, or more as needed

1 tablespoon chopped green onions

1 tablespoon chopped cilantro

1 tablespoon Deep-Fried Minced Garlic (see Chapter 2)

Ground white pepper for garnish

1. Heat a medium saucepan over medium heat, add oil, and fry garlic until golden brown, about 10 seconds. Add pork and sauté until pork is brown on the outside but not cooked, about 1 minute.

2. Add chicken stock, rice, and soy sauce and let simmer for about 10–15 minutes until rice is open and starts to become less grainy. Add more stock or water if needed. The soup should be thick, but with enough stock to reach about 2" above the rice. Taste and adjust with more soy sauce if needed.

3. Serve garnished with chopped onions, cilantro, fried garlic, and ground white pepper.

Panang Fried Rice with Salted Egg

Any curry can be used in this recipe. Panang Curry is great for fried rice because it is thick and creamy. Salted duck eggs add depth to the dish.

INGREDIENTS | SERVES 2

1 cup Panang Curry with Beef (see Chapter 7)

2 cups cooked Jasmine Rice (see Chapter 2)

½ cup Thai basil

1 Salted Duck Egg (see Chapter 2)

2 teaspoons sifted all-purpose flour

2 tablespoon vegetable oil

1. In a deep frying pan, bring Panang Curry with Beef to a boil over medium heat, add rice, and stir-fry until incorporated. Add Thai basil and fold the basil in until wilted, about 30 seconds.

2. To fry salted duck egg, crack the egg in a bowl. Separate egg white, add flour to the white, and beat to combine. Cut egg yolk into small pieces. Scoop egg white mixture onto a spoon, place one piece of egg yolk in the middle, drop both the yolk and egg white in hot oil and fry for 1–2 minutes, until egg starts to crisp. Continue until the mixture is gone.

3. Serve with eggs on top of rice.

Rice Congee (*Joak*)

Rice congee is an early-morning and late-night treat that is usually sold from a street vendor. People will gather at the famous Rice Congee stand waiting to order at all hours of the day. This is certainly not a home-cooked meal, although it is very easy to make at home.

INGREDIENTS | SERVES 4

1 cups broken rice, available at Asian grocery stores. Alternatively, put rice in a food processor and pulse until rice is broken

6 cups water

1 teaspoon plus 1 pinch salt, divided

1 pandan leaf, bundled

4 ounces minced pork

2–3 tablespoons light soy sauce

2 cups chicken stock

2 eggs

2–4 tablespoons finely shredded ginger

1 tablespoon chopped onions

Pinch of ground white pepper

Making Plain Rice Congee

Plain Rice Congee can be frozen for up to one year. If you are planning to make more of this dish, double the amount of the plain congee recipe, combining the first 3 ingredients and follow step one in this recipe to make plain rice congee. The plain rice congee can be frozen for later use.

1. Soak broken rice for 1 hour. Drain. In a thick, large saucepan, bring 6 cups water, 1 teaspoon salt, and pandan leaf to a boil. Add rice and simmer for 30–45 minutes on low heat, stirring occasionally to prevent the rice from sticking to the bottom of the pot (this is the plain congee).

2. Mix pork, pinch of salt, and soy sauce together in a bowl.

3. Add stock to the plain congee and bring to a boil. Roll pork into small dumplings and add to the simmering congee. Let cook for a few minutes over medium-low heat until pork is cooked. Add more stock or water if needed. Taste and adjust with salt if needed.

4. Turn off the heat, crack two eggs into the cooked congee, and let sit for a few minutes, allowing the eggs to cook from the heat of the congee. Sprinkle ginger, green onions, and white pepper over the dish and serve.

Rice Soup with Snapper

This dish is a late-night meal eaten mainly in Chinese communities in Thailand.

INGREDIENTS | SERVES 4

3 cups chicken stock

2 tablespoons soy sauce

¼ teaspoon salt

6 ounces red snapper fillet, cut into bite-size pieces

1 cup cooked Jasmine Rice (see Chapter 2)

1 tablespoon chopped Chinese celery or cilantro

1 teaspoon Chinese preserved cabbage

Pinch of ground white pepper

1 tablespoon Deep-Fried Minced Garlic (see Chapter 2)

1 tablespoon chopped green onions

Soybean Sauce

3 tablespoons salted soybean sauce or yellow bean sauce

1 tablespoon white vinegar

1 teaspoon sugar

2 minced Thai chilies

1. In a heavy, medium saucepan, bring stock to a boil. Season with soy sauce and salt. Add fish to the stock and simmer on low heat for 3–5 minutes, until the fish is cooked.

2. Add cooked rice to the pan and turn off the heat. Alternatively, scoop rice in a soup bowl and add the cooked fish and stock over the rice. This rice soup is supposed to be served with the rice still grainy.

3. Prepare sauce by combining sauce ingredients in a mixing bowl.

4. Garnish soup with celery, preserved cabbage, white pepper, fried garlic, and onions. Stir in about 1 tablespoon of soybean sauce per bowl to serve.

American Fried Rice

This dish was created for Americans by Thais during the Vietnam War. Ingredients that are commonly used in American food (by the Thai standard) are combined. This fried rice is the most popular breakfast item at hotels in Thailand.

INGREDIENTS | SERVES 4

8 small, low-sodium hot dogs, or cut larger hot dogs into 3" pieces

2 cups and 3 tablespoons vegetable oil, divided

2 garlic cloves, minced

Pinch of salt

3 cups cooked Jasmine Rice (see Chapter 2)

2 tablespoons ketchup

1 tablespoon light soy sauce

1 teaspoon dark soy sauce

Pinch of sugar

¼ cup raisins, soaked in room temperature water for 15 minutes

2 Fried Eggs (see Chapter 2)

1 tomato, sliced

1 cucumber, sliced

1 tablespoon chopped cilantro

1. Quarter hot dog pieces lengthwise halfway through so that the pieces are still in one piece. In a deep frying pan, deep-fry in 2 cups oil heated to 350°F, for 2 minutes or until they start to float. Set aside.

2. Heat a deep sauté pan or a wok over medium heat. Add 3 tablespoons oil and fry garlic and salt over medium heat until fragrant and brown, about 10 seconds.

3. Add rice, ketchup, soy sauces, and sugar and stir-fry until rice is heated up and starts to color, about 1 minute. Add raisins and stir-fry for another minute. Taste and adjust seasoning.

4. Put rice on a plate, top with Fried Eggs, and serve with fried hot dogs, slices of tomatoes, and cucumber. Garnish with cilantro.

Basil Fried Rice with Beef

For this fried rice, ground beef with some fat is usually used in order to spread the flavor, so you taste it in every bite.

INGREDIENTS | SERVES 4

Drunken Noodle Paste Mix

3–5 Thai chilies

1 shallot

4 cloves garlic

Beef

4 ounces beef sirloin, sliced thinly

1 tablespoon oyster sauce

¼ cup vegetable oil

¼ cup chopped yellow onions

3 cups cooked Jasmine Rice (see Chapter 2) or leftover rice

1–2 tablespoons fish sauce

2 tablespoons dark soy sauce

2 teaspoons sugar

2 cups Thai basil

1. Marinate beef with oyster sauce for 20 minutes.

2. Make the paste using a mortar and pestle, food processor, or mince all the paste ingredients well and mix together.

3. Heat a wok or a deep sauté pan over medium heat. Add the oil and fry the paste for 10 seconds, until fragrant. Add beef and stir-fry until beef is mostly cooked, about 1 minute.

4. Add yellow onions and sauté until translucent, about 30 seconds. Add rice and season with fish sauce, soy sauce, and sugar. Add basil and stir for another 30 seconds, folding in the basil until wilted. Serve.

Chili Jam Fried Rice

Most spicy relishes are great for fried rice. A lot of the time, this dish is served without any protein, and with just fresh vegetables on the side.

INGREDIENTS | SERVES 2

3 tablespoons vegetable oil, divided

3–4 tablespoons Chili Jam (see Chapter 3)

2 cups cooked Jasmine Rice (see Chapter 2)

2 eggs, beaten

1 Salted Duck Egg (see Chapter 2)

Fresh vegetables like carrots, cucumbers, and iceberg lettuce

1. Heat a deep frying pan over medium heat and add 1 tablespoon oil. Fry chili jam until fragrant, about 15 seconds. Add rice and-stir fry until incorporated.

2. Heat a skillet and add 2 tablespoons oil; add beaten eggs and swirl to cover the pan to make a thin omelet. When the eggs are cooked, let cool and roll the omelet and cut into thin strips. Cut Salted Duck Egg in half, scoop out the yolk and egg white, and chop into smaller pieces.

3. Serve fried rice with omelet strips, chopped Salted Duck Egg, and fresh vegetables on top.

Sardines in Tomato Sauce Fried Rice

Another great dish using canned sardines in tomato sauce.
Sardines are already seasoned, and the sauce adds depth to fried rice.

INGREDIENTS | SERVES 4

3 tablespoons vegetable oil

2 garlic cloves, minced

Pinch of salt

½ cup sardines in tomato sauce

3 cups cooked Jasmine Rice (see Chapter 2)

1 tablespoon fish sauce, more if needed

Pinch of sugar

¼ cup thinly sliced shallots

2 tablespoons chopped green onions

3 Thai chilies, sliced

1. Heat a deep sauté pan or a wok over medium heat. Add oil and fry garlic and salt over medium heat until fragrant and brown, about 10 seconds.

2. Add sardines with sauce and fry until sardines are heated through, about 30 seconds.

3. Add rice, fish sauce, and sugar and stir-fry until rice and sardine sauce are incorporated, about 1–2 minutes. Taste and adjust seasoning. Add more fish sauce if desired. Add shallots and green onion, and fold in. Turn off the heat and serve with sliced chilies.

Fried Rice with Chinese Salted Olives

This fried rice is always eaten out at a restaurant rather than made at home. If available, shredded green mango makes a great accompaniment to the fried rice. You can substitute grapefruit for the green mango.

INGREDIENTS | SERVES 4

3 tablespoons vegetable oil

2 teaspoons minced garlic

6 ounces medium shrimp, peeled and deveined

3 ounces ground pork

8 Chinese salted black olives, pits removed, finely chopped

1 teaspoon thin soy sauce

1 teaspoon sugar

4 cups cooked Jasmine Rice (see Chapter 2)

2 eggs

¼ cup roasted cashews

2 tablespoons Salted Shrimp (see Chapter 2), deep-fried

½ cup shredded or julienned green mango or grapefruit meat

6–8 Thai chilies cut into thin rounds

2 tablespoons chopped cilantro

1. Heat a deep sauté pan until hot. Add oil and fry garlic over medium heat until fragrant, about 10 seconds. Add shrimp and stir-fry until shrimp is cooked, about 1 minute. Remove shrimp (garlic will be with the shrimp, too) from pan and set aside. Add ground pork and stir-fry, breaking up the pork as it cooks. When most of the pork is brown, add chopped salted olives, soy sauce, and sugar. Stir-fry until the pork is cooked through about 30 seconds. Add rice and stir-fry for 3–5 minutes, until the rice is heated through. Turn off the heat.

2. Beat the eggs and make two to three thin omelets in a fry pan. When the omelets have cooled, roll them up, and slice thinly into strips.

3. Place the cooked rice on a plate. Add cashews, Salted Shrimp, fresh shrimp, omelet strips, julienned green mango, and Thai chilies. Top the rice with cilantro.

CHAPTER 10

Stir-Fries

Spicy Green Beans with Chicken

Other vegetables like bamboo shoots, broccoli, or mushrooms can be used in this dish.

INGREDIENTS | SERVES 4

2 garlic cloves

Pinch of salt

1 shallot (optional)

4 Thai chilies

1 tablespoon vegetable oil

6 ounces minced chicken or thinly sliced chicken

6 ounces green beans, sliced on an angle into 1½"-long pieces

1–2 tablespoons fish sauce

Pinch of sugar

1 cup Thai holy basil or Thai sweet basil

2 cups cooked Jasmine Rice (see Chapter 2)

1. Pound garlic, salt, shallot (if using), and chilies into a paste using a mortar and pestle. Alternatively, put all ingredients in small food chopper. Add salt later if using the chopper.

2. Heat a wok or a saucepan over medium-high heat. Add oil and then fry the paste for 1 minute. Add chicken and continue to stir-fry for another minute. Add green beans and stir-fry until almost cooked, about 1 minute. Add fish sauce and sugar. Taste for seasoning.

3. Sprinkle Thai basil in pan. Stir-fry until basil is soft, about 30 seconds, and take it off the heat. Serve over cooked Jasmine Rice.

Pad Prik King with Chicken

A dried version of this curry uses oil to fry the curry paste.
The result is a spicier and drier curry dish with a touch of sweetness.

INGREDIENTS | SERVES 4

3 tablespoons vegetable oil

¼ cup red curry paste

2 cups sliced chicken, cut into bite-size pieces

½ cup water

5 cups green beans

1–2 teaspoons fish sauce

2 tablespoons sugar

1 tablespoon kaffir lime leaves, thinly julienned

2 cups cooked Jasmine Rice (see Chapter 2)

1. Heat a sauté pan or wok over high heat until it is hot. Add oil and wait until the oil is hot. Add the curry paste and turn the heat down to medium. Fry the paste until fragrant over medium heat, about 15 seconds. Add chicken and sauté until chicken is cooked, about 1–2 minutes. Add about ½ cup of water to help cook the chicken.

2. Add green beans and continue to cook until green beans are done, about 1–2 minutes. Season with fish sauce and sugar. Add kaffir lime leaves and sauté for about 30 seconds. Serve over cooked Jasmine Rice.

Spicy Basil with Ground Turkey

Any ground meat can be used for this dish. If you'd like, you can substitute beef or pork for turkey. The level of spice can be adjusted by adding more or less Thai chilies.

INGREDIENTS | SERVES 4

2 garlic cloves

Pinch of salt

1 shallot (optional)

4 Thai chilies

1 tablespoon vegetable oil

12 ounces minced turkey

1–2 tablespoons fish sauce

Pinch of sugar

1 cup Thai holy basil or Thai sweet basil

2–3 cups cooked Jasmine Rice (see Chapter 2)

1. Pound garlic, salt, shallot (if using), and chilies into a paste using a mortar and pestle. Alternatively, put all ingredients in a small food chopper. Add salt later if using the chopper.

2. Heat a wok or a sauté pan over medium-high heat. Add oil and then fry the paste for 1 minute. Add ground turkey and continue to stir-fry for 2 minutes or longer until the meat is done. Add fish sauce and sugar. Taste for seasoning.

3. Sprinkle the Thai basil over the top. Stir-fry until basil is soft, about 30 seconds, and take it off the heat. Serve over rice.

Ginger with Chicken (*Pad King*)

This dish is perfect for ginger lovers. Pork or beef can be used as a substitute for chicken. If you do end up using pork or beef, thinly sliced or ground meat is best.

INGREDIENTS | SERVES 4

½ pound chicken breast, sliced thinly

5 teaspoons light soy sauce, divided

3 tablespoons vegetable oil

2 teaspoons minced garlic

½ cup sliced yellow onions

½ cup chicken stock

1 teaspoon dark soy sauce

1 tablespoon salted soybeans

1 tablespoon sugar

1 cup thinly julienned ginger

½ cup green onion, chopped into 1½" pieces

2–3 cups cooked Jasmine Rice (see Chapter 2)

1. Marinate chicken with 2 teaspoons soy sauce for 15 minutes.

2. Heat a wok or deep sauté pan over high heat. Add oil and fry garlic over medium heat until fragrant, about 10 seconds. Add chicken and sauté until chicken is brown and almost done, about 1 minute. Add onions and sauté for 2 minutes until onions are translucent. Add chicken stock.

3. Season with remaining light soy sauce, dark soy sauce, salted soybean, and sugar and stir to mix. Add ginger and stir for 2 minutes until ginger is done. Add green onions and fold in until slightly wilted, about 30 seconds. Turn off the heat. Serve with rice.

Stir-Fried Mixed Vegetables with Chicken (*Pak Kai*)

You can change up the vegetables depending on the season if you'd like, but be sure to add vegetables that take longer to cook to the pan first. Try replacing the chicken with 8 large shrimp.

INGREDIENTS | SERVES 4

2 tablespoons vegetable oil

2 garlic cloves, minced

¾ pound boneless, skinless chicken breast, cut into 1" cubes

½ cup sliced carrots

1 cup chopped asparagus, cut into 2"-long pieces

½ cup snow peas

2 tablespoons chicken stock or water

1–2 tablespoons light soy sauce

Pinch of sugar

Pinch of ground pepper

1. Heat the wok over high heat until hot and add oil. Add garlic and fry over medium heat until fragrant, about 10 seconds. Add chicken and stir-fry until chicken is cooked through, about 5 minutes.

2. Add the carrots and stir-fry for 1 minute. Add the asparagus and snow peas and sauté for another 2 minutes until the vegetables are almost done. Add stock, soy sauce, and sugar and fry for another minute. Serve sprinkled with pepper.

Asian Eggplant with Pork (*Pad Ma Kua Yao*)

Salted soybean or soybean paste is the key player in this dish. Peppers can be omitted entirely if desired.

INGREDIENTS | SERVES 4

2–3 tablespoons vegetable oil

4 cloves garlic, chopped

4 ounces ground pork

2 jalapeños, or Serrano peppers, cut lengthwise in thin slivers

3 Asian eggplants, cut into wedges or quartered lengthwise and cut 1½" long

½ cup chicken stock or water

1 tablespoon soybean paste

1 tablespoon sugar

2–3 teaspoons fish sauce

1–2 teaspoons dark soy sauce

½ cup whole Thai sweet basil leaves

1. Heat a wok or deep sauté pan until hot. Add oil and fry garlic over medium heat until fragrant and brown, about 10 seconds. Add pork and stir, breaking up the pork. Sauté for 1 minute. Add chopped peppers. Sauté for a few more seconds and add eggplant. Add chicken stock or water and sauté until eggplants are soft, about 3–5 minutes.

2. Add soybean paste; stir and mix well. Add sugar, fish sauce, and dark soy sauce. Add more stock if needed to cook eggplant longer. There should be a little bit of sauce left once the eggplants are done. Add basil and stir for a few seconds until soft. Serve.

Beef and Broccoli with Oyster Sauce

This is a very quick stir-fry dish that is great when cooked with other meats or mushrooms. Adding vegetables like carrots, bell peppers, or green beans will give this dish more texture.

INGREDIENTS | SERVES 4

12 ounces beef sirloin, sliced thinly
1 tablespoon tapioca flour
2 tablespoons light soy sauce
3 tablespoons vegetable oil
1 tablespoon minced garlic
2 cups quartered button mushrooms
4 tablespoons oyster sauce
2 teaspoons white sugar
½ teaspoon ground black pepper
½ cup chopped green onions

1. Marinate beef with tapioca flour and light soy sauce for 20 minutes.

2. Heat a deep sauté pan or a wok until hot. Add oil and fry minced garlic over medium heat until golden, about 10 seconds. Add beef and sauté for 2 minutes. Add mushrooms and stir-fry until mushrooms are soft, about 2 minutes.

3. Season with oyster sauce, sugar, and pepper. Add green onions and fold in until wilted, about 30 seconds. Turn off the heat and serve.

Chicken with Pepper and Garlic (*Kai Kratium Prik Thai*)

Freshly cracked pepper is best for this dish. It will give it a much a more robust flavor and aroma.

INGREDIENTS | SERVES 4

3 tablespoons vegetable oil
5 cloves garlic, minced
2 teaspoons minced cilantro stems or roots
Pinch of salt
2 teaspoons cracked black or white pepper
8 ounces chicken breast or chicken thighs, cut into bite-size pieces
2 tablespoons light soy sauce
Pinch of sugar
2 tablespoons chopped cilantro

1. Heat a deep sauté pan or wok until hot. Add oil, and when oil is hot, add garlic, cilantro stems, salt, and pepper and fry over medium heat until fragrant, about 10–15 seconds.

2. Add chicken and fry until chicken is cooked on the outside, about 2–3 minutes. Season with soy sauce and sugar. Stir-fry until chicken is done, about 2–3 minutes. Remove from heat and garnish with cilantro.

Salty and Sweet Chicken

If desired, vegetables like bell peppers can be added to the dish at the end of preparation.

INGREDIENTS | SERVES 6

2 tablespoons chopped garlic

2 tablespoons chopped shallots

1 tablespoon chopped cilantro stem

¼ tablespoon chopped Thai chilies

3 tablespoons vegetable oil

3 cups chicken, cut into bite-size pieces

1 cup chicken stock

1 tablespoon white sugar

2 tablespoons palm sugar

2 tablespoons light soy sauce

1 tablespoon dark soy sauce

1 cup sliced onions

½ cup chopped green onions

Pinch of chopped cilantro

Pinch of ground black pepper

2–3 cups cooked Jasmine Rice (see Chapter 2)

Chicken Breast and Chicken Thighs

In order to get the most nutrients from chicken, both the thighs and breast should be consumed. Chicken breast contains more niacin, a B-vitamin substance that helps the body use the energy consumed from food. On the other hand, chicken thighs contain double the iron than the breast.

1. Combine garlic, shallot, cilantro stems, and chilies in a mixing bowl. Heat a wok or deep sauté pan until hot. Add oil and fry the garlic mixture over medium heat for 10 seconds until fragrant.

2. Add chicken and stir-fry. Add water or stock, sugar, palm sugar, and both soy sauces. Simmer for about 15 minutes over medium-low heat until the meat is darkened. Add more water or stock if needed.

3. Add all onions and stir-fry until translucent, about 2 minutes. Taste and adjust seasoning. It should taste sweet and salty. Turn off the heat and sprinkle cilantro and black pepper. Serve with rice.

Sweet and Sour Stir-Fry with Pork

This dish doesn't hold up very well over time. It has to be served immediately when it is hot. If you are planning on having leftovers, omit the cucumbers.

INGREDIENTS | SERVES 4

12 ounces sliced pork shoulder or tenderloin

1 tablespoon light soy sauce

2 tablespoons vegetable oil

2 teaspoons minced garlic

½ cup quartered mushrooms

½ cup cucumbers, halved and sliced on an angle

¼ cup sliced yellow onions

½ cup chopped tomatoes

¼ cup sliced red and green bell pepper

1 cup chopped green onions, cut into 1"-long pieces

2 tablespoons ketchup

1 tablespoon white vinegar

2 tablespoons sugar

1–2 tablespoons fish sauce

½ cup chicken stock, divided

1 tablespoon tapioca flour

Pinch of white pepper

2–3 cups cooked Jasmine Rice (see Chapter 2)

1. Marinate pork with soy sauce for 15 minutes. Heat a deep sauté pan or a wok. Add oil and fry garlic over medium heat until fragrant, about 10 seconds. Add pork and sauté until pork is mostly cooked, about 1 minute.

2. Add mushrooms, cucumbers, yellow onions, and tomatoes and sauté until the vegetables are wilted, about 1–2 minutes. Add bell pepper and green onions and mix.

3. Season with ketchup, vinegar, sugar, fish sauce, and half of the stock and stir to mix.

4. Meanwhile, mix tapioca flour with the second half of the stock in a mixing bowl and add to the pan. When the sauce has thickened slightly, turn off the heat, taste, and adjust with pepper. Serve with rice.

Cashew Chicken

Cashew Chicken is the most popular tourist dish in Thailand.
Sliced water chestnuts can be added for extra crunch.

INGREDIENTS | SERVES 4

2 tablespoons vegetable oil

¼ cup Thai long dried chilies, chopped into ½"-long pieces

½ tablespoon minced garlic

½ pound chicken, sliced

1 small onion, sliced into 1" pieces

½ cup fried or roasted cashew nuts

1 cup chopped red bell pepper

1½ tablespoons fish sauce

1 tablespoon dark soy sauce

1 tablespoon sugar

Pinch of salt

⅓ cup chopped green onion

Cilantro to garnish

2–3 cups cooked Jasmine Rice (see Chapter 2)

Frying Nuts

To fry nuts, blanch the nuts starting with cold water and then bring to a boil. Strain and let dry for 5 minutes. In oil that has been heated to 300°F, deep-fry for 1 minute or until brown. The nuts have already been cooked from blanching; frying them is just to brown the outer layers.

1. Heat a deep sauté pan or a wok until hot. Add 2 tablespoons vegetable oil and fry chilies until they just change color, about 1 minute. Keep moving the chilies around or they will burn. Remove chilies from oil and set aside.

2. Add minced garlic and fry over medium heat until golden, about 10 seconds. Add chicken and sauté until almost cooked, about 1–2 minutes. Add onion, cashew nuts, fried chilies, and bell pepper and stir-fry for about 1–2 minutes.

3. Season with fish sauce, dark soy sauce, sugar, and salt. Add green onion and fold until onions are wilted, about 30 seconds to 1 minute. Turn off the heat. Garnish with some cilantro and serve over rice.

Old-Style Chinese Chicken with Steamed Rice

Twice-cooked chicken is tender and flavorful. If you prefer, chicken thighs are also great for this recipe. Also try bone-in chicken (simmer the pieces longer, up to 45 minutes for bone-in thighs).

INGREDIENTS | SERVES 4

12 ounces chicken breast, sliced into bite-size pieces

3 teaspoons tapioca flour

2 tablespoons light soy sauce

1 tablespoon dark soy sauce

3 tablespoons oyster sauce, divided

1 tablespoon pure sesame oil

3 tablespoons vegetable oil

1 cup chicken stock

1 teaspoon sugar

Pinch of ground white pepper

1 fried Chinese sausage, sliced

2 finger or Serrano peppers, sliced in rounds

½ cup chopped green onions

2–3 cups cooked Jasmine Rice (see Chapter 2)

1. Marinate chicken with tapioca flour, light and dark soy sauce, 2 tablespoons oyster sauce, and sesame oil overnight in the fridge.

2. Heat a deep sauté pan or a wok until hot. Add vegetable oil and fry marinated chicken over medium heat. Do not stir the chicken; let sit in oil for 3–5 minutes. When the chicken starts to cook and the sauce thickens slightly, add chicken stock. Bring to a simmer and add 1 tablespoon oyster sauce and sugar. Taste to see if more light soy sauce is needed.

3. Add ground pepper and serve with sliced Chinese sausage, sliced peppers, and green onions over rice.

Tapioca Flour in Marinade

Tapioca helps to bind liquid ingredients to the meat, and therefore makes the meat taste more flavorful when marinated. The flour also tenderizes the meat. Cornstarch can be used in place of tapioca flour if you cannot find it.

Baked Shrimp and Bean Thread Noodles
(*Kung Op Woon Sen*)

For best flavor, use a stovetop-proof clay pot, found at Asian grocery stores.
Let the noodles steam on the stove covered for 15 minutes at very low heat.

INGREDIENTS | SERVES 4

1 pound large shrimp, heads and shell on, or at least with shell on

2 tablespoons vegetable oil

10 cilantro stems, bruised

3 slices fresh ginger

¼ teaspoon salt

1 small onion, thinly sliced

1 tablespoon crushed black peppercorn

6 ounces bean thread noodles, soaked for 20 minutes in room temperature water

3 tablespoons light soy sauce

1 tablespoon whiskey

1 tablespoon sugar

1 tablespoon sesame oil

3 slices bacon or thinly sliced pork belly strips

Green onion for garnish

1. Wash shrimp thoroughly. Heat the wok or deep sauté pan and add vegetable oil. When the oil is hot, add cilantro stems, ginger, salt, onion, and peppercorn, and stir-fry over medium heat until fragrant, about 10–15 seconds. Set aside in a large mixing bowl. Add bean thread noodles, light soy sauce, whiskey, sugar, sesame oil, and shrimp to the mixture and mix well.

2. Lay bacon in ovenproof container and pour the mixture on top. Bake at 350°F for 20 minutes with a lid or foil on top. Check to see if the shrimp is cooked. Shrimp should be pink in color all the way through. If not, let it cook a little longer. Add green onions and steam for another 30 seconds. Take off the heat.

Chicken and Chili Jam

Milk can be omitted from this recipe if a dairy-free dish is preferred.
Substitute with the same amount of coconut milk.

INGREDIENTS | SERVES 3

2 tablespoons milk

3 tablespoons Chili Jam (see Chapter 3)
or purchase at Asian grocery store

8 ounces chicken breast, sliced thinly

½ cup sliced red bell pepper

1 teaspoon sugar

Fish sauce to taste

1 tablespoon chopped cilantro

Heat a deep sauté pan on high and when hot, turn the heat down to medium-low. Add milk and chili jam and bring to simmer. Add chicken and stir-fry until chicken is cooked, about 1–2 minutes. Add bell pepper and season with sugar and fish sauce if needed. Garnish with cilantro.

Stir-Fried Pumpkin

Kabocha squash is a good choice for this dish, since the skin can be partially peeled.
Once cooked, the skin will be softer. Larger and meatier pumpkin can also be used.

INGREDIENTS | SERVES 3 OR 4

3 tablespoons vegetable oil

2 tablespoons minced garlic

½ cup ground pork

2 eggs

4 cups sliced pumpkin, cut into bite-size
pieces

6 tablespoons chicken stock or water

2 tablespoons oyster sauce

2 tablespoons fish sauce

½ teaspoon sugar

Add oil to a hot wok or sauté pan over medium heat. Add garlic and fry until fragrant, about 30 seconds to 1 minute. Add pork and stir-fry until pork is done. Add eggs, break the yolk, and cook without stirring until eggs are firm, about 1–2 minutes. Add pumpkin and chicken stock, and stir-fry until pumpkin is soft, about 5 minutes. Season with oyster sauce, fish sauce, and sugar. Taste for seasoning and turn off the heat.

Pad Cha with Fried Catfish

"Cha" is the sizzling sound chilies make when they are fried in oil. This recipe can be made spicier by adding more chilies. Sliced mushroom can be added with the bamboo shoots to add more texture.

INGREDIENTS | SERVES 4

2 garlic cloves

Pinch of salt

1 shallot

4 Thai chilies

3 cups vegetable oil for deep-frying

12 ounces catfish, cut into bite-size pieces

2 sprigs green peppercorn

3 or 4 kaffir lime leaves, torn

1 cup sliced bamboo shoots

½ cup thin strips lesser galangal (wild ginger, "grachai")

1–2 tablespoons fish sauce

Pinch of sugar

1 cup Thai basil

2–3 cups cooked Jasmine Rice (see Chapter 2)

1. Pound garlic, salt, shallot, and chilies into a paste with a mortar and pestle. Or put all ingredients in small food chopper and blend until smooth.

2. Heat 3 cups oil in a saucepot. Bring to 350°F; deep-fry catfish pieces until brown and crispy, about 4 minutes. Set aside.

3. Heat a wok or a pot over medium-high heat. Add 2 tablespoon of frying oil and then fry the paste for 10–20 seconds.

4. Add fried fish and continue to stir-fry for another minute. Add peppercorn, kaffir lime leaves, bamboo shoots, and lesser galangal. Add fish sauce and sugar and taste. Sprinkle the Thai basil. Stir-fry until basil is soft, about 30 seconds, and take it off the heat. Serve over rice.

Stir-Fried Green Curry with Chicken

This recipe does not call for coconut milk and uses oil to stir-fry the paste. This method gives the curry a more robust flavor of fresh green chilies.

INGREDIENTS | SERVES 4

2 tablespoons vegetable oil

2 tablespoons Green Curry Paste (see Chapter 2)

1 cup sliced chicken, cut into bite-size pieces

½ cup water (if necessary)

2 cups bamboo shoots

2–3 teaspoons fish sauce

1 teaspoon sugar

5 kaffir lime leaves, torn

½ cup Thai basil

2–3 cups cooked Jasmine Rice (see Chapter 2)

Liven Up Canned Green Curry Paste

Adding freshly ground white pepper to the paste before using makes the curry taste even fresher.

1. Heat a pan or wok over high heat until it is hot. Add oil and wait until it is hot. When hot, add the curry paste, and turn the heat down to medium-low. Fry the paste over medium heat until fragrant, about 30 seconds.

2. Add chicken and sauté until chicken is cooked, about 1–2 minutes. Add about ½ cup of water to help cook. Add bamboo shoots and continue to cook until bamboo shoots are all heated, about 1–2 minutes.

3. Season with fish sauce and sugar; add kaffir lime leaves and sauté for about 30 seconds. Fold in Thai basil until basil is wilted, about 30 seconds. Serve over rice.

Scallop and Chili Jam

Other seafood like clams, fish, mussels, or shrimp can also be used to replace the scallops in this recipe.

INGREDIENTS | SERVES 4

2 tablespoons vegetable oil

3 tablespoons Chili Jam (see Chapter 3)

1 pound scallops

3 or 4 kaffir lime leaves, torn

1 tablespoon fish sauce, plus more to taste

1 sliced jalapeño pepper

½ teaspoon white sugar

½ cup Thai basil leaves

1. Heat a sauté pan or wok over high heat until it is hot. Add oil and wait until it is hot. Add the chili jam and turn the heat down to medium. Fry the jam over medium heat until fragrant, about 1 minute.

2. Add scallops and stir-fry until well incorporated and scallops are cooked, about 2–3 minutes. Add kaffir lime leaves, fish sauce, sliced jalapenos, and sugar. Fold in Thai basil. Adjust seasoning with fish sauce or sugar if needed. Remove from heat and serve.

Spinach with Soybean Paste

Traditionally, morning glory is used for this recipe, but spinach makes a great substitution. Snow pea leaves are another great choice.

INGREDIENTS | SERVES 2

2 tablespoons vegetable oil

4 cloves garlic, bruised

4 bruised chilies

6 cups spinach

1 teaspoon soybean paste

2 tablespoons light soy sauce

½ cup chicken water or stock

2–3 cups cooked Jasmine Rice (see Chapter 2)

Heat a deep sauté pan or wok over high heat. When hot, turn heat down to medium and add oil. Fry garlic and chilies until fragrant, about 10 seconds. Add spinach, soybean paste, soy sauce, and water or stock, and stir-fry until vegetables are wilted, about 2–3 minutes. Check seasoning and serve immediately over rice.

Pork with Red Curry Stir-Fry

This stir-fried curry allows the red curry paste to show off its smoky flavor.

INGREDIENTS | SERVES 4

10 ounces pork tenderloin or pork chop, sliced in thin pieces

2 teaspoons soy sauce

2 tablespoons vegetable oil

2 tablespoons Red Curry Paste (see Chapter 2), or store-bought red curry paste

½ cup coconut milk

1 tablespoon fish sauce

2 teaspoons sugar

4 kaffir lime leaves, torn

3 sprigs green peppercorn

1 fresh long red chili, cut into thin strips

1. Marinate pork in soy sauce for 15 minutes. Heat a deep sauté pan and add oil. Fry curry paste until fragrant at medium-low heat, about 15 seconds. Add pork and sauté until pork is cooked, about 2 minutes.

2. Add the coconut milk and continue to stir until coconut milk releases some oil to the surface. Season with fish sauce, sugar, kaffir lime leaves, and green peppercorn. Stir in red chilies and turn off the heat.

Pad Prik King with Fried Fish

Any kind of fish can be fried this way to make Pad Prik King. Sometimes, fish is steamed and broken up into small pieces with a fork and then deep-fried for use in this recipe.

INGREDIENTS | SERVES 4

12 ounces catfish, cut into 2" × 2" pieces

¼ teaspoon salt

2 cups and 3 tablespoons vegetable oil

¼ cup Red Curry Paste (see Chapter 2)

½ cup water (if necessary)

1–2 teaspoons fish sauce

2 tablespoons sugar

1 tablespoon thinly julienned kaffir lime leaves

2–3 cups cooked Jasmine Rice (see Chapter 2)

1. Rub catfish with salt. In a deep frying pan, deep-fry catfish in 2 cups oil at 350°F until golden and crispy, about 5 minutes.

2. Heat a sauté pan or wok until it is hot. Add remaining oil and wait until it is hot, then add the curry paste and turn the heat down to medium. Fry the paste until fragrant over medium heat, about 1 minute. Add fried catfish and sauté about 1–2 minutes. Add about ½ cup of water to help cook. Season with fish sauce and sugar. Add kaffir lime leaves and sauté for about 15 seconds. Serve over rice.

Stir-Fried Chicken with Chestnuts

Replacing the meat with Fried Tofu (see Chapter 5) makes a great vegetarian version of this simple recipe.

INGREDIENTS | SERVES 2

3 tablespoons vegetable oil

3 teaspoons minced garlic

4 slices ginger

8 ounces chicken breast, cut into thin strips

2 tablespoons light soy sauce

2 teaspoons sherry or Chinese cooking wine

1 teaspoon sugar

½ cup water or chicken stock

1 tablespoon chopped Chinese or regular celery

10 water chestnuts, sliced

1 stalk green garlic, split in fourths lengthwise and cut into 2"-long pieces

1. Heat a deep sauté pan or a wok over medium heat. Add oil and fry garlic and ginger for 30 seconds until fragrant. Add chicken and sauté for 3–5 minutes until chicken is almost cooked. Add light soy sauce, sherry, sugar, and water and simmer for 5 minutes with the lid on.

2. Add celery, water chestnuts, and green garlic, and sauté for another 3 minutes. Turn off the heat. Taste and adjust seasoning if necessary.

Chinese Broccoli with Fried Pork Belly

This dish can be made with or without the crispy pork belly. Chinese broccoli is tender and sweet once cooked, but be careful not to overcook it. It should still have a bite to it when it is done.

INGREDIENTS | SERVES 4

2 tablespoons vegetable oil

1 tablespoon minced garlic

1 cup Crispy Pork Belly (see Chapter 11)

5 Chinese broccoli stalks, chopped into 2"-long pieces, with the stems sliced thinly

2–3 tablespoons oyster sauce

1 teaspoon sugar

¼ cup chicken stock or water

Pinch ground white pepper

Heat a deep sauté pan over medium-high heat and add oil. Fry garlic until fragrant, about 10 seconds. Add Crispy Pork Belly and sauté for a minute. Add Chinese broccoli, oyster sauce, sugar, and water. Stir-fry until broccoli just turns bright green, about 1 minute. Taste and adjust seasoning. Serve sprinkled with ground white pepper.

Garlic Shrimp

This is a very versatile recipe because you can use different kinds of seafood to make it.

INGREDIENTS | SERVES 4

¼ cup vegetable oil

2 tablespoons minced garlic

1 tablespoon minced cilantro stems

1 teaspoon ground white pepper

2 teaspoons fish sauce

1 teaspoon sugar

1½ pounds large shrimp, peeled and deveined

¼ cup minced ginger

¼ cup thinly sliced green onion

1. Heat oil in a large skillet over medium-high heat. Fry garlic, cilantro stems, and pepper until fragrant, about 10 seconds. Add fish sauce and sugar and mix well.

2. Add shrimp and sauté until shrimp is almost done, about 1–2 minutes. Add ginger and green onion. Stir to combine. Serve hot.

Chive Flowers with Shrimp

Chive flowers are available at Asian grocery stores. The whole stalk, including the flowers, is used. The flavor is mild and goes well with a combination of shallots and garlic.

INGREDIENTS | SERVES 4

2 tablespoons oil

2 garlic cloves, minced

8 large shrimp, peeled and deveined

4 cups chive flowers, cut into 1½" pieces with the ends cut off

2 tablespoons chicken stock or water

1–2 tablespoons light soy sauce

Pinch of sugar

Pinch of ground pepper

2–3 cups cooked Jasmine Rice (see Chapter 2)

Heat a wok over medium-high heat until hot. Add oil, and when the oil is hot, add garlic. Fry garlic until fragrant and starting to turn color, about 10 seconds. Add shrimp and stir-fry until shrimp just turn pink, about 1–2 minutes. Add chive flowers, stock, soy sauce, and sugar and fry for another 2–3 minutes. Serve sprinkled with pepper over steamed rice.

Stir-Fried Pork Liver and Onions

Pork liver has the bitterness that balances the sweetness of onions.
Other vegetables like chive flowers or snow peas can be added to the dish.

INGREDIENTS | SERVES 4

2 tablespoons vegetable oil

2 garlic cloves, minced

6 ounces pork liver, sliced into ⅛" pieces

1 cup chopped yellow onions

2 tablespoons chicken stock or water

1–2 tablespoons light soy sauce

Pinch of sugar

Pinch of ground pepper

2–3 cups cooked Jasmine Rice (see Chapter 2)

Heat a wok over medium-high heat until hot. Add oil, and when oil is hot, add garlic. Fry until fragrant and starting to turn color, about 10–15 seconds. Add pork liver and stir-fry until the outside of the liver is brown, about 1–2 minutes. Add onions, stock, soy sauce, and sugar and fry for another 2–3 minutes until onions are translucent. Serve sprinkled with pepper over steamed rice.

Clams with Chili Jam

Any seafood can be used in this recipe. Mussels in their shells are commonly used for this style of stir-fry.

INGREDIENTS | SERVES 4

¼ cup chicken stock or water

1 pound clams in shells

1 stalk lemongrass, cut in half and bruised

4 slices of galangal, ¼" thick

3 kaffir lime leaves, torn

1 teaspoon palm sugar

2 teaspoons fish sauce

3 tablespoons Chili Jam (see Chapter 3)

½ cup Thai basil leaves

2–3 cups cooked Jasmine Rice (see Chapter 2)

1. Bring stock to a boil in a medium saucepan. Add clams, lemongrass, galangal, and lime leaves. Cover and simmer over medium heat until clams are open. Discard clams that remain closed.

2. Season with palm sugar, fish sauce, and Chili Jam. Stir to mix. Fold in Thai basil and serve with rice.

CHAPTER 11

Steamed, Grilled, and Fried Dishes

Garlic Pepper Frog Legs

Butter is called for in this recipe to add a different flavor to this classic Thai dish. Any oil can be used in its place if you'd like. If you are using unsalted butter, add more salt at the end of preparation.

INGREDIENTS | SERVES 4

8 frog legs

2 tablespoons light soy sauce

½ teaspoon freshly ground white pepper

½ teaspoon ground turmeric

1 tablespoon rice flour

3 cups vegetable oil for deep-frying

3 tablespoons salted butter

½ teaspoon sugar

3 tablespoons Deep-Fried Minced Garlic (see Chapter 2)

1 tablespoon finely shredded lemongrass

1 tablespoon finely sliced celery

1 tablespoon oyster sauce

1 sprig green peppercorn

Making Your Own Turmeric Powder

Purchase fresh turmeric and slice into small rounds. Dry in the sun or by the windowsill, and then grind in a coffee grinder. Make sure to not use the same grinder to grind your coffee or it will be spicy and bitter!

1. Marinate frog legs with soy sauce, pepper, and turmeric for 1 hour in the fridge.

2. Dust marinated frog legs with rice flour. In a deep frying pan, deep-fry in oil that has been heated to 350°F until golden, about 4–5 minutes.

3. In a different pan, melt butter over low heat and add sugar, fried garlic, shredded lemongrass, and celery, and mix well. Season with oyster sauce and add green peppercorn and continue to stir until fragrant, about 1–2 minutes.

4. Plate fried frog legs and top with the garlic mixture.

Steamed Fish with Lime Sauce and Garlic
(*Pla Nueng Manao*)

Fish fillets can be used in this dish if a large steamer is not available to steam whole fish.

INGREDIENTS | SERVES 4

1 whole red snapper (about 1 pound), cleaned

4–6 Thai chilies, finely minced

½ cup chicken stock or water

1–2 tablespoons light soy sauce

3 tablespoons lime juice

4 cloves garlic, mashed but still whole

½ cup chopped green onions

½ cup chopped Chinese celery or regular celery, julienned

1. Score the fish 3 times on each side. Place on a platter.

2. Combine Thai chilies, stock or water, light soy sauce, and lime juice in a bowl. Pour over the fish. Top with mashed garlic, green onions, and celery. Steam for 15 minutes at a rapid boil.

Fried Fish with Mango Salad

Cotton fish is usually used in this recipe; however, it is not widely available in the United States. Salmon is a great substitution.

INGREDIENTS | SERVES 4

1 pound salmon fillets with skin on

3 cups vegetable oil for deep-frying

1 recipe Mango Salad (see Chapter 4)

Green Mango

Green mangoes are mangoes picked when they are green and firm. They will not ripen any further. They are very tart and not at all sweet. When buying green mangoes, make sure they are hard. If it is soft, it is not suitable for green mango salad. They will be too mushy and not as tart.

1. Score salmon fillets into crisscrosses all over the skin on one side. Sun-dry for 3 hours on a rack or place in the oven at 200°F for 4 hours.

2. In a frying pan, deep-fry salmon in hot oil at 350°F until golden brown, about 5–6 minutes.

3. Serve fried salmon topped with the Mango Salad.

Thai Omelet with Pork (*Kai Jiew*)

This well-done omelet is great on its own or when served with rice. If making it as an omelet served without rice, use ¼ less fish sauce. Serve with Sriracha Sauce (see Chapter 2).

INGREDIENTS | SERVES 2

4 eggs

1 tablespoon fish sauce

¼ cup minced pork

1 shallot, sliced

1 tomato, chopped

¼ cup vegetable oil

2–3 cups cooked Jasmine Rice (see Chapter 2)

¼ cup Sriracha Sauce (see Chapter 2)

1. Crack eggs into mixing bowl, and beat well until they are fluffy and the egg whites are completely mixed in. Add fish sauce, pork, shallot, and tomato and mix well.

2. Heat frying pan over medium-high heat until hot. Add oil and make sure that the oil is very hot. Add the egg mixture to the pan, and roll the pan so that egg mixture spreads out. After 1 minute, the omelet will begin to cook. Turn the heat down to medium. Pull the sides into the middle and tilt the pan for the eggs to run to the side. Do this all the way around the pan. Wait another minute until one side is cooked and brown, then flip to cook the other side.

3. Flip parts of omelet back if there are uncooked eggs or pork, until all the way done and brown. When the egg is cooked and slightly crispy, transfer it to a plate. Serve rice and a side of Sriracha Sauce.

Fried Pork Ribs

Ask your butcher to cut the ribs for you. It is almost impossible to cut them up into small pieces at home, even with a meat cleaver.

INGREDIENTS | SERVES 4

2 pounds pork ribs, cut into 2" pieces
2 tablespoons oyster sauce
2 tablespoons light soy sauce
1 teaspoon sugar
Pinch of salt
3 cups plus 3 tablespoons vegetable oil
1 tablespoon minced cilantro stems
2 tablespoons minced garlic
1 tablespoon cracked white or black peppercorns

1. Marinate pork ribs with oyster sauce, soy sauce, sugar, and salt for 4 hours in the fridge.

2. In a frying pan, deep-fry pork in 3 cups oil that has been heated to 350°F, until golden, about 4–5 minutes.

3. Mix cilantro stems, garlic, and peppercorns to make a paste. Heat a sauté pan over medium heat, and add 3 tablespoons vegetable oil. Fry the mixture until golden and fragrant, about 10–15 seconds. Top pork ribs with the fried mixture and serve.

Steamed Egg with Pork (*Kai Toon*)

This is a great dish for kids and adults alike. The soft custard-like texture can be eaten alone or with steamed rice.

INGREDIENTS | SERVES 4

4 eggs, beaten
3 tablespoons ground pork
2 tablespoons thinly sliced green onions, both white and green parts
1 tablespoon thinly sliced shallot
¼ teaspoon ground white pepper
¼ teaspoon salt
2 tablespoons light soy sauce
1 cup chicken stock or water
1 tablespoon chopped cilantro

1. Combine all ingredients, except the cilantro, in a mixing bowl and stir to mix.

2. Transfer the mixture into four 6-ounce ramekins and steam for 15 minutes at medium boil.

3. Check to see if the eggs are cooked. When cooked, it should have a custard-like texture. Continue to cook if the eggs are still runny. Serve garnished with cilantro.

Fried Fish with Turmeric

Fresh turmeric works best for this dish, but turmeric powder will do a good job as well. If using powder, make sure that it is 100 percent turmeric powder with no additives. Frozen fresh turmeric can also be purchased at Asian grocery stores.

INGREDIENTS | SERVES 4

1 teaspoon turmeric powder, or fresh turmeric the size of the tip of your thumb

2 teaspoons salt

2 teaspoons garlic powder

1 pound fish fillets, any kind, skin on if possible

3 tablespoons rice flour

1 cup vegetable oil

1. If using fresh turmeric, pound turmeric and salt using mortar and pestle. If using powder, mix the powder with salt. Add garlic powder and mix.

2. Rub fish with the mixture until coated and let sit for 30 minutes.

3. Dust the fish with rice flour and deep-fry in a frying pan with oil that has been heated to 350°F, until golden, about 6 minutes, 3 minutes on each side. Remove from oil and serve.

Steamed Snapper with Ginger (*Pla Nueng*)

*This is a no-fat dish that doesn't sacrifice flavor.
The fish is moist and tender with robust flavors from the ginger and green onions.*

INGREDIENTS | SERVES 4

1 whole red snapper, flounder, or perch (about 1 pound of fillets is fine too)

3 tablespoons light soy sauce

Pinch of sugar

1 cup shredded ginger, divided

4 spring onions, minced

1 tablespoon chopped cilantro

Large pinch of ground white pepper

1. Clean fish. Score three slits on each side. Place on plate and cover with soy sauce, sugar, and half the ginger. Steam until cooked, about 15–20 minutes.

2. When the fish is done, add the remaining ginger and spring onions and steam for 1 minute longer, until onions are softened. Remove the plate and serve sprinkled with cilantro and ground pepper.

Son-in-Law Eggs (*Kai Look Kuey*)

Duck eggs are best for this recipe because the egg whites of duck eggs hold up better when fried. The story goes that a son-in-law was trying to impress his mother-in-law and made this recipe. Hence the name.

INGREDIENTS | SERVES 4

5 Boiled Eggs (see Chapter 2)
¼ cup vegetable oil
½ cup sliced shallots
¼ cup Tamarind Water (see Chapter 2)
3 tablespoons palm sugar
1 tablespoon fish sauce or more to taste
5 fried dried small Thai chilies
2 tablespoons chopped cilantro
2–3 cups cooked Jasmine Rice (see Chapter 2)

1. Peel the eggs and let cool. Heat up a deep frying pan over medium-high heat, add oil, and fry eggs until golden brown and slightly crispy on all sides at 350°F, about 2–3 minutes. Place on paper towels to drain.

2. Using the same oil, fry shallots until brown and crispy, about 1 minute. Add more oil if needed. Take the shallots out. Add tamarind water, sugar, and fish sauce to the oil and stir to mix.

3. To serve, cut eggs in half, top with tamarind sauce, fried shallots, fried chilies, and cilantro. Serve with rice.

Crispy Pork Belly

The robust flavor of salt and vinegar make this crispy pork belly a great addition to any stir-fry dish. The oil left from deep-frying can be used to stir-fry.

INGREDIENTS | SERVES 4

12 ounces pork belly
2 teaspoons salt
3 teaspoons white vinegar
4 cups vegetable oil

1. In a large saucepan, bring water to a boil. Blanch pork belly in simmering water for 15 minutes until tender. Let dry and rub with salt and vinegar and cut the piece in half. Allow to air dry for another 3 hours.

2. Heat oil in heavy frying pan (cast iron is ideal). Fry pork belly in oil heated to 350°F until the skin is crispy, about 4–6 minutes. Continue to fry if the skin is not crispy. The skin should be golden brown color, but the meat will still be moist. Remove from oil and let sit on paper towels to drain before serving.

Three-Flavored Fish (*Pla Sam Rod*)

Whole fish can also be used for this dish. Deep-fry the fish in a large wok and follow the same steps below. Once fried, fish is easy to work around the bones.

INGREDIENTS | SERVES 4

Paste

1 teaspoon chopped cilantro stems

Pinch of salt

3 Serrano peppers, deseeded and chopped coarsely (red is better, but green is fine)

4 garlic cloves, chopped

3 red shallots, chopped

Fish

1 tablespoon oil

½ cup palm sugar

2–3 tablespoons water

2 tablespoons Tamarind Water (see Chapter 2)

1 tablespoon fish sauce

12 ounces fish fillets (any kind of fish), cut into 2" × 2" pieces

1 tablespoon light soy sauce

3 cups oil for deep-frying

2 dried long chilies, deep-fried and broken into small pieces

1 cup Thai basil leaves, deep-fried

Deep-Frying Basil

To deep-fry basil, heat 1 cup vegetable oil to 350°F and drop basil in hot oil. Let fry for 1 minute and place on paper towels to drain.

1. Make the paste either with food processor or a mortar and pestle, adding the ingredients one by one until smooth.

2. In a large sauté pan, fry the paste over medium heat in 1 tablespoon of oil until fragrant, about 10–15 seconds. Season with palm sugar, and then add 2–3 tablespoons of water and simmer until thick. Add tamarind water and fish sauce and continue to simmer until reduced, about 3–5 minutes. Check the seasoning: the sauce should be sweet, sour, spicy, and salty.

3. Marinate the fish in light soy sauce for about 10 minutes. In a frying pan, heat oil to 350°F. Deep-fry fish until crisp, about 4 minutes. To serve, coat the fish with the sauce, and sprinkle with fried dried chilies and fried Thai basil.

Red Sauce Chicken

Ketchup is a magic ingredient used in several Thai recipes.
The sweet, sour, salty, and spicy flavors add depth and flavor to many dishes.

INGREDIENTS | SERVES 4

1 pound bone-in chicken thighs

1 teaspoon salt

¼ teaspoon cracked black pepper

2 cups vegetable oil for deep-frying

¼ cup sliced yellow onions

¼ cup ketchup

2 tablespoons light soy sauce

1 tablespoon Worcestershire sauce

2 tablespoons Sriracha Sauce (see Chapter 2), or bottled

2 tablespoons sugar

3 bay leaves

1 cup chicken stock

2 tablespoons chopped cilantro

2 tablespoons chopped green onions

1 cup blanched vegetables of your choosing

Using Seasonal Vegetables

Visit your farmers' market and browse around to see what you can use for vegetables in this recipe. When substituting vegetables, think about the textures and flavors that are similar to the ones you are substituting.

1. Rub chicken with salt and pepper. In a cast iron or carbon steel wok, heat oil to 350°F and deep-fry chicken until golden, about 8 minutes.

2. Measure ¼ cup of oil used for deep-frying, and add to sauté pan. Sauté onions over medium heat until translucent and fragrant, about 2 minutes. Season with ketchup, soy sauce, Worcestershire sauce, Sriracha Sauce, sugar, and bay leaves and stir-fry until incorporated, about 1 minute.

3. Add chicken and stock to the pan, and simmer for 30 minutes at low heat. Keep checking the liquid. If it's too dry, add more stock as needed. Serve topped with cilantro and green onions and a side of blanched vegetables.

Thai Beef Jerky (*Nuer Daed Deaw*)

Traditionally, the beef in this dish is sun-dried for 4 hours on a rack, with the pieces flipped after 2 hours to dry evenly. Alternatively, dry the meat on a rack in the oven at 165°F for 6 hours. Dried beef can be stored in the refrigerator up to two weeks.

INGREDIENTS | SERVES 6

1 pound beef roast
1 tablespoon minced cilantro roots or stems
5 cloves minced garlic
½ teaspoon ground white pepper
1 tablespoon fish sauce
1 tablespoon oyster sauce
4 tablespoons whiskey
1 tablespoon sugar
1 teaspoon curry powder
3 cups vegetable oil for deep-frying
Sticky Rice (see Chapter 2)

1. Cut beef roast into ½" × 5" pieces, about ¼" thick.

2. Make the marinade by first pounding cilantro roots or stems, garlic, and pepper until smooth with a mortar and pestle. Add the paste, fish sauce, oyster sauce, whiskey, sugar, and curry powder to the beef. Let marinate for 1 hour.

3. Dry beef with your preferred method, until dry but still a little moist.

4. In a frying pan, heat oil to 350°F. Deep-fry beef until cooked all the way, about 2–3 minutes. Serve with Sticky Rice (see Chapter 2).

Fried Pork with Sesame Seeds

This is a great snack, or you can make a meal out of it by serving with Sticky Rice (see Chapter 2) and a side salad.

INGREDIENTS | SERVES 6

1 pound pork loin or roast
1 tablespoon minced cilantro roots or stems
5 cloves minced garlic
½ teaspoon ground white pepper
1 tablespoon fish sauce
1 tablespoon oyster sauce
4 tablespoons whiskey
1 tablespoon sugar
1 teaspoon curry powder
½ cup white sesame seeds
3 cups vegetable oil
Sticky Rice (see Chapter 2)

1. Cut pork roast into ½" × 5" pieces, about ¼" thick.

2. Make the marinade by pounding cilantro roots or stems, garlic, and pepper until smooth with a mortar and pestle. Add the paste, fish sauce, oyster sauce, whiskey, sugar, and curry powder to the beef. Let marinate for 1 hour.

3. Roll pork in sesame seeds.

4. In a fry pan with oil heated to 350°F, deep-fry pork until cooked all the way, about 2–3 minutes. Serve with Sticky Rice (see Chapter 2).

Chicken Wings

Marinated chicken wings can be frozen for later use.
When frying frozen wings, add 1 minute to the frying time.

INGREDIENTS | SERVES 4

1 pound chicken wings

4 tablespoons soy sauce

1 tablespoon sugar

1 tablespoon salt

2 tablespoons vegetable oil

1 tablespoon cilantro stems

2 teaspoons crushed black peppercorn

4 cloves minced garlic

4 cups vegetable oil

1. In a bowl, marinate chicken wings with soy sauce, sugar, salt, vegetable oil, cilantro stems, black peppercorn, and garlic for at least 6 hours or overnight in the refrigerator.

2. In a frying pan with oil heated to 350°F, deep-fry wings for 5 minutes. Drain on paper towels and serve.

Crying Tiger (Grilled Beef and Roasted Chili Sauce with Shallots)

Crying Tiger references the fat that drips when you are grilling the beef. The cut of steak depends on your preferred level of fat, but a fattier cut of beef is usually preferred for this dish.

INGREDIENTS | SERVES 4

Sauce

3 tablespoons lime juice

2 tablespoons fish sauce

1 teaspoon sugar

Large pinch of roasted chili flakes

1 shallot, finely sliced

1 tablespoon chopped coriander

Steak

12 ounces rump steak or rib-eye or sirloin steak, sliced into big, ½"-thick pieces

¼ cup light soy sauce

Roasted Chili Dipping Sauce with Shallots (see Chapter 3)

1. Make the sauce by combining all the sauce ingredients in a small mixing bowl.

2. Marinate the steak in soy sauce for 1 hour.

3. Grill steak over high heat for 5–10 minutes, depending on your preferred doneness. Let rest for another 10 minutes. Slice into small ⅛"-thick pieces and serve with dipping sauce.

Grilled Chicken with Sticky Rice (*Kai Yang*)

In Thailand, this is a street food favorite. The vendors that sell this dish are often found right next to a vendor selling Green Papaya Salad (see Chapter 4).

INGREDIENTS | SERVES 4

1 small whole chicken (about 2 pounds)
2 tablespoons minced ginger
2 tablespoons minced lemongrass
1 tablespoon black peppercorn
2 tablespoons minced cilantro roots or stems
2 tablespoons light soy sauce
2 teaspoons sugar
1 tablespoon curry powder
Sticky Rice (see Chapter 2)

1. Cut chicken in half lengthwise.

2. Pound together ginger, lemongrass, black peppercorn, and cilantro roots or stems using a mortar and pestle. Add soy sauce, sugar, and curry powder to the paste and rub the chicken pieces with it. Marinate for 6 hours in the refrigerator.

3. Grill chicken over hot flame until done, about 5–7 minutes on each side. Serve with Sticky Rice (see Chapter 2).

Grilled Prawns

This dish is all about the sauce. Fresh seafood doesn't need much seasoning. When grilled, its natural sweetness complements the sauce very well.

INGREDIENTS | SERVES 4

Sauce

1½ tablespoons minced garlic
2 teaspoons minced Thai chilies
1 teaspoon minced cilantro
¼ teaspoon salt
1 tablespoon sugar
2 tablespoons lime juice
⅓ cup water
1 tablespoon fish sauce

Seafood

4 large prawns or 2 lobsters

1. Make the sauce by mixing all the sauce ingredients in a small bowl. Stir to dissolve sugar.

2. Wrap prawns in aluminum foil or banana leaves and grill over medium flame until cooked, about 8–10 minutes. Serve with the sauce.

Mussels with Thai Basil

Cooking mussels this way is very easy, and not much seasoning is needed because the mussels have a natural saltiness and sweetness when steamed.

INGREDIENTS | SERVES 2

1 pound mussels in shells

½ cup water or chicken stock

3 sprigs Thai basil

1 stalk lemongrass, cut in half and bruised

Wash the mussels. Place stock, mussels, Thai basil, and lemongrass in a large saucepan or soup pot. Bring to a simmer and simmer with the lid on for 3 minutes, or until the mussels open. Discard the unopened shells and serve.

Steamed Shrimp with Soy Sauce

This recipe is very easy and can be made with fish. This is a great example of the Chinese influence on Thai cuisine.

INGREDIENTS | SERVES 4

10 large shrimp, butterflied

1 tablespoon thinly chopped green onions, green and white parts

1 cilantro root or 4 cilantro stems, minced

2 tablespoons minced garlic

2 tablespoons light soy sauce

1 tablespoon oyster sauce

½ teaspoon sugar

¼ teaspoon freshly ground black pepper

1. Place shrimp on a platter for steaming. Do not stack the shrimp.

2. Combine most of chopped green onions (save some for garnish), cilantro roots or stems, minced garlic, light soy sauce, oyster sauce, and sugar in a bowl. Pour over shrimp and steam for 5 minutes. Serve sprinkle with pepper and the rest of the onions.

Roast Duck

Roast duck goes great with rice or noodle soup.

INGREDIENTS | SERVES 6

3 teaspoons minced ginger

1 teaspoon ground roasted cinnamon

½ teaspoon ground roasted nutmeg

1 teaspoon ground black pepper

1 whole duck (about 3–4 pounds)

4 tablespoons light soy sauce

Pineapple slices and lettuce to garnish

Fresh vegetables like cucumbers, tomatoes, or carrots

¼ cup sweet soy sauce

Cutting Duck

Duck is not a very meaty poultry. It is almost impossible to carve duck like chicken. To cut the duck to serve, cut duck in half lengthwise and start cutting pieces with the bones. Let guests work around the bones with hands.

1. Heat the oven to 450°F. Make a paste with ginger, cinnamon, nutmeg, and pepper. Split the paste in half and rub half of the mixture inside the duck and the other half on the outside.

2. Wrap duck with aluminum foil and place in a roasting pan on a rack. Roast at 450°F for 1 hour and then remove from the oven. Turn the oven down to 350°F and let duck rest for 10 minutes. Remove the aluminum foil.

3. Place duck back on the roasting rack, poke the duck with fork all around, and roast for 30 minutes at 350°F. Remove the duck from the oven and turn the oven up to 400°F.

4. Rub duck with light soy sauce and return to the oven at 400°F for another 5 minutes until the skin is crispy. Serve with pineapple, lettuce, or other fresh vegetables with a side of sweet soy sauce.

Mussels Pancake (*Hoy Tod*)

In Thailand, these are always seen sold next to Pad Thai.
A heavy skillet like cast iron or carbon steel will work best for this dish.

INGREDIENTS | SERVES 1

2 tablespoons tapioca flour

1 tablespoon rice flour

¼ cup water

3 tablespoons oil

2 teaspoons chopped garlic

¼ cup mussel meat, preferably raw

1 tablespoon fish sauce

1 teaspoon oyster sauce

1 egg, slightly beaten

1 tablespoon chopped green onions

2 tablespoons chopped cilantro

1 cup bean sprouts

Pinch white pepper

2 tablespoons Sriracha Sauce (see Chapter 2)

1. Mix the two flours together and add the water. Heat a skillet over medium heat and add oil. Add the garlic and fry until fragrant, about 30 seconds to 1 minute. Stir the flour mixture and add the mixture to the pan. Add mussels, fish sauce, and oyster sauce and fry for 20 seconds without stirring.

2. Pour the egg on the side of the batter and let fry for 1 minute. When the egg begins to crisp, mix it with the mussels. Fry for 3–5 more minutes, until parts of the flour mixture turn crispy. Add oil around the edges if needed.

3. Add the chopped green onion, chopped cilantro leaves, bean sprouts, and white pepper, and flip so the vegetables are on the bottom of the pan. When bean sprouts begin to wilt, turn off the heat and serve with Sriracha Sauce.

Snapper with Pickled Garlic

This dish is usually ordered during a sit-down dinner at a restaurant.
Whole fish is served in a hot pot with charcoal to keep the dish warm at the table.

INGREDIENTS | SERVES 4

Sauce

5 Thai chilies

1 tablespoon minced garlic

Pinch of salt

1 tablespoon sugar

2 tablespoons lime juice

1 teaspoon ground roasted peanuts

Fish

1 small red fish, about 1 pound

¼ cup pork belly, sliced into strips

1 stalk celery or Chinese celery, chopped

1 head Pickled Garlic (see Chapter 4), sliced thinly

¼ cup julienned ginger

½ cup thinly sliced red bell pepper

2 cups chicken stock or water

3 tablespoons white vinegar

2 teaspoons sugar

How to Julienne Ginger

Peel ginger and thinly slice ⅛" thick length-wise. Stack ginger pieces, about 3 or 4 pieces at a time, and slice into thin match-sticks. Done!

1. Wash the fish and score both sides. Make the sauce by combining all sauce ingredients in a small mixing bowl and set aside.

2. Place the fish on a platter and top with pork belly. Steam for 10 minutes or until done. Turn off the heat, and top with celery, Pickled Garlic, ginger, and bell pepper. Combine stock with vinegar and sugar and pour over the fish. Steam for another 5 minutes. Remove from heat and serve.

Thai Omelet with Oyster

This is a very simple dish to make. Clams or shrimp make a great substitution for oyster.

INGREDIENTS | SERVES 2

3 eggs, beaten until foamy
3 tablespoons oyster sauce
1 tablespoon soy sauce
3 tablespoons vegetable oil
Sriracha Sauce (see Chapter 2) to garnish

1. Combine all ingredients, except oil and Sriracha Sauce, in a bowl.

2. Heat a skillet over medium-high heat, add oil, and wait until oil is very hot. Add the egg mixture and fry until one side is done, about 1 minute, tilting the pan to spread the egg evenly. Flip and cook on the other side. Add more oil if needed.

3. Remove from heat and serve.

Drunken Fried Eggs

Thais like to combine different dishes to make a new dish, like this one. Serve with or without rice.

INGREDIENTS | SERVES 2

½ cup oil
2 eggs
1 cup Spicy Basil with Ground Turkey
(see Chapter 10)

1. Heat a skillet over medium-high heat until very hot. Add oil and wait until oil is hot. Add eggs, one at a time, and let fry, without moving, for 1 minute. Flip to fry the other side until egg is crispy.

2. Top eggs with Spicy Basil with Ground Turkey.

Shrimp with Tamarind Sauce

Tamarind has a tangy flavor with a bit of sweetness, different than common lime juice. Tamarind sauce is great over any meat or seafood.

INGREDIENTS | SERVES 4

2 tablespoons vegetable oil

2 tablespoons finely diced yellow onion

2 tablespoons palm sugar

1 tablespoon fish sauce

⅓ cup tamarind water

¼ cup chicken stock or water

1 pound large shrimp, peeled and deveined

1 tablespoon Deep-Fried Minced Garlic (see Chapter 2)

2 tablespoons fried shallots (bought at Asian grocery store)

5 small fried dried chilies

1 long red chili, thinly sliced

2 tablespoons chopped cilantro

1. Heat oil in a large skillet over medium-high heat. Add onions and fry until fragrant and translucent, about 5 minutes. Add palm sugar, fish sauce, tamarind water, and stock or water and stir-fry for 3 minutes.

2. Add shrimp and stir-fry until shrimp is cooked, about 2 minutes. Turn off the heat.

3. Transfer shrimp to a platter and top with fried garlic, fried shallots, fried chilies, sliced red chili, and cilantro.

Grilled Fish with Lemongrass

Any whole fish can be used for this recipe—just make sure the fish is fresh!

INGREDIENTS | SERVES 2

1 stalk lemongrass, chopped into 2" pieces

10 white peppercorns

3 cloves garlic

2 teaspoons salt

10 cilantro stems

1 whole red snapper, cleaned

Banana leaves for grilling

Make a paste using a mortar and pestle with lemongrass, white peppercorns, garlic, salt, and cilantro stems. Rub the outside and inside of the fish with the paste. Wrap in banana leaves and grill over medium heat until the fish is done, about 20 minutes. Check and grill longer if not done. When it is done, fish will peel off the bones.

Grilled Turmeric Chicken

This easy and delicious grilled chicken is influenced by southern cuisine using a few dried spices to marinate the chicken. It is similar to Chicken Satay with Peanut Sauce (see Chapter 5) with a few different ingredients.

INGREDIENTS | SERVES 8

2 tablespoons finely chopped cilantro stems

10 white peppercorns

2 teaspoons whole coriander seeds

4 cloves garlic

¼ teaspoon salt

3 pounds boneless, skinless chicken thighs, cubed into 2" × 2" pieces

2 tablespoons fish sauce

2 tablespoons oyster sauce

1 tablespoon ground turmeric

2 tablespoons palm sugar, melted with 1 tablespoon water in a microwave or on the stove

Bamboo skewers, soaked for 1 hour to prevent burning

1. Make a paste using a mortar and pestle combining cilantro stems, white peppercorns, coriander seeds, garlic, and salt. Pound until smooth.

2. Combine chicken with the paste, fish sauce, oyster sauce, turmeric, and sugar. Refrigerate for 4 hours.

3. Thread the chicken pieces onto bamboo skewers. Grill the chicken over a medium flame, turning after 1 minute. Turn the chicken again after 1 more minute. Turn the pieces again if the chicken is still raw on the outside., Flip a few times until thoroughly cooked through and slightly charred, about 3–4 minutes total.

Black, White, and Green Peppercorn

Thais use mostly white peppercorn in their dishes; black peppercorns are rarely used. Green peppercorns are used in curries and stir-fries. Using frozen green peppercorns results in a better flavor than if you were to use the ones in brine.

CHAPTER 12

Vegetarian Dishes

Homemade Seitan

*Seitan is a meat substitution made from vital wheat gluten.
It is somewhat porous and absorbs flavors very well.*

INGREDIENTS | YIELDS 6 CUPS

1 cup vital wheat gluten

1 teaspoon ginger powder

1 teaspoon garlic powder

1 teaspoon onion powder

2 tablespoons plus ½ cup light soy
  sauce, divided

¾ cup water or vegetable broth

6 cups vegetable broth for cooking

Seitan

Because seitan is so high in protein, it is a great choice for a meal addition for vegetarians. Try adding or substituting other spices for seasoning before cooking. Seitan freezes really well, but be sure to thaw for an hour before using.

1. Mix wheat gluten, ginger powder, garlic powder, and onion powder in a mixing bowl. In another bowl, add 2 tablespoons soy sauce to the ¾ cup broth or water.

2. Pour broth and soy sauce mixture over dry mixture, and combine well with hands.

3. Knead the dough for 2 minutes and let sit for 5 minutes. Knead for another 1 minute. Cut the dough into small pieces or use your hand to pinch small amounts, making somewhat flat balls.

4. Use a large saucepan or soup pot, as seitan will expand as it's cooking. Bring the dough pieces to a boil with 6 cups of broth. Add the rest of the soy sauce and simmer with a lid for 1 hour or more. Check the seitan regularly, making sure there is enough broth. Add more if needed.

5. Seitan is done when expanded and firm to the touch. The texture is somewhat bouncy. Store in the fridge for two weeks or freeze up to six months.

Soy Protein Cashew

Soy protein is another great meat substitution for vegetarians.
It usually comes in dry form, but to use it, you'll have to soak it in water for 20–30 minutes first.

INGREDIENTS | SERVES 4

1 cup dry soy protein

1 cup and 1 tablespoon vegetable oil

2 tablespoons plus 1 teaspoon light soy sauce

1 teaspoon sugar

½ cup water or vegetable stock

1 cup rice flour to coat

3 dried long chilies, chopped into 1"-long pieces

2 teaspoons minced garlic

2 cups mixed color bell peppers, chopped into 1" x 1" pieces

½ cup fried or roasted cashew nuts (see sidebar in Cashew Chicken, Chapter 10)

1 teaspoon sugar

1 teaspoon pure sesame oil

2–3 tablespoons oyster sauce

2 teaspoons tapioca flour

½ cup water

1 recipe Jasmine Rice (see Chapter 2)

Sesame Oil

When buying sesame oil, make sure it is 100 percent sesame oil. There are a few brands out there that sell sesame oil "blend," which has other oils as ingredients. Pure sesame oil is much more fragrant and worth every penny.

1. First prepare the soy protein. Soak soy protein in water until soft, about 30 minutes.

2. Heat a sauté pan and add 1 tablespoon oil. Sauté soy protein with 2 tablespoons of soy sauce, sugar, and water or stock over medium heat until all the liquid is absorbed.

3. Dust seasoned soy protein in rice flour. Using a frying pan, heat 1 cup of oil to 350°F and deep-fry soy protein for 3 minutes. Set aside.

4. Reserve 3 tablespoons of oil in the pan. Add dried chilies and fry for 1 minute over medium heat. Set aside.

5. Add minced garlic and fry until fragrant, about 30 seconds. Add fried soy protein, bell pepper, cashew nuts, 1 teaspoon light soy sauce, sugar, sesame oil, and oyster sauce, and stir-fry until incorporated, about 2 minutes.

6. Mix tapioca flour with ½ cup water and add to the pan. Sauté for another minute until sauce thickens. Taste and check the seasoning. Turn off the heat and serve with rice.

Tofu Stew

This dish can be made into a soup by adding more liquid and adjusting the seasoning accordingly.
It is great when served with steamed rice as well.

INGREDIENTS | SERVES 4

2 cups vegetable oil for frying

1 pound silken tofu, cubed to ½" × ½" pieces

2 tablespoons vegetable oil from deep-frying

2 teaspoons minced garlic

½ cup minced seitain

1 tablespoon Chinese chili sauce or Sriracha Sauce (see Chapter 2 or store-bought)

1 tablespoon light soy sauce

1 teaspoon salt

1 cup vegetable stock

1 tablespoon tapioca flour

2 tablespoons water

1 teaspoon pure sesame oil

1 tablespoon chopped green onion

1 teaspoon ground Szechuan peppercorns

1. Heat 2 cups oil in a deep pan or wok over high heat. Fry tofu pieces for 1 minute, remove from pan, and set aside.

2. Pour out the oil, reserving 2 tablespoons, and lower the heat to medium. Add garlic and fry until fragrant and brown, about 10 seconds. Add minced seitan and sauté for 15 seconds. Season with chili sauce, soy sauce, and salt.

3. Add stock and tofu, and stir to mix well (be careful not to break up tofu pieces). Simmer for 3 minutes.

4. Mix tapioca flour with 2 tablespoons water, pour into the pan, and mix well. Simmer for 1 minute until the sauce is slightly thickened. Turn off the heat and top with sesame oil and green onions. Sprinkle with ground Szechuan peppercorn.

Vegetarian Thai Omelet

The vegetarian version of this well-done omelet uses soy sauce instead of fish sauce.

INGREDIENTS | SERVES 2

4 eggs
1 tablespoon light soy sauce
¼ cup chopped mushrooms
1 shallot, sliced
1 tomato, chopped
¼ cup vegetable oil

1. Crack eggs into mixing bowl. Beat well until they are fluffy and the egg whites are completely mixed in. Add the rest of the ingredients, except oil, and mix well.

2. Heat frying pan over high heat until hot and add oil. Make sure that the oil is very hot, and add the egg mixture into the pan. Roll the pan so that the egg mixture spreads out. After 1 minute, the omelet will begin to cook. Pull the sides into the middle and tilt the pan for the eggs to run to the side. Do that all the way around the pan. Wait another minute until one side is cooked and brown, and then flip to cook the other side. Flip parts of omelet back if there are uncooked eggs until all the way done and brown. When the egg is cooked and slightly crispy, transfer it to a plate. Serve with rice.

Tofu Delight

This dish is both salty and sweet. The spice is very subtle.
Seitan or soy protein can also be used in place of tofu.

INGREDIENTS | SERVES 4

2 tablespoons chopped garlic

2 tablespoons chopped shallots

1 tablespoon chopped cilantro stem

¼ tablespoon chopped chilies

3 tablespoons vegetable oil

3 cups Fried Tofu (see Chapter 5)

1 cup water or vegetable stock

1 tablespoon sugar

2 tablespoons palm sugar

2 tablespoons soy sauce

1 tablespoon dark soy sauce

½ cup sliced onions

1 cup mixed red and green bell pepper, chopped into 1" pieces

½ cup chopped green onions

Pinch of chopped cilantro

Pinch of ground black pepper

1 recipe cooked Jasmine Rice (see Chapter 2)

1. Combine garlic, shallot, cilantro stems, and chilies. Heat a wok or deep sauté pan until hot. Add oil and fry the garlic mixture over medium heat until fragrant, about 10 seconds.

2. Add tofu and stir-fry. Add water or stock, sugar, palm sugar, and both soy sauces. Simmer for about 15 minutes until the tofu is darkened. Add more water/stock if needed. Add sliced onions, bell pepper, and green onions and stir-fry until translucent, about 2–3 minutes. Taste and adjust seasoning. It should taste sweet and salty.

3. Turn off the heat and sprinkle cilantro and black pepper. Serve with cooked rice.

Lemongrass Soup with Mixed Mushrooms

Oyster, shitake, chanterelles, King Trumpet, porcini, and button mushrooms are all great choices for this dish.

INGREDIENTS | SERVES 4

4 cups chicken stock

1 stalk lemongrass, chopped into 1½" pieces and bruised

6 slices galangal, sliced and bruised

4 kaffir lime leaves, torn

1 tablespoon soy sauce

Large pinch of salt

4 cups of mixed mushrooms

Sauce

4 tablespoons lime juice

3 tablespoons soy sauce

2 or 3 Thai chilies, minced (about 1–2 teaspoons minced chilies)

½ teaspoon of sugar

½ cup chopped cilantro

1. Bring stock to a boil in a medium saucepan. Add lemongrass, galangal, and kaffir lime leaves to the stock. Simmer for 3–5 minutes. Season with soy sauce and salt.

2. Add mushrooms and simmer until the mushrooms are cooked, about 4 minutes.

3. In a bowl, mix lime juice, soy sauce, chilies, sugar, and cilantro. Turn off the heat, add the sauce to the hot soup, and serve.

Kaffir Lime Leaves

The kaffir lime tree grows limes and produces leaves, both of which can be used for cooking. In Thai cuisine, kaffir lime zest is added to curry paste and kaffir lime leaves are used in curries and stir-fries. In cooler climates like in the Northeast, a greenhouse will provide protection for these trees all year round.

Bean Sprouts with Tofu

This is simple vegetarian dish that can be done with any vegetables.
Serve the dish immediately over cooked Jasmine Rice (see Chapter 2).

INGREDIENTS | SERVES 2

3 tablespoons vegetable oil
3 teaspoons minced garlic
1 cup Fried Tofu (see Chapter 5)
4 cups bean sprouts
2 tablespoons light soy sauce
1 teaspoon sugar
½ cup water or stock
1 bunch chopped green onions
Pinch of ground white pepper

1. Heat a deep sauté pan or a wok over medium heat. Add oil and fry garlic until fragrant, about 10 seconds. Add tofu and sauté until tofu is hot, about 1 minute.

2. Add bean sprouts, light soy sauce, sugar, and water and stir-fry for 1 minute, until bean sprouts are wilted but still firm. Add green onions and fold.

3. Turn off the heat and sprinkle with ground white pepper.

Chu Chee with Seitan

Seitan is a great addition to any curry. In fact, it is the star of this dish!

INGREDIENTS | SERVES 4

1 (13.5-ounce) can coconut milk
⅓ cup Red Curry Paste (see Chapter 2)
1½ pounds seitan, chopped into bite-size pieces
2 tablespoons palm sugar
3 tablespoons soy sauce
2 kaffir lime leaves, finely julienned

1. Do not shake the coconut milk. Scoop the cream on top of coconut milk can, about halfway down, into a medium saucepan. Bring coconut cream to a boil over medium heat. Stir in curry paste and turn down the heat to low. Simmer over low heat, without stirring, until fragrant and coconut cream starts to release some oil, about 3–5 minutes.

2. Add seitan to the fried paste and simmer for 2 minutes. Season with sugar and soy sauce. Add the rest of coconut milk to the saucepan and bring to a boil.

3. Add kaffir lime leaves and turn the heat off. Taste and adjust seasoning as needed.

Soy Protein and Spicy Sauce (*Pra Ram Long Song*)

This dish is great on its own without any starch. Keep in mind that other greens can be used instead of spinach (traditionally morning glory is used).

INGREDIENTS | SERVES 2

Paste

10 dried long red chilies, seeded and soaked

1 tablespoon chopped lemongrass

1 tablespoon chopped galangal

1 teaspoon salt

Protein

1 (13.5-ounce) can coconut milk

1 tablespoon light soy sauce

1 tablespoon palm sugar

1 tablespoon Tamarind Water (see Chapter 2)

½ cup ground roasted peanuts

5 tablespoons all-purpose flour or gluten-free flour substitute

¼ cup water

4 ounces oyster mushrooms, blanched

1 pound spinach, blanched

1 cup chopped soy protein, deep-fried

1. Make the paste by grinding all paste ingredients with a mortar and pestle.

2. Don't shake coconut milk can; scoop top creamy part of the can into a pot and bring to a boil. Add the paste and stir to mix well. Reduce heat to low and simmer for 3 minutes until fragrant. Add the rest of the coconut milk and bring to a boil. Season with light soy sauce, sugar, and tamarind water. Add peanuts and stir to mix well.

3. Mix the flour with ¼ cup water and add to the mixture. When boiled, turn off the heat.

4. Boil water in a saucepan and blanch mushrooms and spinach for 30 seconds.

5. To serve, place blanched vegetables on a plate, top with fried soy protein, and pour the curry sauce over.

Chinese Broccoli with Oyster Sauce

Baby bok choy is a good substitution for Chinese broccoli in this recipe. Other hardy greens like kale or collard greens will also work for this dish.

INGREDIENTS | SERVES 4

2 tablespoons vegetable oil

1 tablespoon minced garlic

8 Chinese broccoli stalks, chopped into 2"-long pieces with the stems thinly sliced

4 tablespoons oyster sauce

1 teaspoon sugar

¼ cup stock or water

Pinch ground white pepper

1. Heat a deep sauté pan over medium heat and add oil. Fry garlic until fragrant, about 10 seconds.

2. Add Chinese broccoli, oyster sauce, sugar, and water. Stir-fry until broccoli just turns bright green, about 1 minute. Taste to adjust seasoning.

3. Serve sprinkled with ground white pepper.

Green Curry with Seitan and Mushrooms

Seitan is like sponge. It will take on the flavor of green or other curry very well. If cooking for a meat eater, replace soy sauce with fish sauce for extra flavor.

INGREDIENTS | SERVES 4

2 (13.5-ounce) cans coconut milk

½ cup Green Curry Paste (see Chapter 2)

2 cups chopped seitan

2 cups chopped mixed, wild mushrooms

3–4 tablespoons light soy sauce

2 teaspoons sugar

1 cup Thai basil

3 kaffir lime leaves, torn

1. Do not shake the coconut milk. Scoop the cream on top of coconut milk cans into a saucepan. Bring it to a boil over medium heat. Stir in curry paste and turn down the heat to low. Simmer over low heat, without stirring, until fragrant and coconut cream starts to release some oil, about 3–5 minutes.

2. Add the rest of coconut milk and bring it back to boil.

3. Add seitan and mushrooms and bring back to boil. Let simmer for 5 minutes. Season with soy sauce and sugar. Taste and adjust seasoning. Add Thai basil and kaffir lime leaves and turn the heat off. Serve.

Fried Rice with Tofu and Shitake Mushrooms

Mushrooms always add great flavor to any vegetarian dish.
Dried shitake mushrooms add a deeper flavor than fresh ones.

INGREDIENTS | SERVES 4

3 tablespoons vegetable oil

2 garlic cloves, minced

¼ teaspoon salt

½ cup sliced Fried Tofu (see Chapter 5)

½ cup sliced dried shitake mushrooms, soaked in warm water for 25 minutes and drained

2½ tablespoons light soy sauce, divided

¼ cup sliced yellow onion

2 eggs, lightly beaten

4 cups cooked Jasmine Rice (see Chapter 2)

2 teaspoons dark soy sauce

½ teaspoon pinch of sugar

1 cup Chinese broccoli, chopped

2 tablespoons chopped green onions

1 tablespoon chopped cilantro

⅛ teaspoon ground white pepper

1 cup sliced cucumbers

1. Heat a deep sauté pan or a wok over medium heat. Add oil and fry garlic and salt over medium heat until fragrant and brown, about 10–15 seconds.

2. Add tofu, mushrooms, and ½ tablespoon light soy sauce, and fry until tofu and mushrooms are cooked and heated through, about 1–2 minutes. Add onion and fry until translucent, about 8 minutes.

3. Add eggs to the pan and let cook without stirring for 1 minute (don't scramble the egg). Add rice, remaining light soy sauce, dark soy sauce, and sugar and stir-fry until rice is heated through, about 10 minutes.

4. Add Chinese broccoli and stir-fry for about 5 minutes. Taste and adjust seasoning. Stir in green onion and cilantro. Turn off the heat. Serve sprinkled with ground pepper and sliced cucumbers.

The Truth about Shitake Mushrooms

There is a naturally occurring glutamate in shitake mushrooms that has the same effect on people's senses as MSG. Glutamate gives the unique savory taste sensation called *umami* that acts as a taste enhancer.

Coconut Rice

*Coconut Rice is served with Green Papaya Salad (see Chapter 4) or
Southern Dried Red Curry with Chicken (see Chapter 7).*

INGREDIENTS | SERVES 6

2 cups uncooked jasmine rice

2 cups coconut cream

1 cup water

½ teaspoon salt

1 tablespoon white sugar

2 pandan leaves, folded

1. Soak rice in enough water to cover by 3" for 1 hour. Drain.

2. In a heavy, medium saucepan, mix coconut cream, water, salt, sugar, and pandan leaves, and stir to dissolve salt and sugar.

3. Add rice to the pot, stir, and bring to a boil, stirring occasionally. When the rice comes to a boil, turn the heat down to a very low simmer. Cover and let cook for 15 minutes. When done, remove from heat and let rest for 5–10 minutes before serving.

Brussels Sprouts with Garlic and Chili

This is a very easy dish to make with any kind of vegetables. If you are cooking for meat eater, chicken stock can be used in place of water.

INGREDIENTS | SERVES 2

2 tablespoons vegetable oil

4 cloves garlic, bruised

4 bruised chilies

4 cups Brussels sprouts

1 teaspoon soybean paste

2 tablespoons light soy sauce

½ cup water

2 cups cooked Jasmine Rice (see Chapter 2)

Heat up a deep sauté pan or wok over medium heat, add oil, and fry garlic and chilies until fragrant, about 10 seconds. Add Brussels sprouts, soybean paste, soy sauce, and water and stir-fry until vegetables are wilted, about 30 seconds. Check seasoning and serve immediately over rice.

Banana Blossom Salad with Tofu

Add shredded boiled chicken or blanched shrimp to the salad to replace tofu for a meat dish.

INGREDIENTS | SERVES 4

1 cup coconut cream

1 tablespoon soy sauce (or fish sauce if making with meat)

1 teaspoon palm sugar

1 (19-ounce) can banana blossoms available at Asian grocery stores

1 cup sliced Fried Tofu (see Chapter 5)

3 shallots, thinly sliced

2 tablespoons chopped cilantro

Banana Blossom

Banana blossoms are the baby bananas that didn't grow into bananas. They can be used in coconut soup. They have the texture and flavor similar to artichokes.

Heat coconut cream in a saucepan over medium heat and season with soy sauce and palm sugar. Drain banana blossoms and tofu pieces and add to the coconut milk. Garnish with shallots and cilantro.

CHAPTER 13

Thai-Inspired Dishes

Soy Dressing

*This is a great salad dressing for any salad, and you can
make it low-fat by changing the ratio of oil to water.*

INGREDIENTS | YIELDS 1 CUP

½ cup salted soybeans

1 tablespoon sugar

1–2 tablespoons light soy sauce

2 teaspoons lime juice

1 tablespoon Dijon mustard

1 teaspoon white vinegar

½ cup water

½ cup vegetable oil

1. Mix all the ingredients, except the oil, in a bowl. Whisk until incorporated.

2. Slowly add oil, whisking at the same time. Store in a jar in the refrigerator for three months.

Chicken Satay Sandwich

A full-flavor sandwich that will blow your guests away. Chicken satay and peanut sauce can be frozen, so you can pull them out anytime to make this wonderful sandwich.

INGREDIENTS | SERVES 4

1 ciabatta loaf, cut into 4 sandwich-sized pieces

Chicken Satay with Peanut Sauce (see Chapter 5)

1 cup Pickled Cabbage (see Chapter 4)

2 tablespoons chopped cilantro

1. Toast ciabatta bread. Spread peanut sauce on each piece of the bread.

2. Put satay pieces to cover the bottom piece of bread, and top with pickled cabbage and cilantro. Serve.

Pulled Pork Sandwich

This southern-style sandwich takes a twist using full flavor five-spiced pulled pork and spicy pickled cabbage.

INGREDIENTS | SERVES 2

1 cup Stewed Pork (from Stewed Pork over Rice and Broccoli, see Chapter 9)

2 whole-wheat hamburger buns

½ cup Pickled Cabbage (see Chapter 4)

1 tablespoon chopped cilantro

1. Shred pork finely. Cut hamburger buns in half and toast all pieces.

2. Place pork on the bottom bun and top with pickled cabbage and cilantro.

Thai Basil Dressing

Thai basil is fragrant with a hint of star anise in it. This green dressing will become your new favorite.

INGREDIENTS | YIELDS 2 CUPS

4 cups Thai basil

6 cloves garlic

⅓ cup lemon juice

1 tablespoon salt

4 teaspoons sugar

2 teaspoons ground black pepper

⅔ cup water

1⅓ cups vegetable oil

1. Combine all ingredients, except oil, in a blender and blend until smooth.

2. Add oil slowly while the blender is on until all the oil is added. Store in a lidded jar for two weeks in the refrigerator.

Ceviche

Many different versions of this dish can be made. Explore your options with different vegetables or fruits like jicama, peaches, mangoes, or bell pepper.

INGREDIENTS | SERVES 4

2 pounds shrimp, chopped into small, ¼" pieces

1 cup fresh-squeezed lime juice

¾ cup fish sauce

½ red onion, finely diced

1 teaspoon minced garlic

1 cup chopped fresh, seeded watermelon

Pinch of salt

2 teaspoons minced Thai chilies

2 tablespoons chopped cilantro

4 leaves iceberg lettuce

Combine all ingredients except lettuce in a bowl and let sit for 1 hour in the refrigerator. Serve with iceberg lettuce.

Spicy Tuna Salad

This salad can also be made into a sandwich just like a regular tuna salad sandwich. This oil-free version of tuna salad makes it a healthy choice for lunch, while Thai chilies add a punch for your taste buds.

INGREDIENTS | SERVES 2

1 (6-ounce) can tuna in water, drained and crumbled

½ cup diced red and green bell pepper

1 shallot, thinly sliced

1 celery stalk, chopped finely

2 tablespoons lime juice

1½ tablespoons fish sauce

1 teaspoon sugar

2 tablespoons minced fresh cilantro

½ teaspoon minced chilies

Combine all ingredients in a mixing bowl. Toss to combine and serve.

Green Curry Pizza

This pizza can also be made with red curry paste.

INGREDIENTS | SERVES 4

½ cup coconut cream (can be bought in store or scoop out just the top of the can)

2 tablespoons Green Curry Paste (see Chapter 2)

1 cup thinly sliced chicken breast or thigh

1 Asian long eggplant, sliced

2 teaspoons fish sauce

½ teaspoon sugar

1 cup Thai basil

1 tablespoon vegetable oil

1 thin prebaked pizza crust

½ cup shredded mozzarella cheese

½ cup red bell pepper, julienned into thin strips

1. Preheat the oven to 450°F. Heat coconut cream in a small sauté pan and add curry paste to fry. Fry over medium-low heat for about 2 minutes until fragrant and oily.

2. Add chicken and sauté until chicken is almost cooked, about 2 minutes. Add eggplant and continue to stir until eggplant is cooked, about 3 minutes. Season with fish sauce and sugar. If the mixture becomes too thick, add more coconut cream. Add half of the basil and cook until basil is wilted, about 30 seconds.

3. Brush vegetable oil on pizza crust. Spread the curry all over the crust and sprinkle cheese on top of the curry.

4. Bake for 10 minutes and top with bell pepper and remaining basil. Bake another 2 minutes to wilt the basil and pepper.

Thai-Inspired Hamburgers

This is a classic Thai seasoning for grilled or fried meat dishes. The five flavors of salty, sweet, spicy, sour, and bitter are all present in this burger.

INGREDIENTS | SERVES 4

1½ pounds ground beef

1 medium-size onion, diced

3 eggs

1 tablespoon chopped cilantro roots or stems

1 tablespoon light soy sauce

1 tablespoon sugar

1 tablespoon rice flour

1 tablespoon tapioca flour

Pinch of salt

1 teaspoon black pepper

4 burger buns

Toppings

4 slices cheddar cheese (optional)

Green leaf lettuce

Sliced tomatoes

Chopped cilantro

Ketchup to taste, optional

Mustard to taste, optional

Sriracha Sauce (see Chapter 2), optional

1. Combine all ingredients (except buns and toppings) in a mixing bowl and fold to combine.

2. Roll into hamburger patties, about 3 or 4 patties.

3. Heat up the grill until hot. Spray or brush oil on the grill. Grill at high heat until inner temperature of meat reads 165°F, or about 4 minutes on each side for medium-rare. Only flip the burger once. Add sliced cheese if desired. If adding cheese, add at the end while cooking the second side at the last minute.

4. Assemble the burger by toasting the buns; then place green leaf lettuce on the bottom half of the bun, top with hamburger patty, tomatoes, and chopped cilantro. Add ketchup, mustard, or Sriracha Sauce (see Chapter 2) if desired.

Butternut Squash Soup

This classic winter soup is spiced up with red curry paste.
Using coconut cream instead of regular cream makes this soup vegan.

INGREDIENTS | YIELDS 6 CUPS

1 tablespoon vegetable oil
2 teaspoons red curry paste
2 shallots, chopped
1 carrot, sliced
1 stalk celery, chopped
4 cups chopped butternut squash
2 (13.5-ounce) cans coconut milk
½ cup water
1–2 teaspoons salt
Fresh ground white pepper
2 tablespoons cilantro leaves

How to Cut Butternut Squash

It always seems challenging to cut butternut squash. First, peel butternut squash with sharp peeler. Cut butternut squash in half and scoop out the seeds with a spoon. Cut into cubes. Make sure to cut them in a somewhat uniform size for even cooking.

1. In a saucepan over medium-low heat, add oil, and then fry curry paste until fragrant, about 15 seconds. Add shallots, carrots, and celery and sauté until the vegetables are softened, about 4–5 minutes. Add butternut squash and continue to stir to season the squash.

2. Reserve ½ cup of the cream on top of coconut milk can for garnishing, and add the rest of coconut milk, water, and salt to the pot. Bring to a boil and simmer on low heat until butternut squash is tender, about 20–30 minutes.

3. Blend the soup with an immersion blender or let cool and then add to a blender. Add more salt if needed. To serve, garnish with ground white pepper and a scoop of coconut cream. Place cilantro leaves on top of the cream.

Omelet Tacos

Tacos are an ingenious invention. You can put anything in them, roll the tortilla up, and done! Both delicious and convenient, what more can you ask for? A Thai omelet makes an excellent taco. Different sauces can be used to season the taco.

INGREDIENTS | SERVES 2

Thai Omelet with Pork (see Chapter 11)

3–5 tortillas

Sriracha Sauce (see Chapter 2) or Chili Jam (see Chapter 3)

½ cup chopped cilantro for garnish

1. Heat tortillas by placing them on the grate over a flame on the stovetop. Be careful not to burn them. Flip tortillas several times.

2. Place Thai omelet on the tortilla, top with Sriracha Sauce or Chili Jam, and garnish with cilantro. Serve hot.

Thai-Style Pico de Gallo

Use watermelon pieces for this recipe in place of cucumbers for a different taste. You can also blend the mixture in a food processor to make salsa.

INGREDIENTS | YIELDS 3 CUPS

1 pickling cucumber, diced with seeds

2 medium tomatoes, diced

3 shallots, diced

½ cup chopped cilantro stems

1 tablespoon fish sauce

¼ cup lime juice

½ teaspoon minced garlic

¼ teaspoon salt

1 teaspoon minced Thai chilies

1 teaspoon sugar

Combine all ingredients in a mixing bowl. Toss to mix well and let marinate for 20 minutes before serving.

Penne Pasta with Garden Tomatoes

This recipe is a classic dish for kids. It has been around for so long that it can be called a Thai recipe, rather than a Thai-inspired recipe. Moms know this dish very well. What's better than ketchup and noodles with some vegetables?

INGREDIENTS | SERVES 4

4–5 cups cooked pasta

2 tablespoons vegetable oil

1 teaspoon minced garlic

6 ounces chicken breast, cut into bite-size pieces

½ cup chopped yellow onion

½ cup chopped tomatoes

3–4 tablespoons ketchup

1–2 teaspoons fish sauce, or to taste

Pinch of sugar

½ cup chopped green onions

1. In a large saucepan, bring water to a boil and add pasta. Simmer for about 8 minutes, strain, and set aside.

2. Heat a wok or a sauté pan over medium heat. Add the oil and fry garlic until fragrant and it starts to change color, about 10 seconds. Add chicken and stir-fry until chicken is cooked, about 1–2 minutes. Add yellow onions and fry for about 1 minute. Add pasta, chopped tomatoes, ketchup, fish sauce, and sugar and stir-fry for 2 minutes until tomatoes are cooked. Taste and adjust seasoning.

3. Add chopped green onions. Fold the onions in and turn the heat off. Serve.

Thai Cole Slaw

Crisp vegetables are cut in a fine julienne and then tossed in a tangy dressing.
Serve the cole slaw as a side dish, a salad, or as a topping for sandwiches.

]INGREDIENTS | SERVES 4

½ cup chopped cilantro

2 tablespoons chopped roasted peanuts

2 teaspoons toasted sesame seeds

1 cup peeled and finely julienned jicama

1 cup julienned carrots

4 cups shredded cabbage

2 tablespoons lime juice

2 tablespoons fish sauce

½ teaspoon minced Thai chilies

2 teaspoons sugar

Combine all ingredients in a large mixing bowl. Using your hands, mix well to ensure all vegetables are coated. Taste and adjust seasoning as needed.

Basil Bean Dip

This is a twist on hummus, the classic garbanzo bean dip.
Serve it with fresh vegetables, crackers, or bread.

]INGREDIENTS | SERVES 4

2 (15-ounce) cans garbanzo beans,
  rinsed and drained
2 tablespoons sesame oil
2 tablespoons smooth peanut butter
2 teaspoons lime juice
2 cloves garlic, minced
¼ cup fresh basil leaves
1 teaspoon Sriracha Sauce (Chapter 2)
1 teaspoon salt

Blend all ingredients in food processor or blender. Add hot water, a tablespoon at a time, if the mixture becomes too thick to blend.

CHAPTER 14

Desserts and Drinks

Sweet Sticky Rice with Mango (*Kao Neaw Ma Muang*)

When mangoes are in season in Thailand, you will see this dessert sold everywhere on the street. Long-grain rice is preferred for this recipe, but if you have short grains, they work just as well; keep in mind that short-grain rice will take longer in the steamer.

INGREDIENTS | SERVES 4

2 cups sweet or glutinous rice

2 cups coconut cream

1¼ cups sugar

1 teaspoon salt

1 pandan leaf, or ¼ teaspoon vanilla
   extract

2 medium ripe mangoes, peeled,
   seeded, and sliced

How to Cut Mangoes

With a sharp paring knife, hold mango in the palm of your hand with the tail facing away from you. Cut off the tail attached to the stem. Peel off the skin with the knife blade facing toward you, starting from the left side. Continue to peel until half of the mango is peeled. Place mango's flat tail on the cutting board, slice off the peeled side as close to the seeds as possible. Flip the mango and continue to peel on the other side, and then slice off the other side of mango. Cut it into bite-size pieces.

1. Soak rice overnight for at least 4 hours.

2. In a saucepan, heat the coconut cream over medium heat; add sugar and salt. Stir until dissolved. If using pandan leaf, add it to the sauce and simmer for about 2 minutes to let it infuse into the sauce. Let cool completely. The sauce can be made and refrigerated a day ahead.

3. Drain, rinse, and steam rice over medium heat in a steamer for about 15–20 minutes. Check if the rice is cooked from the thickest part of the pile. If a steamer is not available, put soaked sticky rice in a bowl and cover with a dish or cheesecloth. Cook for 3 minutes in the microwave without adding any water. Check if the rice is cooked. If it is still hard, cook for another 1 minute and check again.

4. When the rice is cooked, pour the prepared coconut cream over rice, a little bit at a time. The rice should be covered with sauce but not drowning in it. Stir to mix thoroughly. Add more sauce if needed. Cover and set aside for 15 minutes in a warm place.

5. Serve with sliced mangoes.

Egg Custard (*Sang Ka Ya*)

Egg custard is similar to flan, but it has a fluffier texture. Serve with sweet sticky rice (from Sweet Sticky Rice with Mango in this chapter) or on its own.

INGREDIENTS | SERVES 4

1 cup thick coconut cream
1 pandan leaf
1 cup palm sugar
5 eggs
Sweet Sticky Rice (from this chapter)

1. Heat the coconut cream, pandan leaf, and palm sugar in a saucepan over medium heat, just enough to dissolve the sugar and blend with the cream into a smooth mixture, about 2 minutes. Remove from heat and allow to cool to room temperature.

2. Beat the eggs well until foamy and mix with the cooled, sweetened coconut cream. Strain the mixture through a dampened muslin cloth, or through a fine wire mesh colander. Spoon out any bubbles that may have formed over the top.

3. Pour the mixture into a heatproof dish. Steam over medium-high heat until the custard is set, about 20 minutes. When you serve it, use a spoon, shave off the custard, and top with the sweet sticky rice.

Egg Custard in Pumpkin

This dessert has amazing texture. Once cooked, cut the pumpkin in half and cut into wedges to serve. Keep in mind kabocha squash is what Thais call pumpkin.

INGREDIENTS | SERVES 4

1 cup thick coconut cream

1 pandan leaf

1 cup palm sugar

5 eggs

1 or 2 kabocha squash (pumpkin)

1. Heat the coconut cream, pandan leaf, and palm sugar in a saucepan over medium heat, just enough to dissolve the sugar and blend with the cream into a smooth mixture. Remove from heat and allow to cool to room temperature.

2. Beat the eggs well until foamy and mix with the cooled, sweetened coconut cream. Strain the mixture through a dampened muslin cloth, or through a fine wire mesh colander. Spoon out any bubbles that may have formed over the top.

3. Cut off the top of the squash and spoon out the stringy meat and the seeds. Pour the mixture into the squash until the cream reaches to about 2" below the opening. Steam over medium heat until the custard is set, about 20–30 minutes. Make sure your heat is not too high or the squash will split.

Banana in Coconut Cream (*Kluey Buad Chee*)

This dessert is great served hot or cold. When choosing bananas, make sure they are ripe but firm. Taste one to make sure they are sweet.

INGREDIENTS | SERVES 4

6 small sugar bananas (or 4 regular bananas)
1 cup coconut milk
1 cup white sugar
Large pinch of salt
2 cups coconut cream

Thai Desserts

Coconut cream is the main ingredient in Thai desserts. It is rich and creamy and does not burn or curdle as easily as heavy cream does.

1. Peel bananas, cut in half lengthwise, then cut into 2" pieces widthwise. Bring coconut milk to a boil. Add bananas and simmer over low heat until tender, skimming and reserving any foam that has formed on top. Once bananas are cooked, about 5 minutes, add sugar and salt, stirring gently. Be careful not to break up the banana pieces. Simmer for 3–4 more minutes.

2. In a separate saucepan, bring coconut cream to a boil, stirring constantly to prevent it from separating, about 3 minutes. Remove from the heat and allow to cool. Skim off the cream that has floated to the top and add to the bananas. Also stir in the reserved coconut "foam" to enrich and thicken dessert. Serve.

Thai Coffee (*Ka Fae Yen*)

Any coffee can be used to make Thai coffee, although
Thai coffee mix can be purchased at Asian grocery stores.

INGREDIENTS | SERVES 4

6 cups strong brewed coffee

1 can sweet condensed milk

Thai Coffee

Thai coffee mix can be found at any Asian grocery store. The mix has coffee, corn, and soybeans. Other coffees like chicory mixed coffee, good quality French roast, Vietnamese coffee mix, or other dark roast coffee are all great to make Thai coffee. It all depends on your preference. Brewing it with a French press makes a more flavorful coffee, while a Vietnamese metal press can also be used if you are only making one serving of coffee. Add 1½ tablespoons coffee grounds to the chamber, level coffee grounds, and place the press over the coffee. Place the chamber on top of the glass, pour in ¼ cup water, and let sit for 1 minute for the coffee to become fully saturated. Pour hot water over to fill up the chamber and let sit over a glass with 2 tablespoons sweet condensed milk. Watch it drip.

Add sweet condensed milk to the coffee, stir, and serve hot or over ice. If serving over ice, let cool a little so coffee won't be diluted.

Thai Iced Tea (*Cha Yen*)

The orange color of the tea comes from food coloring in the tea mix. In the old days, the color was not so intense, and it came from crushed tamarind seeds mixed in with the tea leaves.

INGREDIENTS | SERVES 8

5 tablespoons Thai tea mix

8 cups boiling water

1 cup sugar

1 cup evaporated milk, coconut milk, half-and-half, or cream

Thai Tea Mix

Thai tea mix is made with black tea leaves and spices like star anise, cloves, or tamarind seeds. It can be served hot or iced, with or without milk.

1. Brew tea with boiling water for 8 minutes. Strain.

2. Add sugar and stir until sugar is dissolved. Add milk of choice and serve.

Thai Basil Lime Sparkler

This is a refreshing drink that can be made into an adult beverage by adding rum or vodka. It's great on hot summer days.

INGREDIENTS | SERVES 4

4 cups Thai basil

¾ cup lime juice

4 cups simple syrup (see sidebar)

Sparkling water to taste

Make a Simple Syrup

Mix 1 part sugar with 1 part water. In a saucepan, bring to a simmer, or cook until sugar is dissolved.

Put basil, lime juice, and simple syrup in a blender and blend until smooth. Strain it through a fine sieve. Top with sparkling water. Follow the ratio of about ¼ basil lime mix and ¾ sparkling water over ice.

Ginger Peach Fresca

Other fruits like mango or strawberry can be used in this recipe.

INGREDIENTS | SERVES 4

2 cups peaches
¼ cup lemon juice
4 cups ginger simple syrup (see sidebar)
Sparkling water to mix

Ginger Simple Syrup

In order to make this syrup, simmer 6 pieces of sliced ginger in simple syrup, let sit overnight and remove ginger. Done!

Put everything in a blender and blend until smooth. Strain it through a fine sieve. Top with sparkling or still water. Follow the ratio of about ¼ fruit mix and ¾ water over ice.

Coconut Ice Cream (*Ai Tim Kati*)

*This ice cream is a good base for making other ice cream flavors.
And it is rich and delicious without the dairy of traditional ice cream.*

INGREDIENTS | SERVES 4

⅔ cup coconut cream
1 cup coconut milk
2 ounces or ¼ cup palm sugar
⅛ teaspoon salt

1. In a medium-size saucepan, bring all the ingredients to a boil.

2. Reduce the heat to low and simmer gently for 5 minutes, stirring occasionally. Remove from heat, and chill the mixture thoroughly.

3. Once chilled, freeze in your ice cream maker according to the manufacturer's directions.

Pumpkin in Coconut Milk

Sweet potatoes or butternut squash can also be used in place of pumpkin. Once the kabocha squash is cooked, the skin will be soft and crispy, adding extra texture to this dish.

INGREDIENTS | SERVES 4

1 pound kabocha squash (pumpkin)
½ cup sugar
½ teaspoon salt
2 cups coconut milk
½ cup coconut cream

1. Peel squash, leaving a little bit of skin on the meat, and cut into 1" × 2" pieces.

2. Combine sugar, salt, and coconut milk in a saucepan. Bring to a boil to dissolve sugar. Remove from heat. Strain the mixture through a cheesecloth, pour back into saucepan, and bring to boil again. Add squash pieces and simmer over low heat for 15 minutes. Add coconut cream, bring to boil, and take off the heat. Serve.

Corn Tapioca

*Corn often appears as an ingredient in Thai desserts.
Sometimes it is even mixed in with coconut ice cream. You usually see this dessert served
at Chinese restaurants in small portions as a complimentary dessert after the meal.*

INGREDIENTS | SERVES 4

2¼ cups water, divided

3 cups shaved corn kernels

1 cup sugar

¼ cup tapioca flour

1½ teaspoons salt

1 cup coconut cream

Fresh Corn

Nothing beats the taste of fresh corn in season. Shuck the husk and shave corn directly into the bowl. Shaved corn kernels have more flavor than frozen whole kernels because they are more broken, allowing the sweetness of the corn to be released.

1. Bring 2 cups water to a boil over high heat and add corn. Stir occasionally until corn is cooked, about 3 minutes. Add sugar and make sure sugar is all dissolved.

2. In a mixing bowl, add ¼ cup water to tapioca flour and stir to mix. Add the mixture to the pot and stir until tapioca turns clear and is cooked, about 15–20 minutes.

3. Combine salt and coconut cream in a saucepan and bring to a boil to dissolve salt. Remove from heat. To serve, scoop corn mixture into a small bowl, and top with coconut cream sauce.

Sweet Potato Ginger

This is a great dessert to serve in the winter months when it is cold and frosty outside.

INGREDIENTS | SERVES 4

4 cups water

1 pound sweet potatoes, peeled and chopped into 2" × 2" pieces

5 slices ginger

1 cup sugar

Bring water to a boil over high heat and add sweet potato pieces. When water returns to a boil, add ginger. Boil until sweet potatoes are done, about 25 minutes. Add sugar and stir to dissolve. Serve hot.

Growing Ginger

Growing ginger is easy. Find a good-sized ginger root (if you can find one with the end of the root starting to grow a green shoot, that's great) and bury ginger in the soil about 2" deep. Water every few days. The plant will shoot above ground. When you need some ginger to cook with, dig the soil and find the root, cut however much root you need to use, and let the rest keep growing.

Pineapple Ice

If you visit Thailand, everywhere you go you will see stalls on the streets selling different fruit drinks.

INGREDIENTS | SERVES 2

2 cups chopped pineapple

1 cup simple syrup (see sidebar in the Thai Basil Lime Sparkler in this chapter)

½ teaspoon salt

1 cup crushed ice, no block ice

Combine everything in a blender and blend until smooth.

Orange Ice

Freshly squeezed orange juice is the key for this drink.
Texas sweet oranges are great for this recipe.

INGREDIENTS | SERVES 2

2 cups orange juice

½ cup simple syrup (see sidebar in the Thai Basil Lime Sparkler in this chapter)

Pinch of salt

1 cup crushed ice

Combine all ingredients in a blender and blend until smooth.

Limeade

Lemons are not widely used in Thai cuisine. You can make this drink into a slushie by adding ice and a little more simple syrup and blending in the blender.

INGREDIENTS | SERVES 4

2 cups sugar

4 cups water

3 cups fresh lime juice

1 teaspoon salt

1. Make syrup with 2 cups sugar and 4 cups water. Bring the mixture to simmer and turn off the heat. Stir to dissolve the sugar. Let cool.

2. Combine syrup, lime juice, and salt and stir to mix.

Lemongrass Tea

Lemongrass is fragrant and makes excellent tea. If growing lemongrass in the garden, use the stalk to cook and cut the leaves off to make tea. It is great hot or iced.

INGREDIENTS | SERVES 6

1 stalk lemongrass or the leaves of 2 stalks

6 cups filtered water

Sweetener of choice

1. If using the stalk, cut the stalk into 4" pieces. Bruise the pieces with a pestle or meat tenderizer. If using the leaves, fold them into bundles.

2. In a saucepan, bring water to a boil, add lemongrass, and let simmer for 3 minutes. Remove lemongrass and add sweetener of your choice for your desired level of sweetness.

Pandan Tea

This drink can be enjoyed either sweetened or unsweetened. Many Thai restaurants in Thailand serve pandan tea in place of plain water.

INGREDIENTS | SERVES 6

6 cups water
2 pandan leaves
Sweetener of choice

In a saucepan bring water to a boil, add pandan leaves, and let simmer for 3 minutes. Remove pandan leaves and add sweetener of your choice for your desired level of sweetness.

Tamarind Drink

This is a very refreshing drink for the summer. It's a perfect balance of sweet, salty, and sour in a drink.

INGREDIENTS | SERVES 8

4 tablespoons tamarind concentrate, not paste
8 cups water
1 cup sugar
1 teaspoon salt

Combine all ingredients in a large saucepan or soup pot and bring to boil to dissolve sugar. Let cool and serve over ice.

Black Beans in Coconut Milk

Red beans can also be used in this recipe.

INGREDIENTS | SERVES 4

1 cup black beans
2½ cups coconut milk
¼ teaspoon salt
1 cup palm sugar

1. Soak beans overnight. Cook beans in a saucepan over medium-low heat with enough water to cover the beans, about 30–45 minutes. Drain.

2. In a separate saucepan, combine coconut milk, salt, and sugar and bring to a boil over high heat. Remove from heat and strain through a fine strainer into a different saucepan. Bring back to a boil. When boiling, add black beans. Bring the mixture to a boil and turn off the heat. Serve hot.

Mung Beans with Sugar

This is as simple as it gets as far as dessert goes.

INGREDIENTS | SERVES 4

1 cup mung beans
5 cups water
1 cup brown sugar

Soak mung beans overnight. In a saucepan, bring water to a boil, add mung beans, and boil over medium-low heat until the beans are done, about 45 minutes. When done, add sugar. When sugar is dissolved, turn off the heat. Serve hot.

Corn with Fresh Coconut Meat

This dessert or snack is all about texture. Simple ingredients with different textures make this dish taste more complicated, even though it is really quite easy to make.

INGREDIENTS | SERVES 4

2 ears of corn

2 pandan leaves

¼ teaspoon salt

1 cup grated coconut

3 tablespoons sugar

1 tablespoon toasted white sesame seeds

Buying Fresh Coconut

You can buy frozen fresh grated coconut meat or you can cut a young coconut open and slice the meat into thin strips. The flesh of young coconut is not yet firm. More mature coconuts are a little harder to cut open, but you won't know until you cut it. If the meat of the young coconut is firm, it can be julienned and used in this recipe.

1. In a saucepan, boil corn in water over medium-high heat with pandan leaves until corn is cooked, about 10–15 minutes. Allow to cool. Remove from water, drain, and shave off corn kernels into a bowl.

2. In a bowl, mix salt and shredded coconut meat. Add sugar and shaved corn kernels and mix well. Mix in sesame seeds and save some to sprinkle on top for garnish.

Mixed Fruits with Chili Sugar Salt

You read it right. Fruit in Thailand is often served with a side of chili, sugar, and salt mix. The combination of the three flavors and the sweetness and tartness from the fruit creates the balance.

INGREDIENTS | SERVES 4

1 tablespoon salt

3–4 tablespoons sugar

1 or 2 Thai chilies

2 cups peeled, cored, and chopped fruits like green mango, pineapple, or guava

Combine salt, sugar, and chilies in a mortar. Pound until chilies are finely ground. Alternatively, dried red chilies can be used. Serve fruit on a platter with seasoning on the side.

Fruits for Dessert

Because it is blessed with tropical weather, Thailand has a variety of fruits, and every season brings different kinds. For dessert, Thais usually opt for fruit instead of sweeter desserts like cake.

Watermelon Freeze

This drink is so easy and extremely refreshing, perfect for midsummer when watermelon is at its peak.

INGREDIENTS | SERVES 6

1 small seedless super-sweet watermelon

1–2 tablespoons lime juice

1. Put watermelon pieces and lime juice in a blender. Blend until smooth.

2. Chill in the freezer for about 30 minutes. Serve.

Tamarind Candy

The combination of spicy, sour, salty, and sweet in a dessert is rare.
The candies will keep indefinitely in an airtight jar.

INGREDIENTS | YIELDS 3 CUPS

2 dried small Thai chilies

½ teaspoon salt

2 cups concentrated tamarind paste

2 cups tamarind meat, seeds and pulp removed

2 cups sugar, divided

Concentrated Tamarind Paste

Concentrated tamarind paste is available in Asian grocery stores, or you can make it using the recipe for Tamarind Water in Chapter 2 (use half of the water to make tamarind concentrate).

1. Pound chilies and salt using a mortar and pestle.

2. Mix tamarind concentrate, tamarind meat, 1½ cups sugar, and chili mixture in a heavy medium saucepan. Stir to mix with a wooden spoon over low heat until thick and sticky, about 5–10 minutes.

3. Remove from heat and let cool. Form mixture in ½" balls and roll in remaining ½ cup sugar. Store in an airtight jar.

Banana Candy

Brass woks or a sauté pan will work well for this recipe. A stainless steel pot will work, too. Fruits like mangoes, peaches, and strawberries will also work well in this recipe.

INGREDIENTS | YIELDS 2 CUPS

2 cups coconut cream

¼ teaspoon salt

1 cup palm sugar

2 cups puréed bananas

½ cup hydrolyzed lime water

Making Lime Water

Prepare lime water by mixing 2 tablespoons lime paste (available at Asian grocery stores or online) with 5 cups water. Stir well and leave until the lime crystals sink to the bottom. Then pour the clear liquid into another container. Discard the solids.

1. Simmer coconut cream in a small saucepan over medium heat for 3–5 minutes until separated. You will see oil rising to the surface of the cream.

2. Add salt and sugar to the pan and stir to dissolve. Add bananas to the pan and stir. Slowly add lime water while stirring.

3. Cook banana mixture over low heat, stirring constantly, until banana mixture starts to peel off the pan, about 15 minutes. Transfer to a shallow pan and let cool. Cut into 1" squares to serve.

Mango Coconut Ice Cream

This recipe can be adapted to use other fruits like peaches, strawberries, or blackberries.
Replace lime juice with lemon juice when making with other fruits.

INGREDIENTS | YIELDS 2 QUARTS

6 cups coconut milk

2 cups sugar

1 teaspoon salt

3 tablespoons lime juice

3 mangoes, peeled, seeded, and cut into small pieces

1. Place coconut milk, sugar, salt, and lime juice in a medium saucepan and bring to a boil. Reduce heat to medium-low and simmer for 5 minutes. Let cool for 5–10 minutes.

2. Reserve a few pieces of mango and add the rest to the coconut milk mixture. Pour mixture in a blender and blend until smooth.

3. Make ice cream in an ice cream maker, following manufacturer's instructions. Add reserved mango chunks to the ice cream at the end as it finishes churning.

Black Sticky Rice Pudding

This recipe is very easy to make and keeps quite well in the fridge.
The combination of salty and sweet makes this dessert totally irresistible.

INGREDIENTS | SERVES 4

1 cup black sticky rice
Water to cover the rice
½ cup sugar
½ cup coconut cream
2 teaspoons salt
2 teaspoons sesame seeds

1. Add sticky rice and water to a heavy, medium saucepan. Bring to a boil, reduce heat to low, and let simmer until rice is cooked and mushy, about 1 hour. Add more water as needed.

2. Stir in sugar. Mix well to dissolve sugar.

3. In a small saucepan, heat coconut cream with salt over medium heat for 5–8 minutes.

4. To serve, put scoops of sweet black sticky rice in small bowls and top with salted coconut cream and sesame seeds.

Strawberry Tapioca Pudding

This is a spiced-up version of classic tapioca pudding. Any seasonal fruit can be used in this recipe.

INGREDIENTS | SERVES 6

2 cups water

⅓ cup small tapioca pearls

1 cup coconut cream

6 tablespoons sugar, divided

Pinch of salt

1 teaspoon anise seeds

4 cups coarsely chopped strawberries, trimmed

Tapioca

Tapioca is a starch made from cassava roots. Tapioca starch or flour is used mainly to thicken soups or sauces. Tapioca pearls come in different sizes and are boiled to use in desserts.

1. Bring water to a boil in a heavy saucepan and add tapioca pearls. Stir occasionally to prevent the pearls from sticking to the bottom of the pan. Cook until tapioca is mostly clear, about 15 minutes.

2. Add coconut cream and stir. Add 4 tablespoons sugar and salt and simmer, uncovered, until tapioca is cooked through, about 3 minutes. Make sure to stir often. Turn off the heat and cool in an ice bath, stirring occasionally.

3. Grind anise seeds in spice grinder or with a mortar and pestle. Purée strawberries, the remaining 2 tablespoons sugar, and ground anise seeds in a blender. Divide strawberry mixture among six glasses. Spoon tapioca over strawberries and chill before serving.

Grilled Bananas with Coconut Sauce

These charred bananas with a creamy, salty, sweet coconut sauce make for a perfect snack or dessert.

INGREDIENTS | SERVES 4

4 Thai bananas or 2 regular bananas (if using regular bananas, cut bananas into 2 short pieces)

½ cup coconut cream

2 tablespoons palm sugar

¼ teaspoon salt

Thai Bananas

Thai bananas are best for this dish. They are less creamy and are denser, making them easier to cut. They can be found at Asian or Mexican grocery stores. Don't confuse them with the very small ones from South America.

1. Grill bananas over low flame until charred, about 5 minutes on each side. Be careful not to burn the bananas.

2. Heat coconut cream in saucepan over medium heat. Add sugar and salt and stir to dissolve the sugar. Drizzle over grilled banana to serve.

Ice Cream Dog

This is the perfect way to eat ice cream. Hot dog buns hold the ice cream really well, making it a handheld treat. You can put as many ice cream flavors as you want on them!

INGREDIENTS | SERVES 2

2 hot dog buns

½ cup Sweet Sticky Rice (from Sweet Sticky Rice with Mango in this chapter)

6 scoops ice cream, any flavor

2 tablespoons roasted peanuts

¼ cup evaporated milk

Cut the hot dog buns and split open. Lay Sweet Sticky Rice on the bottom of the bun. Top with 3 scoops of ice cream and roasted peanuts, and drizzle evaporated milk on top of everything.

Online Resources

Online Resources for Thai Ingredients

Asian Food Grocer
www.asianfoodgrocer.com

Asian Supermarket 365
www.asiansupermarket365.com

eFood Depot
www.efooddepot.com/ethnics/thai.html

Grocery Thai
www.grocerythai.com

Import Food
http://importfood.com

Temple of Thai
www.templeofthai.com

Online Resources for Thai Cooking

Thai Fresh
Jam Sanitchat started the Thai Fresh blog in 2007 around the idea of cooking authentic Thai food using local ingredients. There are recipes, information about Thai cooking, seasonal ingredients, and beautiful photographs.
http://thai-fresh.com/blog

Joy's Thai Food
Joy is based in Thailand. She writes this blog while working full time.
www.joysthaifood.com

Marion's Kitchen

Marion created her own food range business called Marion's Kitchen, which is a collection of Asian ingredient kits containing "real" ingredients and a step-by-step guide to perfecting each dish. Follow Marion on her journey through Thailand and make the delicious Thai and Asian recipes from her blog.

http://marionskitchen.com.au/blog

Rachel Cooks Thai

Recipes and great stories from an American girl who fell in love with Thai food.

http://rachelcooksthai.com

Rasa Malaysia

A wealth of Asian cooking, especially Thai, Chinese, and Malaysian. Bee's blog is an encyclopedia of Asian recipes.

http://rasamalaysia.com

She Simmers

A great resource for Thai food and travel. Leela Punyaratabandhu spends most of her time either in Chicago or Bangkok. She is a freelance writer and recipe developer with a passion for the culinary history of Thailand.

http://shesimmers.com

Thai Food Tonight

A free online cooking channel, Thai Food Tonight is the only Thai cooking channel aired in the United States. Watch as Dim Geefay guides you through different Thai dishes with the help of her daughter, Cathy.

www.thaifoodtonight.com

Thai Food and Travel

Kasma Loha-Unchit began teaching Thai cooking classes in 1985 and is still teaching out of her home kitchen in Oakland, California. Her website is very informative with tips on Thai cooking and stories on Thailand. Her Thai Food and Travel blog has information about food and travel written by Kasma and her husband Michael Babcock.

http://thaifoodandtravel.com

Thai Cooking Classes in the United States

Thai Fresh
909 West Mary Street
Austin, TX 78704
Jam teaches hands-on Thai cooking classes in a commercial kitchen at Thai Fresh, a restaurant that focuses on using local seasonal ingredients to create authentic Thai dishes.

Fantastic Thai
New Jersey/New York
Phensri is a Thai cuisine consultant, a restaurant owner, and chef in central New Jersey. She teaches Thai cooking class in the New Jersey and New York area.

I Love Thai Cooking
Seattle, Bellevue, and Eastside Area, Washington
Chef Pranee is a member of IACP, the International Association of Culinary Professionals, and enjoys teaching Thai cooking throughout Washington.

Mama Thai Cooking Club
San Francisco, California
415-572-3001
Mama Thai Cooking Club teaches both private and public classes in the San Francisco area.

Supatra Thai Cuisine
St. Paul, Minnesota
Supatra Johnson is a Thai cooking instructor and author of the Thai cookbook, *Crying Tiger*. She teaches many of her cooking classes in the Minnesota area.

Thai Essence
San Francisco Bay Area, California

Chef Phant is from Thailand and grew up in a food business family watching his mother and sisters cook daily. Phant offers Thai cooking workshops, cooking sessions, chef-for-a-day services, and cooking demonstrations to various culinary schools and events in California.

Thai Food and Travel

Oakland, California

Kasma is a cooking instructor and Thai cookbook author based in the San Francisco Bay Area. Kasma has offered classes for the last 20 years at her own home-based cooking school in Oakland, California.

Thai Gourmet House Cooking School

Scottsdale, Arizona

Praparat Sturlin is a formally trained teacher and culinary professional from Thailand. She founded the Thai Gourmet House Cooking School in 1989 in Scottsdale, Arizona.

APPENDIX B

Useful Thai Ingredients

Bamboo Shoots

Bamboo shoots are excellent in curries and stir-fried dishes. Raw bamboo shoots are a little bitter, but the bitterness is reduced after cooking. If you buy canned bamboo shoots, rinse them before using.

Banana Blossoms

Banana blossoms come in a can, and can be found in Asian grocery stores. They are cut off of the banana plants before the fruit forms. Typically they are served fresh as a garnish for relishes or boiled to make soup or salads.

Basil

There are different types of basil. The type most commonly available in Asian supermarkets is Thai sweet basil (*bai horapa*). The leaves are used in red and green curries. They can also be used in egg rolls or spring rolls. The other type that is commonly used in stir-fried dishes is holy basil (*bai grapao*). Holy basil is sharp and hot. It is difficult to grow in nonhumid weather. Asian supermarkets carry bottled holy basil, garlic, and chili paste for stir-fried dishes. The paste works well when you want to maintain the intense flavor of holy basil.

Bean Sprouts

Bean sprouts are used in many noodle dishes, soups, and stir-fries. Bean sprouts won't keep longer than a day or two, but growing your own mung bean sprouts is easy. There are many directions online on how to grow bean sprouts.

Bok Choy

Also known as Chinese cabbage, bok choy resembles Swiss chard in looks and regular green cabbage in taste. Stir-frying softens its flavor slightly.

Cardamom

This relative of ginger grows in most tropical environments. Its pods release a pungent, sweet-spicy flavor, somewhat similar to cinnamon.

Chili Peppers

Chilies come in three basic forms: fresh, dried, and powdered. Botanists have named hundreds of different varieties, making chilies one of the most diverse plants on the planet. With that said, there are a few generalities that seem to hold true with all chilies. Chilies sweeten as they ripen, so a red chili (of the same variety) will be sweeter than a green one. And the bigger the chili pepper, the milder it usually is. So beware of chilies that come in small packages! The seeds and the veins pack the most punch, so to tone down your chili, don't use the seeds or veins.

Chili Sauce

Bottled chili sauce is a smooth combination of salted fish, red chilies, fish sauce, lime juice, and palm sugar. It is served with almost everything in Thailand. It comes in red and yellow varieties, and in various strengths.

Cilantro

Cilantro, or coriander leaves, is an important component in Thai cooking. Thais use all parts of coriander plants. The end of the stem is used in soups, while the leaves (and stems that the leaves are attached to) are chopped for garnish and extra flavor.

Coconut Milk

Coconut milk can be made fresh by grating and pressing fresh coconut meat, but the canned variety works just as well and is a lot less work! Coconut milk is not the same as coconut water, which is simply the liquid inside the coconut itself.

Coriander

Also known as cilantro, this herb is a cousin to parsley and is used as such. The seeds are also dried and ground and have a semisweet aroma.

Curry

Curry powder is not a specific spice but rather a combination of spices that vary depending on the desired effect. Some are sweet, while others are scorching hot. Basic commercial curry powders usually contain six to eight various ingredients.

Curry Leaf

The leaves of an indigenous Southeast Asian plant that have no relation to curry powder or curry paste. The leaves do, however, release a curry-scented fragrance when crushed and are often added to various Asian dishes.

Curry Paste

Various combinations of spices and chilies, which can be either homemade or store-bought. They are super to keep on hand because they can be stored for long periods of time and help make quick, simple meals.

Dried Fish

Crispy salt-preserved fish used as a snack and in soup.

Dried Shrimp

Tiny shrimp that are preserved in brine and then dried and used as a flavoring agent. Just a few go a long way. They are usually soaked in water for a few minutes before being added to a recipe, which both softens them and reduces their bite.

Eggplant (*makeua*)

The most common eggplant found in Asian supermarkets is the long purple eggplant (*makeua yao*). Thai long eggplants are green and not found as easily as the purple ones. Eggplants are used in green curry, grilled to make salad, or stir-fried with soybean paste and chilies. There are also Thai apple eggplants, a round green eggplant with white stripes, as well as Thai pea eggplants, a small dark-green eggplant used in curries and stir-fries. The latter is very bitter.

Fermented Rice

Fermented rice comes in small packets and can be purchased at an Asian grocery store or an online Asian grocery store. It is mostly used in relishes to counterbalance the sweet and sour ingredients. It is also used in some desserts.

Fish Sauce

Fish sauce, or *nam pla* is one of the most used ingredients in Thai cuisine. It has a flavor similar to soy, although somewhat less salty. Salted, fermented fish or shrimp gives the sauce its characteristic aroma and complex flavor. Beware—it doesn't smell very good to the Western nose, but it is well worth getting used to.

Five-Spice Powder

A Chinese spice mixture that contains cinnamon, star anise, fennel, clove, ginger, peppercorns, and dried citrus peel.

Galangal

Galangal is a more pungent, fiery relative of ginger and is available both fresh and dried.

Garlic

Garlic is a much-used relative of the onion with a sweet, pungent flavor. Pickled garlic is often used as a garnish.

Ginger

Ginger is used in various stir-fries and sauces. Store ginger at room temperature in a plastic bag or in containers to prevent dehydration.

Guava

Also known as the tropical apple, the guava comes in two varieties—green and red. The green is native to Southeast Asia; the red is native to Hawaii. The fruit is especially high in vitamin C, iron, and calcium.

Kaffir Lime

The juice, the zest, and the leaves of this thorny tropical tree are used extensively in Southeast Asian cooking and impart a beautiful tropical fragrance and flavor.

Lemongrass

Lemongrass, or citronella root, is an aromatic tropical grass with a flavor similar to lemon balm. It can be crushed whole or stripped of its fibrous outer leaves and chopped. Placed in a plastic bag, it will keep in the refrigerator for weeks.

Lime (*ma nao*)

Thai limes are smaller than what can be found in the United States. Lemons are never used in Thai cooking. Always freshly squeeze lime juice right before use for the freshest taste.

Mango

A kidney-shaped tropical fruit, mangoes are rich in vitamins A, B, and C. They are also high in sugar, sometimes 20 percent of their weight. Mangoes are used both fully ripe and green in some cases.

Mint

An herb used throughout the world to impart a refreshing, zesty aroma and flavor. Varieties include spearmint, peppermint, and lemon mint.

Mushroom (*hed*)

Fresh and locally grown mushrooms are the best kind to use in Thai cooking. Oyster mushrooms make great soups and curries. Other kinds of mushrooms can also be used. Canned straw mushrooms, although more common in Thai cooking, have a metallic aftertaste.

Oyster Sauce

Oyster sauce is made from oyster extracts, sugar, and other seasonings. It has a sweet-smoky flavor and is available in mild, hot, and "vegetarian" varieties.

Palm Sugar

Palm sugar is a dark, unrefined sugar made from coconut palms. It is usually sold in blocks and must be crushed before it can be used. Dark brown sugar is a good and much easier-to-use substitute.

Papaya

This tropical fruit was introduced to Thailand by the Spanish after they conquered the Americas. Thai cooks use them both as a fruit and a vegetable.

Peppercorn

White peppercorns are commonly used in Thai cooking. Freshly ground peppercorns have a much more robust flavor than preground pepper.

Rice Wine

Rice wine is a fermented concoction made from glutinous rice and millet and is used to add complexity and flavor. In Japan, it is known as mirin, which is a sweetish condiment used as a flavoring agent. If unavailable, dry sherry can be used as a substitute.

Salted Radish

Salted radish is used in Pad Thai and other stir-fries. It is made from daikon, the white Japanese radish. Daikon is pickled and dried. Salted or pickled radish can be stored in the refrigerator indefinitely.

Shallot (*hom daeng*)

Shallots are used in curry pastes or in salads. The flavor of shallots is less pungent than onions. Raw onions are almost never used uncooked in Thai dishes.

Shrimp Paste

A thick, pungent paste made from salted fermented shrimp, which is often used in flavoring other curry pastes.

Soy Sauce

Soy sauce is really not used very much in Thai cuisine. Instead, Thai cooks prefer fish sauce. However, soy can be used as a substitute for fish sauce and is specifically called for in some recipes. Soy sauce can be light or dark, which refers to flavor and color, not salt content. Tamari is a specific type of soy sauce that is strongly flavored, so use it sparingly.

Star Anise

The star anise is an inedible pod with a distinct licorice flavor that is infused into broths and sauces. Slightly crushing the pod helps to release its flavorful oils.

Sticky Rice (*kao neuw*)

Sticky rice is eaten with many salads or is used to make desserts. Although it's also called glutinous rice, sticky rice does not contain any gluten.

Sweet Soy Sauce

This thick dark brown soy sauce is sweetened with palm sugar and star anise and is given piquant overtones with garlic. Sometimes the palm sugar is replaced with molasses.

Tamarind

Tamarind is a large brown podlike fruit that contains both seeds and pulp, although the pulp is the only part used. It is usually sold in dried blocks of pulp, or in concentrates or pastes. If using pulp, soak it in hot water and then press it to release the thick sweet and sour juice. Concentrates and pastes are used straight from the jar. Tamarind has a flavor somewhat reminiscent of prunes and lemon.

Tofu

Tofu, or bean curd, is made from soybeans and water and is highly nutritious, due to its high plant proteins. It doesn't have much of a flavor on its own, but it very quickly takes up the flavors of the dish it is in. It comes in a variety of textures ranging from soft to extra-firm. It is also available smoked.

Yellow Bean Sauce

A sauce made from salted and fermented soybeans.

Index

We Have
EVERYTHING®
on Anything!

With more than 19 million copies sold, the Everything® series has become one of America's favorite resources for solving problems, learning new skills, and organizing lives. Our brand is not only recognizable—it's also welcomed.

The series is a hand-in-hand partner for people who are ready to tackle new subjects—like you!

For more information on the Everything® series, please visit *www.adamsmedia.com*

The Everything® list spans a wide range of subjects, with more than 500 titles covering 25 different categories:

Business	History	Reference
Careers	Home Improvement	Religion
Children's Storybooks	Everything Kids	Self-Help
Computers	Languages	Sports & Fitness
Cooking	Music	Travel
Crafts and Hobbies	New Age	Wedding
Education/Schools	Parenting	Writing
Games and Puzzles	Personal Finance	
Health	Pets	

Made in the USA
Middletown, DE
04 May 2020